Jewish Forerunners
of
Christianity

by

Adolph Danziger

Bloch Publishing Company
New York

First Paperback Printing
New Material Copyright © by
Bloch Publishing Company, 2000

ISBN 0-8197-0706-6

All rights reserved.

Printed in the United States of America

A Word from the Publisher

Danziger's biographical sketches of the primary figures in ancient rabbinic Judaism continue to hold value and interest for today's readers. Written in engaging narrative style, these essays were among the earliest studies in America to reflect the traditions of German Jewish historical scholarship applied to the formative period of Judaism. His notes reflect a sound reading of Jewish sources. In particular, his chapters on Hillel, Akiva, and Judah ha-Nasi illuminate how their sharpness of mind and strength of purpose forged the tools for Jewish survival during the next millennia.

Danziger wrote his text at the dawn of Jewish nationalism before the creation of modern Israel and the discovery of the Dead Sea Scrolls. The tragedy of the Holocaust also recalls the destruction of the Second Temple to which the rabbis had to find a response.

Danziger's book takes us on a journey to an earlier yet strangely familiar time. In our days when the Jewish roots of Christianity are again being studied by Jews and Christians alike, his scholarship and insights remain a useful contribution for a continuing dialogue.

CONTENTS

                                  PAGE

INTRODUCTION vii

CHAPTER I.
HILLEL THE BABYLONIAN, FORERUNNER OF CHRIST; SHAMMAI THE NATIONALIST, OPPONENT OF HILLEL 1

CHAPTER II.
JESUS OF NAZARETH: TALMUDIC EVIDENCES OF HIS LIFE AND DEATH 30

CHAPTER III.
YOCHANAN BEN ZAKKAI, THE "LEAST OF THE DISCIPLES" OF HILLEL 55

CHAPTER IV.
'HANINAH BEN DOSA, THE SECOND SHAMMAI . 73

CHAPTER V.
ELIEZER BEN HYRKANOS, THE DISCIPLE OF BEN ZAKKAI, WHO EMBRACED CHRISTIANITY . 91

CHAPTER VI.
JOSUA BEN HANANIAH, THE BLACKSMITH-JUDGE AND FRIEND OF HADRIAN 122

CONTENTS

CHAPTER VII.

AKIBAH THE REVOLUTIONIST, FORERUNNER OF
    MOHAMMED 152

CHAPTER VIII.

RABBI MAIR THE ILLUSTRIOUS, AND ACHER THE
    AGNOSTIC 185

CHAPTER IX.

SIMON BEN YOHAI, RIVAL OF THE HOUSE OF
    HILLEL; HIS SON ELEAZAR 211

CHAPTER X.

RABBI JUDA THE PRINCE, COMPILER OF THE
    MISHNAH, THE FOUNDER OF TALMUDIC
    LITERATURE 242

NOTES 275

INDEX 319

INTRODUCTION

THE singular position of the Jewish people in the modern world is a fact of supreme interest to the student of history. It constitutes a large and powerful nationality (whatever may be said to the contrary), without political organization or a native land, spread amongst the other nations, yet preserving its own institutions, its own religion, its own language, while mingling in the business, intellectual, and political life of those others.

It is hated in some places, it is flattered in others, but it never is ignored, and it everywhere gives evidence of active national life after an existence of nearly four thousand years. But this is only a part, and not the largest part, of the claims of the Jewish people on the attention of thinkers of every land. It and its literature have been the subject of discussion for centuries by competent and incompetent, by friend and foe, alike. From it have sprung the moulders of religious thought of all the great Western nations. Christianity recognizes the Hebrew Law and the Hebrew patriarchs of three thousand years ago as an integral part of its history. Jesus, recognized by the Christian world as the Mediator between God and man, belongs by parentage to the royal House of David. Mary and Joseph and Peter and Paul and John, all of purest race, are the highest in honor of all in the roll of the Christian Church.

Beyond the wide extent of Christendom, the creed of Mohammed occupies an almost equal portion of the earth from Senegambia to Java, from Siberia to the Sahara and Hindustan. That creed, too, is distinctly traceable to a Jewish source. The Arabian Prophet was of Jewish race by the mother's side; his thought was moulded by Jewish scripture and the teachings of a Jewish master. He recognized the Jewish revelation as a forerunner of that which he claimed was made to himself, and the ceremonial of his law is largely Jewish in form. The strong analogy between his career and that of a Jewish leader five centuries earlier is touched on in the pages following in this work.

The object proposed is to sketch from contemporary Hebrew literature the workings of the Jewish mind during the period when the race was passing from tribal to cosmopolitan existence, and its religion widening from the practice of one land to a worldwide system. Great as has been the part played by the Jewish people in the history of mankind, it has been entirely different from that of other nations generally recognized as leaders. Its distinction is in the moral and mental field, not in that of war or political organization. It is not, then, by records of conquest or legislation, although law has had considerable influence in moulding the religious character of the Jew, that the development of the race can properly be studied. It is rather in the lives of the teachers and thinkers, who, in the democratic theocracy of Jewish society, formed the national policy and shaped the minds of the people. We have chosen a series of the most prominent of these masters in Israel to illustrate the course of events in the Jewish nation during the last two centuries of its separate existence. Their story is mainly drawn from the literature of their own time, as embodied in the great collection of the Talmuds, known as the Babylonian and Jerusalemic. Different as the style of that work is from modern methods and modes of thought, it contains ample foundation of fact to base intelligent historical work on, especially when one seeks to know the nature of mental action of the period, rather than the chronology of external facts.

The Jews in Palestine, under the Asmonean kings, formed a small, independent power between Syria and Arabia. By the outside world they were regarded in the same light as others of the numerous kingdoms of Western Asia. The Roman historian, Tacitus, contemptuously says they were the "most despised of the conquered under Medes, Persians, and Greeks," but they had won some distinction by their successful revolt against the Grecian kings of Syria. In their own minds, however, the Jews regarded themselves as superior to all the other branches of mankind. They were the chosen people of the Most High God, entrusted with the knowledge of his Law, and placed by his special command in the land which they had then possessed for fourteen centuries. During that time they had seen both good and bad fortune. David had extended their rule over Syria, and the wealth and glory of

INTRODUCTION

Solomon was the theme of admiration all through Western Asia still. They had suffered deeply too. The larger part of the sons of Jacob had been dispersed in unknown lands, and the remnant had been carried to Babylon as captives for two generations, but still they had returned. They had increased after the captivity, under Persian and Greek, into a nation of probably two millions in Palestine.

All through their checkered history, the Hebrew people held faith in a future great development of their nation of a permanent and beneficial kind. What its exact nature would be they did not determine. They held that such a development was intended by divine counsel, and the House of Israel was to be a central figure in it. Moreover this beneficent development was to be accomplished by a supernatural person, to appear on earth at some future time, but meanwhile watching over the fate of the Jewish people.[1]

These two ideas were deeply fixed in the minds of the Jewish population, and intensified the patriotic feelings which they possessed in common with other nations. The love of the Jews for their native land and its Law, both given specially by the Lord to them, was far stronger than that of the Spartan or Roman for their respective countries. It was not alone the interests of the present or pride in the

---

[1] כל הנביאים כולן לא נתנבאו אלא לימות המשיח—"All the Prophets had in view the Messianic time in their prophecies."—Talmud Babli, Sanhedrin 99; and Midrash Rabba, Genesis 24, 67: כשישראל חוטאים הוא מבקש עליהן רחמים—"When Israel transgresses He [the Messiah] asks mercy for them."

past that kept up the national spirit, but abiding faith in a future more glorious than any yet seen on earth for the Jewish nation. The land of Palestine was almost as closely connected with that nationality, in the minds of the people, as their own existence, or the Law of which they were the guardians. Jerusalem was to share with the Jew in the future prominence assured by prophecy. In Palestine, alone, the religious rites prescribed by God could be fully accomplished. The descendants of Abraham, away from Palestine, were only exiles. They might keep up their connection with Jewish nationality by observance of the Law and by following implicitly the teachings of the masters of the Law in the Holy Land, but they were distinctively regarded as in an unfortunate position. In fact, the law governing Jewish residents in another land differed essentially in many respects from that applied to those living in Palestine. The man whom circumstances forced to live away from the Holy Land—'Hutz la-Aretz (*ex patria*)—was an object of pity. There was no thought of voluntarily spreading to other lands among the Palestine Jews, when the Asmonean kings held independent sway in Jerusalem and the Temple of the Lord crowned Mount Moriah.

The divine Law itself was moulded under these ideas during many generations of Rabbis. The conditions of life in Palestine were looked on as the normal conditions of humanity in its highest state, and the practical requirements of worship and morals were framed on that theory. The Sanhedrin, the Parliament of the nation, was made up of men trained in the Law in the rabbinical schools of Palestine, and their decisions had the force of law for the people as a part of revelation itself. A narrow and bigoted cast of mind was thus engendered, which made the Jews the object of special dislike to the nations with whom they came in contact. It was the very reverse of the character fitted for a colonizing race or for one destined to intellectual leadership among men.

Hillel, a Jew of Babylonian birth, who came to Jerusalem as a needy student under the reign of Herod, and by sheer force of talent won his way to the Presidency of the Sanhedrin, was the first to see the unfitness of this frame of thought to the conditions and development of the Jewish race. He combated it long and earnestly, and he trained disciples on his own ideas. His personality was strong enough to secure the continuance of his descendants for many generations in the office of President of the Sanhedrin, which, after the suppression of the monarchy, became the highest power in the national organization. A rival school, the House of Shammai, maintained, during two centuries, a vigorous opposition to the policy of the House of Hillel. At times, it was stronger with the nation in virtue of its hot national patriotism, or the superior talent of its professors. The House of Hillel and the House of Shammai were, in fact, in modern language, the Liberal and the Conservative parties in the Jewish nation. The great powers of Akibah, with the help of the Rabbis of the House of Shammai, precipitated the revolt against the Romans under Hadrian. Akibah audaciously proclaimed a leader of his own choice as the divinely sent Messiah, in the person of Bar Kochba, and essayed to found a Jewish Empire of the East by armed force. His failure quenched among the larger part of the people the idea of a Jewish conqueror yet to come. A little later, Rabbi Judah, the Prince, walking in the footsteps of his ancestor Hillel, devoted himself to the work of binding the nation together by the bonds of literature and Law which might preserve its nationality even if scattered through other lands.

Nationalism is common to the people of every land. It was specially developed among the Jews by the exclusive possession of the divine Law revealed to Moses. The maintenance of nationality for the Jew was a religious duty in the fullest sense of the word as well as a human sentiment. Were Israel to pass away, as other nations once greater in power had done, the religious Jews felt that the Lord's work, not man's alone, would be destroyed. But growth and decay are the common lot of nations as of men. Race sympathy, language, country, and common laws are the bonds which maintain the duration of human societies, and each is subject to change with the course of time until the society itself is dissolved and others take its place with new forms.

Under the dominion of the Roman Empire it was evident that the Jewish people could not continue to maintain itself long in its hereditary land. It could not endure the oppression of the Roman tax-gatherer and the Roman soldier. The Roman Government, after the repeated rebellions of the Hebrews, was desirous to scatter them through its dominions, and events helped this political purpose. The keen intelligence of the race made them traders rather than cultivators, and trade naturally led to travel and settlement abroad. Strong as was the race patriotism of the people it had failed to keep up a distinct nationality in the large section of the Jews that had been carried to distant lands by the Assyrian conqueror. The ten tribes were lost forever to national existence when torn from the promised land. That a similar fate did not fall upon Judah seems due largely to the work of Hillel and his descendant, Judah, the Prince.

The work of the latter was to make rabbinic literature a handmaid and protector to the Hebrew Law. The divine Law had been a written one, but the interpretations and deductions which had sprung from it during the course of centuries were only preserved by tradition. Custom had so ruled rigidly. Masters of the Law and Judges in Israel were carefully trained from generation to generation, but it was by the spoken not the written word. The "sayings" of the wise as well as the decisions of the Judges were handed down in the schools of Palestine, and whoever wished to become learned in the law, had to go to Palestine and spend long years there for that end. This is exemplified in the cases of Ben Hyrkanos, Akibah, and Hillel. Those who could not give the time for this exclusive application were forced to remain among the "ignorant," who might, indeed, attain salvation by obedience, but who were regarded as morally and intellectually the inferiors of the Rabbis and students. When the Prince reduced to writing the whole mass of traditional lore, it became possible for the Jewish dweller of any land to acquire the wisdom of his fathers and train his mind in its study. A Jew needed no longer to journey to Palestine to become a scholar or a master in Israel. Thus, in fact, the religious thought first developed in the Holy Land has been kept unchanged through eighteen centuries in every quarter of the globe where Jews dwell.

Three men were specially prominent in the modifications of the Jewish people and customs while they yet dwelt in Palestine: Hillel gave them a cosmopolitan character as opposed to the old tribal one; Akibah, by the failure of his great rebellion, caused the abandonment among his people of the dream of a military supremacy which had almost become part of their creed; Rabbi Judah, the Prince, by the formation of rabbinic literature, gave the race a centre of union which had been strong enough to perpetuate their nationality through centuries of subjection and dispersion. I have tried to show the modern reader what manner of men these Masters in Israel and their fellows were in these sketches.

I cannot refrain from expressing my deep sense of obligation to Miss Henrietta Szold, of Baltimore, whose lucid criticism of another work of mine suggested the writing of this book, and to my friend, Mr. Beyant J. Clinch, of San Francisco, California, who greatly aided me with valuable suggestions and a revision of the manuscript.

ADOLPHE DANZIGER.

JEWISH FORERUNNERS OF CHRISTIANITY

CHAPTER I

HILLEL, THE FORERUNNER OF CHRIST

A BRIEF description of the life and politics of the Jewish people during the last period of its existence as a distinct nation in Palestine is needed for the proper comprehension of the lives of its prominent men.

That period extended from the time when the Persian king, Cyrus, five centuries before Christ, sent back the captives of Babylon to Palestine, down to the middle of the third century after Christ.

The people that returned to the Holy Land after the seventy years' captivity, numbered only a few, probably one or two hundred thousand. They grew in numbers and wealth rapidly, and when the Roman conquerors made them part of their Empire, the Jewish population numbered two or three millions.

When the captives returned the old kingdom of David was not restored. As in the old days before Saul, the people had no ruler but the Law of Moses and its authorized religious interpreters. The Rabbis or teachers of the Law were also the Judges of civil affairs, and practically the rulers of the community.

The priesthood attached to the service of the Temple at Jerusalem had high dignity but no political power. The whole polity of the Jewish people had been formed by Moses on a strictly religious basis, but the priesthood employed in sacrifices and ceremonial was not the guardian of religious doctrines nor the judge in them. These functions were filled by the Rabbis, who were also a clergy, in modern language.

Each generation of Rabbis taught, by word of mouth, the Law to the people and also trained up disciples to fill their own ranks. The intellectual activity of the race was concentrated on the study of the Law, as that of Mediæval Europe was on the study of theology and scholastic philosophy. "Rabbi" and "scholar" were synonymous, as "clerk" (cleric) and "learned man" were in Europe six centuries ago.

Each distinguished Rabbi gathered disciples in proportion to his reputation for learning, and when he deemed any of them thoroughly skilled in the Law, he ordained him Rabbi and gave him the right to teach and preach in the synagogues.

The ruling body of the nation, the Sanhedrin, was a council of the leading Rabbis, who judged the people according to the Law of Moses, both as written in the Scripture and as handed down by tradition of the schools. The Sanhedrin chose its own members and elected its President and Chief Judge, who was of nearly equal authority.

In all important cases the majority vote of the Sanhedrin was the supreme power among the Jewish people, both for making, or rather declaring, laws and pronouncing on their application. The Sanhedrin was practically legislature and Supreme Court. For the enforcement of its decisions it depended on the action of the people. This state of affairs continued, with some slight changes, down to the dominion of the Greek successors of Alexander in Syria. The Antiochid kings tried to Hellenize their Jewish subjects in both religion and language. They intruded High Priests into the Temple for bribes and forbade the practice of the Jewish religion. The revolt of the Makkabees followed, and finally John Hyrkan, the High Priest of the Asmonean family, took the title of King of the Jews, and made Palestine a sovereign state.

Intercourse with the Greek heathens of Syria had lessened the hold of the Jewish faith among the Hebrews. A school, or sect, arose, under the name of Sadducees, which rejected the traditional law accepted by the Jewish people from immemorial time and claimed that the text of the Pentateuch alone, as interpreted by themselves, embodied the whole Law. This teaching was acceptable to Hyrkan, who desired to lessen the influence of the Sanhedrin, then practically the Parliament of the nation, and he became a Sadducee. He persecuted the traditionalist members of the Sanhedrin, in whose stead he put Sadducees, and as he was also High Priest, his office became supreme in every part of religion. The successors of John Hyrkan pursued the same policy toward the Pharisee Rabbis, and when the Asmonean dynasty was succeeded by the Idumæan Herod, the Sanhedrin had lost its power as a political factor altogether, though even Herod leaned more toward the Sadducees than the Pharisees, whom he persecuted bitterly. The priestly office was separated from the kingly, but the High Priests continued to hold Sadducean doctrines. Thus, by a singular combination, the men who to strangers were the heads of religion were heretics to the orthodox Jews themselves.

The Rabbis continued to hold their influence, and were accepted by the bulk of the people as their religious teachers in spite of kingly persecution. A number of the Rabbis, however, especially the writers or *Sopherim* (the scribes of the New Testament) consented to serve the Sadducean kings and priests in the administration of the Law. They were regarded as intermediate between the Sadducees and Pharisees. By their influence among this class, the High Priests succeeded in controlling the Sanhedrin for a considerable period. Their policy was to concentrate the minds of the people on the Temple at Jerusalem as the very centre of religion. By this they increased their own revenues and importance. This special importance of the Temple tended to another result. It intensified the local nationalism and tended to make the people forget the wider brotherhood of man in the local ceremonialism of the Jewish Temple service. Thus Sadducean principles tended to make the Jewish people a mere tribe, which could have no national existence outside of Palestine, the Holy Land.

The orthodox or Pharisee teachers, many of them drawn from Jews born in other lands, taught the broad principles of the Mosaic Law, and lessened the importance of both the Temple and the Holy Land as elements in the religious life of the people. The High Priests of the Temple represented the narrow localism of Palestine and had a contempt for abstract dogma. The Presidents of the Sanhedrin, or Patriarchs, were the heads of the masters teaching Jews of every land. The High Priests perished with the destruction of the Temple by Titus. The Patriarchs of the Sanhedrin continued to exist as recognized religious heads of the Jewish people down to the last Emperor of the Roman world, Theodosius. The man who first made this office hereditary and defined its powers clearly against priestly usurpation was Hillel.

Hillel was born in Babylon among the Jewish colony which had remained there when the "remnant of Israel" was restored to its native land by Cyrus. The Babylonian Jews counted many of the noblest in blood of the race, and Hillel's parents, though poor, traced descent from David.[1] He was advanced in life, forty years old, when he left Babylon to study deeply the Law in the famous schools of Jerusalem, which drew students from many lands to learn. Herod then ruled in Palestine as a subject-king of Rome. The persecution to which the Pharisee Rabbis had been subjected had ceased for a while, and the more famous Rabbis taught in peace, even if the Sadducean High Priests controlled by force or bribery the decisions of the national Assembly. Two famous masters, Shemaiah and Abtalion, were recognized by the faithful in Israel as the wisest amongst the traditional teachers, and to their school Hillel came to learn the precepts of the Law.

He was poor when he came. He had a rich brother in Jerusalem, but he declined his aid when proffered,[2] and preferred to support himself and pay the small admission fee required at the school by daily labor. He fully accepted the rabbinical maxim, "it is better to live by flaying abandoned carcases than by beggary." He went out daily to gather firewood in the forest near, which he sold in the market. The fee for entrance to the school was half a copper shekel. Hillel regulated his labor so that when a shekel was earned for each day, he gave the rest of his time to the studies of the school. The other half defrayed his scanty food.[3] At times he went two or three days without any in his thirst for knowledge.

His example was not a solitary one among the Jewish students of his time. Many of the most eminent Rabbis earned their bread as artisans while giving their energies to the study or teaching of the Law. The Priests of the Temple were rich and honored. The teachers of the Law often had to struggle for the necessaries of life.[4] Honest poverty was no reproach among their class.

It is told of Hillel that one day, when the President of the college was to deliver an important lecture, he lacked the half-shekel to pay the doorkeeper. He mounted the flat roof of the building and listened at a window which looked into the hall below. It was evening and bitterly cold, but the student forgot everything in listening to the words of wisdom which flowed from the great Rabbi's lips. He grew cold and was unable to move when the lecture ended. He fell asleep at last and snow came on, which covered his body with a mantle of white. On the next morning, which was the Sabbath, the students gathered early to hear the morning sermon. They saw the window darkened by the lifeless body, and they carried it into the room. They tried to revive Hillel, but there was no fire, and the Law forbade kindling one on the Sabbath Day. The question whether it was lawful to break it in such a case was keenly debated, but the Masters settled it by declaring the rule, "This man deserves that the Sabbath law be suspended in his behalf."[5] When he recovered and told his story they commanded that thenceforth he should pay no entrance fee.[6]

Independence and perseverance were shown by this conduct, and to these Hillel added a keen and lofty intellect. He profited above all the other students by the lessons of his Masters and after some years he received the rabbinical degree. He then returned to his native land, where he was received with honors by the old Jewish population, and thère he passed some years teaching.

He felt drawn back to Jerusalem by the love of intercourse with the learned and perhaps, also, with a secret ambition of becoming a leader of the people. If so, it was gratified beyond his hopes.[7] The Sanhedrin had been filled with incompetent men after the death of Shemaiah and Abtalion. They were recognized by the people as faithful guardians of the oral law, but when they were gone none was found who could command the same confidence or even remember the text of their decisions, which were the undoubted law of Israel to all believers. Two Rabbis, the Sons of Bethyrah, of high family but little learning, held the offices of President and Supreme Judge, but they were unable through ignorance to decide many of the questions put to them. Hillel gained admission to the Sanhedrin and gradually won respect by his profound and accurate knowledge of the points of the oral law. At length a crisis came. A point of religious observance had to be settled which, small as it appears in modern eyes, was of vital importance to religious Jews. The First Day of the Passover in a certain year fell immediately after a Sabbath, and the question was how to reconcile the laws, one of which commanded the slaying of the Paschal lamb before Passover, and the other that forbade any slaying on the Sabbath. The party spirit between Sadducees and Pharisees, the sticklers for the letter of the Pentateuch as the only law, and the teachers who maintained the value and necessity of tradition, gave the question an importance that may seem incomprehensible to modern minds. It was not so to the Jewish people. They regarded any violation of the Law as among the worst evils that can befall man, and here was a point in which either of two necessary courses seemed to involve such a violation. The people murmured against the ignorance of the Council and asked,

"Are there, then, no Judges in Israel to tell us what is the law so that we may not sin?"

The Sadducee Rabbis of the High Priest's faction were confounded. They had claimed that the Scripture alone was the sole guide for the law, and here the Scripture required two courses to be followed, each of which violated the other. The Pharisees proclaimed tradition as the guide, but none knew the traditional law on this point. Hillel did. He rose and declared the law required that the Passover observance take precedence over the Sabbath Day. At first he was scoffed at as a foreigner,[8] but the scoffers ceased when he quoted the exact decision on this case of his former teachers, Shemaiah and Abtalion. Their authority was recognized by all, and the question was settled to the delight both of the Pharisees and the whole people. Even the Sons of Bethyrah, wearied, perhaps, of the difficulties of their position, voluntarily laid down their office, and the Babylonian Hillel was chosen President of the Sanhedrin "to restore peace in Israel," as the Talmud says.[9]

His election was a triumph for the Pharisees, who had long been overborne by their opponents, backed by the wealth and power of the Saducean High Priests. It was also a triumph for the element among the nation which opposed the narrow-spirited nationalism of Palestine. Hillel was not even born in Palestine. His teachers, whose authority had saved the reputation of the Assembly among the people, were not even of Jewish race, but of the "Proselytes of Righteousness" from the Gentiles.

The election of Hillel was, then, a victory not only over the Sadducees, but over the whole spirit of narrow tribalism which would confine privileges to the natives of Palestine.

Hillel himself recognized this fact, and his quick intelligence and patient tact enabled him to use the power thus placed in his hand to the fullest degree in exalting the dignity of the Presidential office. The court party in the Assembly had been forced to agree in Hillel's election. They tried to offset the power of this foreigner by giving him a colleague who represented Palestine nationalism of the narrowest kind. They chose for Chief Judge, the second officer of the Sanhedrin, a Rabbi named Shammai, famous alike for his learning and his haughty temper. This man, who was attached by many ties to the Sadducean faction, it was hoped, might reduce the power of Hillel to naught in the Assembly.

The position of the latter was assailed by Shammai with the utmost bitterness, though under the regular rabbinical form. As Chief Judge he delighted in reversing decisions rendered by the President, and holding his sayings up to scorn. These assaults Hillel treated with a calmness which shamed even the partisans of his rival. He treated Shammai with scrupulous politeness and extended the same courtesy to his decisions. The curious saying recorded in the Talmud that both these rivals spoke the "words of the living God" sounds like an utterance of Hillel. His work was for something greater than wordy victories.

He evidently realized that the Jewish people

would not long remain in Palestine under existing conditions. Exile was its fate, and in Babylon Hillel had seen and studied how the law of Israel might be preserved intact even though the chosen people were scattered from the Holy Land. He made it his task to prepare the popular mind for the impending changes. As a means to this end he increased the dignity of the office with which he was clothed, so as to make it greater than even the High Priest's functions. He introduced the idea of Davidic descent as a proper qualification for the head of the Assembly of Israel. Hillel himself belonged to that family, and, besides increasing the popular veneration for the office, this new idea made the Presidency practically hereditary in the House of Hillel. As the High Priest was of the House of Aaron so the President of the Assembly, a descendant of the great king, was recognized as the *Nasi*, or Prince, in Israel.

Hillel had no ill-feeling against Rome; at least not in the same degree as the natives of Palestine. The Heathens had not affected him personally nor his family. Jerusalem and the Holy Land were to the Jews in Babylon little more than a memory, a religious sentiment, and re-awakened only when they made a pilgrimage to the land of their fathers. The Hebrews in Babylon were happier than those in the Holy Land. From a religious point, Hillel was satisfied; the Land of the Lord was indestructible, the faith as such was not affected by dynastic changes. He and his people had lived and prayed in Babylon with the same fervor to the same God, as those who lived in Jerusalem. If the Commonwealth was threatened in its religious life, it was wiser to conciliate than to oppose the enemy of the Lord. Love is a greater factor in securing the national and religious stability of a people than hate. God's chiefest law is love, and this the Jew could carry with him to the ends of the world. For this neither Temple nor Palestine was indispensable. What the Jew needed was a clearer understanding of the will of God. Imbued with these ideas, Hillel advocated kindlier feelings towards the Heathens. If the Jews would treat them with consideration they might remain undisturbed in their national existence. Thus thought and acted the foreigner Hillel. It was, therefore, quite natural that the Nationalist party, whose head was Shammai, opposed the conciliatory measures of the President. But in order to maintain this policy, Hillel needed a powerful party behind him, a party of wealth which must be favored to make it stable and responsive.

Here, then, was the contention of the Nationalists. They desired to foster sentimental patriotism among the masses, and they frowned upon the attempt to create a select party of aristocratic diplomatists in opposition to themselves, who held sway over the affairs of the nation for so long.

But the same determination which characterized Hillel's student life was now manifest in his life and work as President of the Assembly. Paving the way for the future, he instructed his disciples how to act in coming events. He put it to them clearly and unmistakably. He taught them the lessons of universal love, unhindered by national

HILLEL, THE FORERUNNER OF CHRIST 13

sentiment, race, or creed. The burden of this mission he placed upon the shoulders of his favorite and famous disciple, Rabbi Yochanan ben Zakkai, whom he taught to look upon learning and the general education of the people as of higher worth than the Temple. This principle was expressed by Hillel's descendant, Judah the Prince, in emphatic terms two centuries later: "Disturb not the training of the young, not even for the sake of rebuilding the Temple," says he.[10]

If Hillel's policy was marked by acts which seemingly favored the rich man against the poor, it must be put to the policy rather than to his character, which was pure and above reproach. That, aided by those whom he thus favored, he became very wealthy must not be accounted a fault to reflect upon his honesty as President of the Sanhedrin. It must be borne in mind that the Presidency was naturally supported in magnificent style, and that Hillel, though personally very frugal, spent vast sums for the support of others and the laying of the foundation for the grandeur of his house, which should not fall, though the walls of the Temple and the city of Jerusalem crumbled to dust. His was not the life of Jesus of Nazareth, who came with a mission of salvation, the prerequisite to which was self-abnegation and a total reliance upon the Father for all things. And yet Hillel was laying the foundation on which the work of Jesus could more easily rise. Hillel was paving the way for a universal faith unhampered by petty national affairs. He was intensely human; had he been otherwise, had he employed other than the simplest and most natural means for his work, who knows how many centuries would have elapsed ere the civilizing influence of Judaism in the guise of Christianity could have made itself felt. None before Hillel ever attempted such a policy. He was the founder and originator—not of the universality of the faith, but of HOW TO MAKE THE FAITH UNIVERSAL.

Withal Hillel was not a reformer in a modern sense. He did not deviate a jot or tittle from the law. His acts stood in no contrast to the Mosaic Law, not even his "Prosbul Act," of which we shall speak farther on. What Hillel attempted was in the nature of a warning note of preparation for the future in case of calamity, so that, when driven from the land of their fathers, the learned men in Israel should carry along the indestructible seed of the sacred faith and plant it upon foreign soil. Dependent upon none but God, they should be ready to go whithersoever His finger pointed. Hillel wanted them prepared to teach and practise love, charity, humility, prudence, wisdom, and forbearance. That Shammai opposed Hillel's work speaks for the power thereof; yet it casts no discredit upon that zealous Nationalist to have had different, though less subtle, ideas.

In matters of doctrine Hillel was even stricter than his opponent Shammai, but when it came to the philosophy of life, to considerateness, to the spreading of Israel's pure religion among the masses, even amongst non-Hebrews; when it came to answering miscellaneous questions by mockers, scoffers, and

Heathens where the peculiar situation demanded skill, patience, and unruffled temper, so that the faith and its adherents might stand glorified before the world; when it came to teaching the principles of human love and forbearance by precept and practice, then Hillel towered above his antagonist as the lofty cedar above the gnarled oak. Then all the gifts of the sage, his amiability and divine patience came into play, and men praised his name and glorified his virtues.

Hillel's sayings show his lofty soul as much as his policy, and the stories in the Talmud, legendary as they may be, always tend to emphasize the latter.

"Be thou of the disciples of Aaron, who loved peace and pursued peace; so that thou love mankind, and allure them to the study of the Law." [11]

That which makes the character of Hillel so admirable to the student of the Talmud is the almost total absence of the miraculous in his work. It seems that the Talmudic fabulists felt that they dared not obscure his splendid personality by petty fantastic stories. Did they understand his policy? Is this a tacit rebuke to Hillel's application of natural means to further a sublime end? There is ground for both suppositions. But thanks be to them, whatever their intention, for the clear-cut pictures they give of his character and manner of acting. These pictures also put into strong relief the nature of Shammai and the policy he pursued.

Once a Heathen, says the Talmud, came to Shammai and said:

"Rabbi, I desire to become a Jew; but I care

nothing for the elucidations of the Rabbis and the ordinances of the Synagogue; I care but for the written Law of Moses, and to it will I adhere."

"Wouldst thou, a Heathen, despise the wisdom of the Rabbis? Go hence, I will have none of thee!" said Shammai angrily.

The Heathen went to Hillel and repeated his request. The Rabbi looked at the stranger quizzically.

"Dost thou know aught of Hebrew?" he asked.

"Nothing whatever," the man replied.

There was a fleeting smile on Hillel's face as he bade the man be seated.

"I will teach thee the Aleph-Beth of the Hebrew language," he said.

It was a simple lesson, merely the reading of the Hebrew alphabet, at which Hillel explained that, unlike the Greek and Latin, the Hebrew language was always read from right to left. The lesson being over, the man went away very much impressed, and on the day following came for another lesson, which Hillel started by reading the alphabet from left to right.

The Heathen was puzzled.

"Rabbi," said he, "thou didst say yesterday that Hebrew is read from right to left."

"Then thou art willing to accept the oral explanation I gave yesterday about the written word as authentic for to-day, and any explanation I should give thee to-day thou wouldst again accept with the same faith for to-morrow? Why? Because thou believest in my ability to teach thee the hidden meaning of words and phrases. Why, then, shouldst thou reject the elucidations and ordinances of the Rabbis, who do no more than I do in thy case, namely, the explanation of the written word, and its proper rendition?" the sage replied.

The Heathen saw the wisdom and justice of Hillel's words and reverently begged for admission into the congregation of Israel, promising to adhere to the written and the oral laws of the Hebrews.[12]

Hillel has some pointed utterances against those who boasted of the position they held by virtue of their names as priests or any other official dignity. Also against those who, having acquired some knowledge, made it a means for sordid ends. "If the Temple is destroyed, where will be your official dignity? If you are despoiled of your ill-gotten wealth, what good will your sham knowledge do you?" To quote his own words:

"Whosoever aggrandizes his name destroys it; and he who fails to increase his knowledge of the Law shall be cut off; and he who does not study the Law is deserving of death; and he who serves himself with the crown of the Law, will be consumed."[13]

In Hillel's day the pomp of the Temple, the high-priestly office, and the wealth and influence of the Jewish aristocracy appeared alluring to some ambitious Heathens, who not infrequently sought Judaism with these ends in view. Shammai, who hated the foreign element in general and the Heathen element in particular, frightened away such applicants with telling harshness. He did not want *Crethi* and *Plethi* in the congregation of Israel. The Jews never had any use for this class of people; they were always a hindrance rather than a help to the development of the national idea. Moses would not give them equality with the Israelites, and accorded them the position of slaves: hewers of wood and carriers of water; and even then they caused great trouble. Such was the position taken by Shammai.

Hillel thought differently. The Heathens' ambition, he argued, was not only natural, but it was encouraged by the boastful Jews themselves. But instead of treating such applicants harshly and making enemies of them, he said, treat them wisely; show them the way to salvation; make them meek and humble; let them see the real beauties of the faith and they will embrace it for its own sake. In this manner you will not only serve the faith in the present, but you may secure for it incalculable benefits for the future.

This thought is clearly illustrated by the following story:

Once, says the Talmud, a Heathen came to the house of Shammai, and said to him:

"Rabbi, I desire to become a Jew on condition that thou make me a High Priest."

Shammai grew very wroth at such a demand, and, threatening the man with his long staff, he cried:

"Away, thou barbarian, lest I chastise thee as thine impudence deserves! An infidel cannot become a High Priest, nor can he come nigh unto the Holy Place."

However, the Heathen's ambition was not so easily thwarted; he went to Hillel, and proffered the same demand.

"Thy desire is not extraordinary, my son," said the sage; "but art thou sincere?"

"I am," said the Heathen.

Hillel's features seemed to change; he became awfully earnest.

"Canst thou approach the Lord God of Israel with proper reverence?" he asked.

"I can," the man replied, somewhat subdued.

"Ah, but knowest thou the law which surrounds the exalted position to which thou aspirest?" Hillel asked with increased solemnity.

"I know it not, oh, Rabbi," the man replied.

"Knowest not the Law?" Hillel cried in evident surprise; "my son, the position of a High Priest is more exalted than that of a king, and even a king must know the laws of his land; how much more then is it incumbent upon the High Priest who stands before the awful sanctuary of the Lord, to know the laws governing the approaches to the sanctuary! Now, my son, listen. This is one of the laws: 'And the stranger who cometh nigh (unto the altar of the Lord) shall die.' " "

The Heathen turned pale.

"To whom doth this refer?" he asked, tremblingly.

"Aye, to whom doth it not refer? Even David, the king, had he lived and dared to go near the altar to serve the offering, would have merited death," Hillel rejoined.

"Your laws are strict," said the Heathen, "but in them is pleasantness. My desire for the exalted position was wrong, but my wish to be of your faith is now keener than before; pray, Rabbi, admit me into the congregation of the Jews."

Thereupon Hillel readily accepted the applicant and put him under the care of his disciples for instruction and ultimate admission into the covenant of Abraham.[15]

Such marvellous wisdom could not fail to bring the Law and its adherents into great respect among the Heathens. But even greater was its effect upon the Hebrew people. The Babylonian who, without financial or political backing, but by mere merit, had become the head of the Sanhedrin, and titular prince, gave to them a higher conception of their own faith and national aspiration. With Hillel rose an appreciation of the laws and the possibility of being released from the burden of dead-letter worship. He also brought a clearer knowledge of tradition; for he had sat at the feet of the masters, Shemaiah and Abtalion, and his keen spirit had penetrated the greatest depths of their discourses; he lost no hint which their words implied. He treasured their teaching regarding the relation between the Law and the needs of human life. The words came to him as a light from heaven, "should one peril his life for the Law, the Law shall be turned to save his life." [16] Was not in this a hint for reform, a point whence to start a form of elucidation of the Law, which shall become, as he himself said, "alluring"? Certainly. None before him saw it so clearly, and none before him set to work so systematically to make the Law of Moses a responsive element, an active principle, and to define the regulations the ignorant application of which wrought unspeakable harm to the people.

Hillel did not care so much for great scholars as for good men. One who knew all the laws and kept none was infinitely more culpable than one who knew none at all. A man's salvation depended not upon his knowledge of every tittle of the law, but in the proper exercise thereof. Nor did he conceal his preference for the kernel to the shell, and when a Heathen, probably to test the Rabbi's patience, asked to be taught all the laws of the Hebrews while he would stand on one foot, the sage did not drive him away as Shammai did. He took that mocker by the hand and spoke to him gently.

"My son," said he, "to be a good Jew thou needest to know but one principle, and that I can teach thee in less time than thou requirest. That which is hateful unto thee, do not unto thy neighbor. This is the fundamental principle of the Mosaic religion: all the rest is mere commentary; go and live up to that." "

Wonderfully enlightened, the erstwhile scoffer became an adorer; he studied the lore and the laws of the Hebrews and became a convert.

In sooth the times and the conditions of society in Palestine were such that a powerful, equipoised factor was needed to stand between the stubborn adherents of the dead letter of the law, and those Hebrews who affected Roman manners and denied the Law altogether, and were even ashamed of being called Hebrews. To break down the barrier erected by stiff-necked zealots, and to bring back into the fold those stray sheep of Israel, whom folly and a contempt for the bigots had driven away, was another aim of Hillel's activity.

Among the first acts of his administration was his "Prosbul Act," which was designed to protect the money-lenders as well as the borrowers during the "Year of Release." For the man who held a mortgage on another man's property was forced to release it on the first day of the seventh year. If the mortgageor was a dishonest man, he simply refused payment, and the mortgagee lost his capital. Thus people resorted to all manner of fraud, in which they were virtually assisted by the law. The money lenders, to protect themselves, would either charge exorbitant rates of interest or refuse to lend money altogether. Ordinarily this would not have been such a great misfortune, but there were times when the people had to have money or feel the scourge of the tyrant. The first year after the accession to the throne of Herod, was a Year of Release; the people had been drained to the last drop by exorbitant taxes the preceding year, which had been followed by bad crops. The people then had neither food nor money to buy it. They took their last possessions and went to the money-lenders; but these refused to advance a single coin; they were afraid to lose their money at the coming Year of Release.

Hillel came to the assistance of both parties by means of the "Script," which was in the nature of a promissory note and which secured to the lender his money even after the Year of Release; for though the property reverted to the borrower, the lender could sue on the "Script" and collect his money by due process of law in judgment and execution.[18]

After the publication of this Act, the people heaved a sigh of relief, and though it favored the lender it gave a fair chance also to the borrower.

Another injurious law was that which provided that a man, having sold a house and desiring to buy it back, which he could do within a year, was forced to pay the original purchase price personally into the hand of the one in possession. But the latter, not desiring to give up the property, often hid himself on the last day and thus defeated the laws of equity.

Hillel made an act which provided that the original owner had the right to deposit the purchase money in a court of justice on the last day of the year within which the property was sold, whereupon he could take immediate possession.[19]

Another evil was found in the borrowing and lending of grain at seed-time. Poor crops frequently forced the people to borrow grain for food or seed, which the rich merchants readily gave; but prior to the expiration of the debt the lenders combined to raise the price of grain and demanded returns equivalent to the increased rates.

Hillel remedied this by providing that cereals shall be returned or paid for at the price it sold for on the day it was loaned.[20]

And so he went on instituting one reform after another; making every Mosaic Law luminous by the brilliancy of his matchless intellect. He was, in sooth, a second Ezra, and, like him, he reconstructed the Law of Moses, making it a moving force for all time."[21]

His knowledge was universal; embracing many languages and the sciences of botany, medicine, astronomy, mathematics, and geography. Speaking in the language of the Talmud: "There was no philosophy and no tongue which he had not learned; he knew the speech of the mountains, hills, valleys, trees, plants, and that of the domestic and wild animals."[22]

As was the man, so was his domestic life, happy to the fullest measure; for his wife was as lovable and tender-hearted as he. The thought of coming evil to the nation which, as we have indicated, mainly directed his policy, never extended to his own house; nor did it manifest itself in his home life. Both were fortified by walls of the purest faith and wisdom. He feared neither the present nor the future. The Talmud illustrates this beautifully and significantly. Hillel was on the way to his home, when a great noise suddenly reached his ear. "I am certain," said he, "that it is not in my house [that no misfortune has befallen me or mine]."[23] This pure optimism ruled all his words and acts, and no amount of personal inconvenience was ever great enough to disturb this wonderful equanimity.

One day a very distinguished man came to see him; Hillel asked his wife to prepare a dinner—probably commensurate with the dignity of the guest. Hour upon hour passed, still the dinner was not brought. Hillel showed not the least impatience; he kept his guest in good spirits by delightful conversation, and at length Hillel's wife appeared with the servants and the steaming food.

"We are late to-day," said Hillel smilingly.

"The food was ready long ere now," said she, "but a poor and hungry man came and asked for something to eat and I gave it to him, and that necessitated the preparation of other food."

"My dear," said Hillel, "thy good heart has prompted thee to do the right thing; for charity is one of the noblest virtues, and the Lord is more pleased with thy work than any other." [24]

His patience was proverbial. It was greater, finer, nobler than that of Job; for Hillel was not called upon to contend with fate, but with the follies of man. But, though tried beyond the ordinary endurance which characterizes wise men, he never lost his temper. This admirable quality is praised by Rabbis who rightly place Hillel above Shammai. "Let every man always be as meek as Hillel and not high-tempered like Shammai." [25] In illustration of Hillel's meekness the following story is given:

On a Friday, while Hillel was in his bath in honor of the Sabbath, a man called to see him. Hillel quickly dried himself, put on his mantle, and, going into the reception-room, asked the man what he desired.

"I have a question to ask," said the visitor.

"Ask, my son," rejoined Hillel.

"Why have the Babylonians round heads?"

"Thou hast asked an important question," said

Hillel, evidently unaffected by the irreverent insinuation. "Because the Babylonians lack skilful midwives."

The man went away without thanking him, and after an hour returned and roughly called for Hillel.

"What desirest thou?" the latter asked.

"I have a question," said the man.

"Ask it, my son," said Hillel.

"Why are the Tharmudians cross-eyed?"

"Thou hast asked an important question," said Hillel, "because they live in a sandy country."

The man went away as before, and after an hour's absence returned, crying: "Is Hillel there? Is Hillel there?"

"He is here," said Hillel pleasantly; "what desirest thou of him?"

"I have a question to ask."

"Ask, my son."

"Why have the Africans flat feet?"

"Thou hast asked an important question; because the Africans are obliged to pass through great swamps," was Hillel's reply.

"I have many more questions to ask," said the man tentatively.

"Ask them, my son," said Hillel.

"But I fear thou wilt become angry," the man remarked.

Hillel drew his mantle closer and sat down.

"Ask all the questions thou hast, my son; I will listen," he said.

"Art thou Hillel whom they call the Prince in Israel?" the man asked.

HILLEL, THE FORERUNNER OF CHRIST

"I am Hillel."

"Then may there be none more like thee in Israel!" the man cried.

"Wherefore this wish, my son?"

"Because I have this day lost four hundred gold pieces on thine account; I wagered that I could make thee angry," the man explained.

"My son, thou mightest lose many hundreds of gold pieces ere Hillel would give way to anger."[26]

He was scrupulous in matters of personal cleanliness, bathing daily, often several times during the day.

"If man taketh such care of statues which he washeth and cleanseth from dust, though these statues are but the images of mortals, how much more eagerly should a man attend to the cleanliness of his person, which was created in the image of the divine!" he often said.[27]

"Man should be clean so as not to offend his guest," he once said to his disciples.

"What guest?" they asked.

"The soul," the Master replied. "The soul is man's most cherished guest; within us to-day, it may be with God to-morrow, and think of it, my children, if the soul should say to God that it had lodged in an unclean dwelling."[28]

None surpassed him in humility; not even in the days of his rising fame, a period when students acquiring a certain degree of recognition are apt to be vain and presumptuous. Hillel was always meek and polite, ready to do a man service, no matter how trifling or how great. If a man needed a service to which he was used, but owing to reverses in his fortune was unable to procure, he would never go without it when Hillel happened to be near. He either hired the services of another, or, if he happened to be without ready money, would do it himself.

It was one of Hillel's principles to prevent humiliation of any person, particularly of impoverished nobles, who, he held, suffered more keenly than others when they had to appear in public and could not afford the means their former position so readily gave them. Such people were Hillel's particular care, and he humored their wants to the smallest degree. The Talmud contains a story in illustration of this feature in Hillel's character.

A certain impoverished noble who used to have a "crier" run in front of his carriage complained that he could now ill afford it. Hillel at once called a "crier," and engaged him for immediate service. Some days later Hillel saw the noble driving, but, alas, without a "crier." Hillel examined his then slender purse and found that he had not the price for a crier's service. Without a second thought, Hillel ran in front of the noble and performed the service of "crier."

Thus by the force of intellectuality and personal service Hillel gradually prepared the Jews, who stood at the threshold of indefinite exile, to bear the great burden which misfortune, deserved or otherwise, put upon them. He wanted them prepared to go into the world and act so that, though assimilated, they might yet retain the power to sway man by the living word.

"Be thou not dressed among the naked, nor among the dressed; sit not when others stand, stand not when others sit; weep not when others laugh, and laugh not when others weep; attempt no changes with the customs of those with whom you dwell."[29]

From this it will be seen that he was possessed of exquisite tact, and had he lived half a century later who knows but that this one amiable intellectual giant might have averted the great calamity which befell the Temple and the city of Jerusalem?

A great deal more might be written about the various disputes between Hillel and Shammai. This, however, would but repeat what we have already said, namely, that Hillel towered above the men of his time an immeasurable height, and that he was the actual founder of Judaism as it appeared after the destruction of the Temple, and that he was practically a new Moses unto the Jews. The former gave the Law, the latter made that law a vital force for all time. Hillel's life and work made the work of Jesus a possibility. Without Hillel the world would have been less receptive to the message of the lowly Nazarene.

Grateful to Hillel's memory and appreciative of his wonderful work, the Talmudists ascribe to his life a value as great as to that of Moses, and in the beautiful hyperbolic form of rabbinical expression, it is said that Hillel lived to the age of one hundred and twenty years. In reality, however, he lived but eighty years, and died about sixty years before the destruction of the Temple by Titus, and ten years before the birth of Jesus of Nazareth, having been president of the Sanhedrin for forty consecutive years."[30]

CHAPTER II

JESUS OF NAZARETH

IN writing of Jesus of Nazareth, I seem to myself to hear a voice such as came to Moses in the desert of old: "Take the shoe from off thy foot, for the place on which thou standest is holy ground." As Moses marvelled at the bush which burned and yet was not consumed, and approached to examine its nature, so I am drawn to examine the wondrous mystery of the life and death of Jesus to my fullest power of mind, and in deep reverence.

I propose to examine the position occupied by Jesus in the history of the Jewish people, to tell the conditions which moulded his life work, and brought about his agony and death.

The sources from which I shall draw mainly in this task are the pages of the Talmud. This remarkable work enshrines the mental activity of the Jewish race during nearly a thousand years. Though embodied in literary form only in the second century after the birth of Christ, by the labors of Rabbi Juda the Prince, the material of the Talmud text was the common property of the Jewish people for centuries earlier.

The history and philosophy of successive generations were handed down by a rigorous system of oral tradition among the Rabbis, as the Koran in after years was handed down by the followers of Mohammed. The earliest traditions embodied in the work of Rabbi Juda the Prince date to at least the third century before Christ, and later writers continued to add to the text down to the ninth century after his birth.

It is rather an encyclopedia than what is styled a history in the common speech of our own day. Juda's object was to embody in writing the traditional law given to Moses as interpreted by later recognized teachers of Judaism. The circumstances under which these decisions were given, as well as the decisions, are related in the customary style of Eastern nations.

The narratives of the Talmud have some resemblance to the legends of the Christian mediæval saints, but they contain a wealth of facts relating to the Jewish people which can be learned from no other source. The difference of language, from pure Hebrew to the patois of Syria and Babylon, in which the Talmud is written, makes its study a task only for scholars, but a task which well repays the labor imposed.

From this record of purely Jewish life and thought, handed down to us like a testament of bygone ages, I seek to gather what it tells of that life, so full of human charm and sweetness, of the individual whose sublime principles might have united all men, Jew and Gentile alike, under the banner of his Messiahship, had it not been for the errors and crimes of those who mistook his word and work and mission, and even in his name were guilty of deeds at which humanity revolts.

I desire to place clearly before the men of our day the community of spiritual thought which, beginning with Hillel, runs through, and is consecrated by, the life and death agony of the Man of Suffering of Galilee. In the sequence of time Jesus follows Hillel, and Hillel's teachings had prepared Hebrew hearts for the gentle message of Him who followed. That many were so prepared, outside history shows. That many of the leading Rabbis, the masters in Israel, knew and approved its doctrine, is attested by the Talmud itself. The name of Jesus of Nazareth and of many of his chief disciples find frequent mention in its pages.[1] His life and work and death are as clearly attested there as is the work of Hillel or his successors in the Patriarchate. Looking exclusively to Jewish historical authority, there can be no more doubt regarding the actual existence of the one than of the other.

"Let none be as Josua ben Perachiah, who repulsed Jesus of Nazareth (Jeshu ha-Notzri) with both hands," is an injunction contained in the Talmud.[2]

The day of his death, the manner of its accomplishment,[3] his age at the time, and the name of the Roman governor, Pontius Pilate (Pinehas Listai), who sanctioned his execution, are also told there.[4]

If Jesus is frequently referred to by other names, as Otho ha-Ish (that man), or Peloni (a certain one), it may easily be understood. After the death of

Jesus his name became a stumbling-block of contention between different portions of the Jewish people. While some used it to heal the sick and give authority to the divine law of love for man,[5] others coupled it with malediction. The bitterness of these dissensions was intense. The followers of Christ were branded by some Jews with the opprobrious name of heretics (Minim), while other Jews, and those often the most learned, echoed the sentiment.[6]

Whether regarded with love or hate, the personality of Jesus fills a large place in the Jewish world of Palestine. It occupied the thoughts and the discussions of the Rabbis to whom everything was centred, at the time, in the affairs of the Holy Land.

The descent of Jesus from David, as set forth in the New Testament, is not disputed in the Talmud, though it must have been publicly proclaimed at the time. It is hardly credible that the hostile High Priest and the Roman governor should have laid such stress on his claims to kingship were not his descent from David an unquestioned fact. Pilate gave the title "King of the Jews" in his sentence in a spirit of no hostility to the victim over whose cross it was written. He even used it as a means of exciting popular sympathy in his behalf, according to the New Testament narrative, and the enemies who sought and compassed his death made no attempt to deny His origin. The Prince of Judaism and the Prince of the Christian world are of one blood, the race of David; and the faith and hopes of mankind, whether Jewish or Christian, spring from a common fountain.

There are many among my people who decline to regard the narrative of the New Testament as worthy attention on their part. At the same time their regard for the Old Testament is not lessened because they accept many things in it in an allegorical or figurative sense. I would ask such why it is not more reasonable to test the statements contained in the New Testament by historical standards. That work has been received as authentic history by the largest part of civilized men during many centuries. Granted even that we as Jews reject certain points cardinal with the Christian faith, it cannot be denied that Christianity is a historical fact, and its existence to-day is directly traceable to Jewish origin through the New Testament. Such a work cannot be ignored nor treated with contemptuous indifference by thoughtful men, be they Jews, Christians, or any other class, but least of all by the Jewish historian.

The first appearance of Christ in public, when, at twelve years of age, he presented himself among the learned doctors of the law in the Temple, was almost in the time of Hillel's life. Whether Hillel himself was one of those who marvelled at the intelligence displayed by a child cannot be told, but certainly the doctors then present were Hillel's followers. Hillel's authority was then supreme among the teachers of Judea. The noble picture of Raffaele is one which may command the fullest sympathy of Christian and Jew alike. The Temple stood in its glory in Jerusalem, and within its precincts the masters in Israel expounded the Law of Moses, which Jew and Christian alike hold in reverence. Hillel had taught it there forty years, and by his words in a great measure the religious thought of the people had been moulded to receive as they might the message which Christ came to offer. That message developed, but did not contradict, the teachings of the great Rabbi. Hillel had come from Babylon in his early days. The boy who appeared among the doctors had been an exile in Egypt from his infancy. Both were Jews even of the noblest blood of the ancient kings, but neither had any part in the narrow local spirit which would make Palestine the only Holy Land in God's world.

The High Priests and their partisans, the self-righteous Sadducees, cared little for either Hebrew learning or Hebrew religion. They rejected the traditional law absolutely, and cared not for the controversies of the learned Rabbis. In the very service of the Temple they were obliged to employ the Scribes or Rabbis, whom they stigmatized by the name of Pharisees, or aliens, but whose knowledge of the Hebrew language was indispensable in the Temple service. But if the Sadducees cared little for Hebrew religion, they were filled with a bitter zeal for the nationality of their land. They were the local aristocracy of Palestine, recognized as such by the Roman governors, and they jealously guarded their official position, while despising the belief of the majority of their nation.

Hillel's teaching was in direct opposition to the bigoted nationalism of the Sadducean High Priests.

They held the Temple as the centre of the law itself: he regarded it as merely an adjunct. "You are lost," he said to them, "if you are separated from the material Temple, but we carry a Temple in our hearts in which the Lord can be served always and everywhere."[7] "A place is only holy if its dwellers make it holy."[8] So close is the analogy between the moral teachings of Hillel and his school with those of Christ, that some of our Jewish writers have asserted that all the sayings recorded in the New Testament may be found in the Talmud. The statement is partially true, but then many of the doctrines so set forth were uttered by Rabbis like Eliezer ben Hyrkanos many years after the death of Christ.

Christ's appearance amid the doctors of the Temple was but momentary. He buried himself in an obscure village for eighteen years afterwards. John the Baptist and others, zealous for the Law, had gone into the desert to live solitary lives of peace and prayer, away from the corruption which reigned even in the Sanctuary of the Most High. They foresaw coming changes in the state of the people of Israel, and the advent of One who would give Judea and the world something greater than a revived empire of David, but a something which the masses of the people could hardly conceive in their narrow range of thought.

The days indeed were evil for the mass of the Jewish people when John came from his desert to raise the minds of men with the hope of a mighty change. Morals had greatly deteriorated during the wars of the two previous centuries. The Talmud gives a proof of this when it records how Ben Zakkai decreed the abolition of the ordeal prescribed in the Mosaic Code in cases of suspected marital infidelity. It says that the change of manners was so great that what had been a protection for innocence was made an engine for its oppression.[9]

Though the populace still gloried in their nationality, and looked forward to indefinite future grandeur for it, the simple faith of a former age had been weakened by the influence of foreign laws and literature. Mention has been made of the Sadducees, a party among the Jews, who sprang into existence under the dominion of the Greek monarchs of Syria, and who proclaimed a new doctrine. They rejected the whole traditional law which had hitherto been accepted unquestioningly as of equal authority with the Scriptures. Their position, doctrinally, was somewhat similar to the Puritans of England. Their innovations in the Jewish religion had indeed an analogy with the Protestant Reformation in Europe afterwards. The Sadducee teachers taught that the Bible alone was the source of all religious truth, and they even rejected belief in a future life because they could not find such expressly set forth in the written word. Their theory found favor with the native Jewish kings, who established an independent kingdom in Palestine during the second century before Christ. These rulers were of the priestly race, and they united in themselves the offices of king and High Priest of the Temple. In the original organization of the Jewish people, law and religion were alike of divine origin, but the priests were entirely distinct from the teachers of the law. The priests were devoted to the service of the Temple exclusively, the law was interpreted and decided by the Rabbis, or masters, who were chosen from all classes on the test of learning alone. It was natural that the kings should seek to lessen the influence of the powerful body of the Rabbis, and the Sadducean doctrine was decidedly favorable to such a result. The Rabbis were branded as Pharisees, or aliens, as a term of reproach. It signified that their place in the nation was less intimately connected with Palestinian nationality than that represented by the hereditary priests, who all descended from Aaron.

Though the office of High Priest was again separated from temporal rule on the extinction of the Asmonean dynasty, it continued to be a high dignity in itself. When the Roman rule was established, the foreign governors treated the High Priest as the head of the Jewish religion, and left him free to deal with his own people in religious affairs. Ishmael Phabi purchased the office from the Roman governor, Gratus, some years before the preaching of Christ. He was not even of the family of Aaron, and was a Sadducee in profession, while the people at large still held the old traditional law, but Roman policy treated such points with scornful indifference. Eight High Priests of Phabi's family retained the priesthood and the profitable guardianship of the Temple of Jerusalem through Roman favor. By it, too, they controlled the Sanhedrin, or Assembly of the Rabbis, which was at once the supreme court and the legislature of the nation in both religion and morals. The Rabbis, scattered through the country, still retained their influence among the people as teachers of the Jewish faith. The members of the Sanhedrin shaped the law to suit the will of the Saducean High Priests. The main object of the latter was to increase their own revenues, and for that purpose they multiplied minute religious observances, and made the breach of them punishable with heavy fines. These fines were part of the revenue of the Temple, and the High Priests drove, besides, a profitable trade in selling the various animals and other articles specified as fines or required for legal sacrifice offerings generally. The demoralizing effect of this traffic in sacred things was deeply felt by the religious part of the people, and its oppressive nature made the office of High Priest odious to the mass of the population, but the favor of the Roman governors maintained the unworthy priests in their purchased power.

The Talmud tells how, shortly before the revolt against Rome which ended in the destruction of Jerusalem, a patriotic member of the Sanhedrin caused a reduction of the prices of the sacrificial cattle and doves as a relief to the people. Subsequently the populace rose in arms, destroyed the bazars of Annas on Mount Olivet, killed the High Priest, and cast his body to the dogs.[10] This illustrates the feelings with which the Saducean Priests were regarded by the people at large in the time of Christ. Their creed and their conduct were alike repugnant to the religious sentiment of the nation.

Of the Pharisees who, for diplomatic reasons, were

employed to do clerical service in the Temple, many were scarcely more esteemed than the High Priest. A large number of others, while affecting unbounded zeal for religion, were grossly corrupt in their lives. The contrast between their preaching and their practice was a public scandal, which finds expression in the Talmud scarcely less strongly than in the Gospel narrative. A remarkable passage in the former enumerates seven classes of Pharisees according to the various manners affected by each, and five of those classes are held up as unworthy of respect. The term *Tzevoim*, "dyed Pharisees," was a common term for hypocrite among the Jews. "You need not fear the Pharisees, who are really such," was the last advice of King Yannai to his wife, "but fear the dyed Pharisees, who do the works of Zimri and seek the reward of Pinehas." [11] The testimony of this king is notable, because of his intense hatred of the Pharisees. In the civil war, and after the capture of their fortress Bethome, about 80 B.C., he caused no less than eight hundred Pharisees and their partisans to be crucified. A deep horror of this form of punishment was left on the minds of all Pharisees for over a century.[12]

It should be remembered that, though Pharisee and Sadducee are names given to two opposite doctrines, they are only applied to the teachers of those doctrines, not to the body of the laity, who accepted either. The common people of Palestine held to the law as given them by the Pharisee Rabbis. They recognized the authority of the Sanhedrin and its president as supreme in matters of

religion, but they are never called Pharisees.
term, both in the Talmud and the Gospels, is ⸤
fined exclusively to the teachers of the law and ⸥
students, from whose ranks these teachers were
recruited.

Such was the religious condition of the Jews of
Palestine when John the Baptist came from his
desert retreat to stir its people to higher spiritual
life. He was looked on as an Essene, a class of men
who devoted themselves to austerity of life and
works of mercy to others. The Jewish people then
as now in many lands recognized the existence of
supernatural powers in individuals, and associated
their possession closely with a stricter rule of life.
John's preaching was received with enthusiasm by
the people at large, and even by many of the Pharisees, who saw nothing opposed to their own belief
in his action. For the Jews always hoped for the
coming of a Messiah, and at no time more fervently
than at the announcement of John. When Christ
presented himself to him for baptism, John recognized him as the Chosen of the Lord, and proclaimed his own inferiority to him at the same time.
There was nothing repugnant to Jewish teaching in
John's proclamation. The idea of a Messiah, a
definite individual, who was to come in the fulness
of time to bring some great beneficial change in the
condition of mankind, was familiar to all Jews. The
prophets promised it; the Rabbis continually taught
it; the Sadducees scoffed at it, but it had gone into
the flesh and bone of the Jewish people, and they
accepted it without any reservation as to its veracity.

Opinions differed about the personality of the Messiah. Some held that the Messiah eternally existed with God, that is, was an emanation of God Himself, and united with the Holy Ghost; that His name, as well as the Law itself, was among the first emanations of God,[13] that is, in the sense of the Logos of the New Testament.

Others held different theories about the person to be expected, but some person was keenly looked for by all Jews to fulfil the glorious promises made by the prophets of God's glory in the Holy Land. When, a century and a quarter after Christ, the famous Rabbi Akibah actually proclaimed the soldier Bar Kochba the Messiah, few objected. The Talmud records but one objection. Yochanan ben Torta said to Akibah: "Sooner will grass grow out of thy chin than this one will be the Messiah."[14] But then this very opposition may have sprung from the faith that the Messiah had already come, that the One crucified was the real Redeemer. Bar Kochba's imposture was recognized after his defeat, and Juda the prince branded his name as *Bar Kozibah*, the son of lies, but Akibah is still regarded as a saint and martyr by the Jewish people.

There seems no evidence that Christ, when he began his mission, made public announcement of any claim to the Messiahship. Even if he had, it would not have been necessarily regarded as an offence against the Law of Moses. He went among the people as a teacher of the Law, and as such he was received into the synagogues of the Rabbis, who saw nothing offensive to their ideas in his mission. He declared he had not come to destroy, but to fulfil the Law of Moses. He bade the people follow the teaching of the Pharisees, as they held the chair of Moses, the inspired lawgiver, while at the same time he cautioned them against the practices in actual life of the same teachers. The questions addressed to him by the Pharisees were, at least in part, addressed to obtain elucidation of the true meaning of the Law. At times they openly approved his answers, as when he declared the falsehood of the Sadducean doctrine that the dead rise not again. On other occasions, the silence with which his answers were received may fairly be interpreted into consent. He was asked to eat in the houses of distinguished Rabbis, and he accepted their invitations. Other Pharisees came to warn him of plots against his life. While individuals occasionally attempted violence or expressed opposition to his teachings, there seem no good grounds to think that the body of the Jewish people, or the larger part of the Rabbis, felt or showed any hostility to him on religious grounds.

Indeed, it is hard to see why they should. If the moral teachings recorded in the New Testament were placed in the mouth of one of the Rabbis canonized in the Talmud, they would seem perfectly conformable to the spirit of the Law of Moses. Christ did not deny the obligation on the Jews of his time of the ceremonial law. When his disciples were rebuked for violating the Sabbath by plucking ears of corn for food, he did not deny that such was forbidden under ordinary circumstances, but excused it on the ground of necessity. The teachers of highest repute in the Talmud used the same reasoning to justify any work on the Sabbath, if needed for the saving of life or even to prevent danger to life. His prohibition of divorce was in accord with the teachings of the Rabbis, "Let no man put away the wife of his youth unless for grievous sin." It is true that Hillel, the president of the Sanhedrin, had sanctioned a laxer application of the law, but there was nothing in the principle laid down by Christ on this subject opposed to the teachings of many orthodox Rabbis. It was, then, neither zeal for the Jewish religion nor opposition to the moral teachings of Christ that instigated the plot to take away his life. The people followed him with ever-growing enthusiasm, during his mission, but the High Priest and his faction saw in the popular movement a twofold danger to their own power and wealth. The revival of the religious spirit among the Jewish people would, they thought, naturally increase the dislike already existing against themselves as unbelievers and intruders into the priestly office. It might provoke popular outbursts, such as that which afterwards did in fact sweep away the second Annas. Another risk was that the popular effervescence over the new Teacher might excite the political jealousy of the Roman rulers in Palestine. Christ was from Galilee, and the Galilean peasantry of that day were a particularly independent and fearless section of the Hebrew people. Local outbreaks had occurred there more than once, and the rulers of the Temple feared that one of national extent might follow. They felt that in such a case the Temple and their own wealth would be involved in a common ruin with the people. To avert such a risk, the unworthy High Priest, Joseph Caiaphas, resolved to make away with the life of the Teacher whose words and deeds were so widely influencing the people.

To accomplish the destruction of Christ with safety to themselves, his enemies must recur either to Jewish or to Roman law. The crowds of followers that surrounded him precluded the possibility of private assassination. By the help of their dependents in the Sanhedrin the High Priest might secure a conviction in that body on some charge that might be capital under Jewish law, but the forms of that law required long delay in such cases, and Caiaphas dared not face the popular feeling that would surely be stirred up against himself by such an attempt. There was absolutely no accusation that could be brought against Christ, under the Law of Moses, of any important kind. It would be different if the Roman authorities could be induced to act. They were heedless of Jewish feeling and popularity if the interests of the empire were involved, but they, too, were wholly indifferent to Jewish religion or questions connected with it. The Sadducees tried, unsuccessfully, to involve Christ in a political charge by asking him whether it were lawful to pay tribute to the heathen cæsar. They were equally unfortunate in trying to interest the tetrarch of Galilee, Herod, in their cause. Finally Caiaphas determined to adopt a middle course to attain his end of destruction. It was to seize his victim suddenly, submit him to a trial before the priestly court, which might be represented to the heathen governor as the usual course of Jewish law, and then obtain from the latter a sentence of death, which it was thought might readily be granted in the case of an individual without wealth or powerful friends to plead his cause. An additional motive might be suggested if the danger of a popular sedition were urgently presented to Roman jealousy.

The plot was put into execution. The great Teacher was seized at night by armed servants of the High Priest, and a patrol of soldiers secured by his influence. No charge had been made against him previously, nor was he brought before the court of the Sanhedrin, the only body competent, under Jewish law, to try a charge involving the death penalty. Almost every rule of that law was, indeed, trampled on in the case of Jesus of Nazareth. It required that a capital charge should be heard in the daytime only, and that two days at least should be given to its investigation. It absolutely forbade the punishment by crucifixion.[16] It gave a culprit, even if convicted, the right of demanding a rehearing of his case during five days in succession. But four crimes were held worthy of death,—idolatry, murder, incest, and blasphemy,—and the last was clearly defined to be coupling the ineffable name of God with an imprecation. Finally, the lawful judge was the vice-president of the Sanhedrin, and the decision rested with him, with no one else, and, least of all, with the High Priest.

Whatever influence Caiaphas and his party may

have had in the Sanhedric Court, they did not venture to bring their destined victim before it. Jesus was dragged by the Temple retainers not to the Court, but to the private house of the High Priest. His captors, who had gone out to seize his person only under cover of night through fear of the people, surrounded the house to keep off any partisans or followers of the illustrious Captive. A gathering of the mercenary scribes of the Temple and of some "elders" proceeded to try him, with the High Priest as their president. No charge had been made to warrant the arrest, and now that Jesus has been seized, his enemies seek to find a colorable pretext for their action. False witnesses attempt in vain to bring forward some point of his teaching which might be twisted into an offence against the Jewish law, but in vain. Even before the High Priest's followers they could not weave any connected story of such.

Then Caiaphas himself rose and by questions sought to draw from Jesus some statement which might be turned into an accusation. Baffled by the reply that the teaching of Christ had been public, and could be learned from his hearers, the High Priest, with affected zeal for the law, which he outraged, asked: "Art thou the Christ, the son of the living God?" The same question had been already publicly asked him, and in answer he had pointed to the works he did. John the Baptist had been publicly asked a similar question three years before. It was no crime under Jewish law, that a man should proclaim himself the Messiah, whom all expected. Much less was it to speak of God as "the Father," and to oneself as the "son of God"; for that term was commonly applied to the whole people of Israel, and Jew and Christian alike address the Almighty as "Our Father."[16] It is uncertain, apparently, whether Jesus replied directly to the question by asserting his Messiahship, or only answered: "So you say,"[17] but neither would have been criminal in the eyes of the Pharisee Rabbis. Even less so would be the prophecy which accompanied the declaration: "Hereafter you shall see the Son of Man sitting on the right hand of the power of God, and coming in the clouds of heaven."

That God had spoken and would continue to speak through the mouths of inspired men, or Prophets, was then, as now, a fixed belief of all who held to the Mosaic Law. A prophecy might be true or it might be an imposition, but its utterance in the name of God Himself was no crime. To assert that would be to stamp the most venerated names in Scripture, Isaiah and Jeremiah and David, as criminals. It was, however, enough for the Sadducee who filled unworthily the seat of Aaron. He tore his robes and proclaimed a blasphemy. His servile partisans echoed the cry and declared the so-called crime worthy of death.

They could only, with safety to themselves, vent their hate in words and blows. The Roman governor held strictly in his own hands the right of capital punishment among the subject race. Accompanied by the gang of his followers, the High Priest goes to the pretorium, the Roman Justice Hall, and there asks Pilate to inflict death on the prisoner he brings to him. The charge is altered to better awaken the political passions of a Roman ruler:

"We have found this man leading astray our nation, and forbidding to pay tribute to cæsar, and saying he is the anointed king."

No shadow of proof is given to these charges, and the governor receives them with coolness, mixed with contempt. Caiaphas urges in vain his own supposed rights and official character. He asks if Pilate supposes he would bring a prisoner to him unless he were indeed guilty of offences against Jewish law.

"Then take and judge him by your Jewish law," was the scornful reply.

Pilate despised the High Priest, whose bribes he had received, with all a Roman's contempt for Asiatic barbarians. But the malice of Caiaphas was not to be baffled by scorn. He urged that Jewish law could not inflict death, and appealed again more eagerly to the Roman fears of sedition by declaring that his prisoner wished to make himself a king, a rebel against the empire. His attendants re-echo the cry, and add that they recognize no king but cæsar. This may well prove that not the people of Judea, but a hired mob, was the public which clamored for the death of Christ.

The Roman governor examines the accused long and earnestly, while the guard checks with spear and sword the noise of the rabble. Pilate was merciless in his rule. He had doomed unsparingly the rioters and zealots of Galilee, and he knew their faces well, but the face now before him is not as theirs. A spiritual light shines there, and universal love for man. The fetters which bind him cannot lower the dignity of his person; the fierce hate of his enemies, who rage for his life, neither daunts him nor affects the mildness of his words. The harsh Pilate softens towards a Hebrew, and he strives hard to release him. He appeals even to the national spirit of his accusers, and asks if they would have him crucify the king of their nation. The appeal to Roman prejudice had fallen in vain even on the Roman Governor.

It was now the turn of the High Priest to pose as the devoted subject of Rome, and to threaten even the Roman governor. "If thou release this man thou art not loyal to the empire," was his final argument, and it succeeded too well. Though Pilate might treat the Jewish dignitaries with haughty indifference, he knew well the power which the wealth of the Temple gave its ruler. Even in Rome itself a charge of disloyalty backed up with gold might be fatal to a Roman governor. He yielded and delivered Jesus into the hands of the High Priest and his followers to deal with as they desired. They led him away to die by the Roman death of crucifixion, absolutely abhorrent to the Jewish religion and, above all, to every true Pharisee.

Over the supreme tragedy let the Angel of Sorrow spread his wings. Veil thy face, Sun! Be darkened, sky; let the earth tremble, and man mourn in tears! The most angelic of men, the most loving of teachers, the meek and humble Prophet, is to die by the death of the cross.

He has made humility honor; he has carried the highest wisdom to the homes of the lowly and ignorant of the world; he has carried it beyond all barriers of schools and Temple, and for this he is to die a death of shame. The Redeemer of the poor, the teacher of the ignorant, the friend of all that faint with toil and are oppressed with cares, must die on the cross.

It is hard to believe that malice and greed could so brutalize the hearts of men; harder, that those men should be the nominal leaders of that people to whom the Lord God himself had given the sovereign commandment: "Thou shalt love thy neighbor as thyself."

But it is only too true. Greed of lawless gain wrung from the people's oppression, low ambition of the venal honors bought from a foreign master, and fear of the wrath of an outraged populace made those leaders craven, apostate to the law of God, and slayers of the noblest spirit of their own and of all times.

Jesus died for the essence of all religion; for purity, charity, and holiness; for a cause in which death itself is a godly thing.

When we place the life and death of Jesus beside that of the greatest of other teachers, as Hillel, the soul expands in admiration. Hillel's was a life of peace. He moulded the minds of his people in the council, and he prepared them remotely for the mission of Jesus, but there was no shadow of sacrifice nor blood in his life. But every word of Jesus points to a tragic end freely accepted for the good of others. It would have been easy for him to raise the bold mountaineers of his native Galilee in his own defence, when his enemies sought his life, and with them to drive the recreant High Priest and his partisans from the Temple, but he would not do it. Bloodshed and human power were repugnant alike to the nature and teachings of this most admirable of men, who freely gave his life for the truth he proclaimed.

His fate is no secret to himself. In his announcement of the kingdom of heaven one can hear the strokes of the hammer on the nails that pierce his hands. The greatness which can speak in the face of torture and death as Jesus spoke; which can return good for evil, love for hate, blessing for curses; which not only preaches the law of love, but lives by it and dies for its sake, is a greatness before which every other fades into nothing.

The man Jesus is the most heroic, the grandest, the noblest personality of all time and age. Even in the shadow of Golgotha let us, however, be just and not lay the charge of the great Crime on those who did not commit it. It was not the Mosaic Law, nor the Jewish people, nor the great body of its teachers, the Pharisees, who steeped their hands in the blood of Christ. That was exclusively the work of the Sadducean High Priest and his servile adherents, of men who had usurped by fraud the succession of Aaron and used it as a means of heaping up wealth by oppression, who were the tools of Rome, not the representatives of the religion of Moses, murderers in the name of Jewish law, which they despised alike in their creed and their lives. The Jewish law did not and could not sanction the death of Christ. The mob which came from the Temple, and the High Priest, with swords and clubs, in the company of Judas, "by night for fear of the people," and which on the following morning yelled, "Crucify the king of the Jews, we have no king but cæsar!" was not the Jewish people that had sung "Hosanah to the Son of David!" a few days before. In truth and justice let not that crowning iniquity be laid to their charge.

Not even the Pharisees or teachers of the law, so frequently rebuked by Jesus for the inconsistency of their precepts with their practice, were the agents of his death. Some of that class undoubtedly co-operated with the Sadducean High Priest, but the mass of the Rabbis had no share in it. Nicodemus, who took down the body of Christ, was himself a master in Israel. Gamaliel, the grandson of Hillel, the president of the Sanhedrin, nowhere appears in the iniquitous proceedings. A short time later, when the High Priest persecuted the disciples of Christ, Gamaliel, according to the New Testament (Acts v.), spoke in their behalf in words that are wholly inconsistent with any hostility towards Christ or his doctrine :

"I say to you, refrain from these men, and let them alone; for if this work be of men it will come to naught. But if it be of God you cannot hinder it, and you may be found yourselves foes of God."

This declaration of the highest authority among

the Jewish teachers shows, we think, that the rabbinical body had no part in the crime of Caiaphas, the High Priest.

The lesson is instructive for Jew and Christian alike, and may well lead both to a better understanding of each other, and an advancement in the charity which Christ taught to men."

CHAPTER III

RABBI YOCHANAN BEN ZAKKAI

AMONG the many disciples who were moulded by the great Hillel to continue his policy, one was specially distinguished, Yochanan ben Zakkai. He had entered the schools late in life, like Hillel himself. He had been a merchant before becoming a student and a Rabbi, and his business ability was shown all through his long life in the discharge of his clerical functions.[1]

Ben Zakkai mastered the learning of the law with an ease not to be expected in a scholar of forty years of age. Hillel's favor was won not less by his diligence than by the systematic power of teaching which he quickly developed. Not only the law, but many languages of the Gentiles, occupied the active mind of Ben Zakkai.[2] He was a natural diplomat as well as a scholar, and at the time diplomatic skill was a matter of vital necessity for Jewish teachers, who would carry on the instruction of their people without exciting the jealousy of their Roman rulers. Ben Zakkai's urbanity, his calmness, which no provocation could disturb, and a quiet dignity which imposed respect on even the haughtiest insolence, made him a model in this respect. Hillel regarded him as his own right hand. He felt that though the arms of Rome might overthrow the walls of Jerusalem, even destroy the Temple, the faith would be safe with men like Ben Zakkai at the head of affairs. The Roman might despise the Jew, but there was one man in Judea he was forced to respect, Rabbi Yochanan ben Zakkai. No Roman could show brutality towards the calm Oriental, whose stately courtesy ever offered the first greeting to even a slave. Even the arrogance of the victorious soldier felt rebuked by the mild patience which marked every act of the Jewish teacher.[3]

In patience, indeed, Ben Zakkai possessed his soul, and in it he both found for himself and pointed out to his people the true secret of success for the Hebrew race. Tenacity of purpose, coupled with meekness of demeanor, has carried the Jew through centuries of struggle, while pride of heart and reckless indifference to principle as surely doomed its conquerors to destruction. The Jewish race was powerless in the field against the disciplined armies of Vespasian or Hadrian. It acknowledged the fact, and bowed to the yoke it could not break, but it never recognized that yoke as other than a passing one. Under the rule of the empire the conquered Jews held still to their own law; they cultivated their minds on the old Hebrew learning, and kept their faith in themselves. They kept aloof from heathen ways and vices, but they avoided disputes or the proclamation of their moral superiority, which they felt to be their own even in physical bondage. Hillel had, all through his life, insisted on the ethical importance of meekness. Ben Zakkai taught the same lesson, not for individuals, but for the public action of the nation. The patient man proved in this field better than the strong man. The Jewish nationality has outlived the empire which destroyed Jerusalem. The religion and morality of Judea have prevailed over the superstitions and the philosophy of Greece and Rome. Whether it was done by Ben Zakkai or by Paul of Tarsus, the moral remodelling of the Roman world was exclusively the work of teachers of Jewish race.

Ben Zakkai's life was lengthened far beyond the ordinary term. He was the favorite disciple of Hillel and a contemporary of Herod the Great, yet he lived to see the destruction of the Temple by Titus, and to reorganize the Sanhedrin after that national catastrophe. His life was cast in a time of factions and disturbances both within and without. Mention has been made elsewhere of how the Sadducean priesthood tyrannized the people and bent their energies to sustain themselves in power. The intruding High Priests of the House of Bœthos, of Cantheros, and of Phabi, in turn, oppressed the people. And as these priests monopolized the traffic in sacerdotal offerings, their influence was naturally directed to multiplying the ceremonial duties connected with the Temple. They had sought and, by bribes to the Roman authorities, obtained a judicial power that did not really belong to their office. Hillel had made a strong attempt to counteract their influence, but he was largely hampered by his opponent, Shammai. In the time of

Christ this pernicious influence was at its height. After his death their influence gradually diminished. In their place another party arose, the Siccarees, the sworn enemies of Rome. Between all these parties and the constant strife amongst them, the very faith of Israel was in danger. The men who had succeeded Hillel—his son Simon, and his grandson Gamaliel the first—were not fitted to cope with the astute diplomats who presided over the Temple; the task then fell to Yochanan ben Zakkai of preserving the Jewish religion, and of carrying out the policy of Hillel. He became the virtual head of the Sanhedrin and the leader of the orthodox, or Pharisee, element of the nation, and no fitter man could have been found.

In multiplying the petty details of ceremonial worship the High Priests exaggerated the importance both of the Temple and the land of Palestine. No fitting worship could be offered anywhere but in the Temple, and by an easy stretch of reasoning the Sadducees argued that a man could hardly be a true Jew if he resided outside the Holy Land, where the Temple stood. This narrow feeling of nationality extended beyond the bounds of Sadducean sectarianism. It grew strong among the masses when Roman oppression became intolerable. It was the special task of Ben Zakkai to moderate the fanaticism of patriotic feeling while cultivating the feeling itself among their people, as well as to preserve the religion of Moses from corruption at the hands of the Sadducean High Priests and their partisans.

Like Hillel, Ben Zakkai felt that a Jewish king-

dom, however glorious, was not the end for which
the divine revelation of the Law had been made to
Moses. He felt it was given for a higher object, to
establish the rule of justice and truth in every part
of God's world, to build up a Temple, not of stone
and mortar, which might be destroyed by human
hands, but of human hearts, freely offering the homage of love to their Creator and to the men made in
his image. He set himself then to lessen the load
of local ceremonial, which had been so notably increased by the greed of the High Priests, and to impress on the minds of the people the spiritual nature
of their religion. The Temple itself, rebuilt by
Herod and profaned by the crimes of its administration, commanded little veneration from his religious
soul. He saw with a prophetic eye that the condition of the people in Palestine had no elements of
stability. A legend represents him as passing the
edifice, when its gates were suddenly opened by invisible hands. "Temple," cried Rabbi Yochanan,
"why wouldst thou frighten me? knowest thou not
that thine own destruction is at hand?"[1]

His task was no easy one, with the Sanhedrin itself
under the sway of the Sadducean High Priests, and
the people handed over to their mercy by the Roman proconsuls. The only influence he could wield
was that derived from his own abilities and learning.
He enlisted the people at large in his cause. Near
the outer wall of the Temple he taught them the
true nature of the law with simple eloquence.
Even in subjection the Jewish people still retained
some influence over its rulers, and Ben Zakkai was

advanced in the Sanhedrin in spite of Sadducean hostility. He was made chief justice, and in that office he had opportunity for carrying out his policy on a larger scale. His boldness was in strong contrast to the timidity of the son and grandson of Hillel. He abrogated one of the oldest regulations of the law, though dating from Moses himself, as a necessity. This was the ordeal of "bitter waters" prescribed as a test in charges of adultery against married women. It was sanctioned alike by the practice of ages, the teaching of the Rabbis, and the doctrine of the Sadducees, who recognized the Scriptures as the sole and infallible guide in religious belief and in practice. It had become an engine of fraud and oppression in the hands of the corrupt administrators of the Temple service, who were charged with its application. As the chief judge in Israel, Ben Zakkai decreed its abolition, and his decision was received with approval by the most religious as well as by the people. It was a signal victory for the Rabbis over the High Priests and their faction.[5]

Even a more significant measure of Ben Zakkai's was his decision that the "Red Cow" as an offering for the sins of the whole people, sacrificed by Sadducean High Priests, was of no worth and void. As there were no other High Priests to offer up the "Red Cow," the decision practically amounted to an abolition of the practice altogether. It is significant of the mould of Ben Zakkai's mind. The Law of Moses had to be shaped to new circumstances if its real life was to be preserved. The Temple observances could not be long maintained if the people were to go forth over the face of the earth, but the spiritual law could if the hearts of the people cherished it. Were this not the case, Ben Zakkai would never have attempted interference with one of the cardinals of the Temple service, though it were performed by less worthy priests.

No doubt the tyranny and corruption of the venal priesthood were evidence sufficient of an approaching catastrophe from without as well as within the land of Palestine. A bitter hatred against the Jewish oppressors existed among all classes. The people cried: "Woe on the house of Bœthos and on the staffs of his hirelings, that beat men to obedience! Woe on the house of Cantheros, because of what their pens have written! Woe on the house of Annas, for their poisoned tongues! Woe on the house of Ishmael Phabi for their heavy hand! They are High Priests, their sons and the husbands of their daughters stand over the Temple, and their servants beat the people with staffs. The Temple cries to them, "Begone ye children of Heli, ye have defiled the House of God."[6] Such are the words preserved in the Talmud as an expression of the popular feeling. But neither the son nor the grandson of Hillel had really penetrated the depth of his teaching. Ben Zakkai alone knew what the master wanted, and he alone foresaw the future.

The corrupt tyranny of the High Priests was not the only foe which the calm yet courageous chief judge had to contend with. A large part of the people who hated the Sadducean doctrines were drunk with fanatical patriotism which they identified with religious duty. A mob rose and slew the High Priest in hate of his extortions, and the act went unavenged by Rome. The hot-blooded among the people felt emboldened, and they believed they could by their own strength overthrow the Roman empire. A conspiracy of murder, not unlike the Italian Carbonari of half a century ago, was organized by the fanatical zealots. These were the Siccarees, the dagger men, or assassins, and their chief was Ben Betiach, a nephew of Ben Zakkai, but far from sharing his mild spirit. Assassination of Roman and of Jewish officials became frightfully frequent. The Jewish people showed a hopeless ignorance of the political conditions around them. They fought bitterly among themselves while exasperating their Roman rulers by their atrocities. There was no council among the patriots, no union. Some looked for supernatural aid in the struggle; others doubted that Rome would even seek to maintain her rule by arms. Others relied on the walls of Jerusalem, the wealth of the people, and the courage of the race to protect them. The fanatics forced the wealthy into their insurrection, and proclaimed war to the death against the rule of the heathen.

The bulk of the Jewish people broke out in insurrection. They lacked not patriotic spirit, nor physical courage such as their fathers had shown in their struggle against the Greek kings of Syria, but there was neither concert, leader, nor discipline among the ill-starred people. There was neither a David nor a Judas Maccabeus to lead them to battle. The ablest men among them foresaw the hopelessness of the cause in which they were engaged, without knowing how to extricate themselves.

A few of the noblest spirits among the nation saw a future beyond the inevitable ruin of the Temple and the city of Jerusalem. They saw the law written in flame on the skies, and its benign light shedding lustre over the world; they recognized a kingdom not of earth but of heaven, as seen by the prophets, and as announced by the meek Nazarene. Among these was Ben Zakkai. Though opposed to the insurrection, he commanded the respect of all among the Jews. He used it to try to bring sane counsels to the hearts of the fanatics. He called his nephew, Ben Betiach, to him, and urged the criminality of a rising which had no prospect of any result but the shedding of oceans of blood. The wisdom of calm age spoke to the senseless fury of passionate youth.

"Unless you desist from your course, you are all doomed to death," said the old Rabbi.

"Better death than dishonor," was the reply.

"But the people will weary of fighting against overpowering enemies. They will seek peace and the enjoyment of what they have, even if under Roman rule."

"They must and shall fight!" replied the fierce zealot.

"They will not," urged Ben Zakkai; "they have food in plenty within the town; they will reflect before famine comes to madden their hearts. Seek peace while yet you may find it."

"We will have no peace with the heathen,

accursed of God! We shall fight this very night or to-morrow!" exclaimed Ben Betiach, and he rushed away from his uncle's counsels.

He did not fight, however, then, but he made the struggle only the more terrible. His uncle's caution had struck him. He would bring hunger to his aid in the desperate struggle. By his command the provisions stored in Jerusalem were burned and the people were called to face death by famine if they did not at once break the lines of the besiegers. The result is too harrowing to repeat here. Through all the agonies that are written on the pages of Jewish history, there is none to match the siege and destruction of Jerusalem. The calamity which still burns the soul of every Jew was caused by disregard of the wise counsels of Ben Zakkai.

When he saw the end approaching, when he recognized that all was lost, he concluded to leave the doomed city. He counselled with his foremost disciples, Eliezer ben Hyrkanos, Josua ben 'Hananiah, and his friend Rabbi Zadok, who had been fasting daily for forty years and had spent his time in prayer to the Lord to save the Holy City and the Temple. At this meeting it was settled that Rabbi Yochanan should leave the city, go to the Roman general, and plead for the people, or at least save the men who had no share in the rebellion. But the rebels slew all who attempted to leave the city. They made no conditions and asked no quarter. They would fight to the death for their rights for independence and the sanctuary.

Ben Zakkai caused a rumor to be spread of his

sudden sickness and, after, of his death. He instructed his disciples to put him in a coffin and carry him out of Jerusalem into the Roman camp. Though the times were such that a life was hardly counted, yet the announcement of the great Rabbi's death caused universal sorrow; even the soldiers, rough-mannered and wild-visaged men, shed tears.

The Rabbi's disciples carried the coffin to the "Death Gate," which opened only for funerals. There they hoped they could pass without difficulty. But the besieged, thinking that members of the peace party might resort to such means of escape, guarded even the Death Gate.

When the funeral procession approached, it was stopped at the gate.

"Whose body have you there?" asked the captain.

"The crown from our head has fallen; we are carrying the body of our master, Rabbi Yochanan ben Zakkai," they cried with wailing and groans.

The captain was affected.

"If Rabbi Yochanan ben Zakkai is dead," he said, "then fallen is indeed the crown of Israel. Open the gate, men, let them pass."

"Art thou sure, captain, that Rabbi Yochanan is dead?" cried a fanatic. "Maybe they are taking away a living traitor. I will make sure that he is dead."

He raised his lance to strike at the shrouded form of the Rabbi.

"Hold, men of Israel!" cried the disciples; "to dishonor the body of the saint would be a sin for which disaster, swift and sure, would fall on all Israel. Let us pass in peace."

"They are right," said the captain; "enough sorrow has already come upon us, let none be added by such a sin. Open the gate."

The fanatic reluctantly desisted; the gate was opened and the procession passed through.

At a distance from the walls of Jerusalem, the disciples halted, Rabbi Yochanan came from his coffin and went to the Roman camp. The guards took him to the tent of Titus,[1] and he bent low before the general.

"Hail, cæsar!" said Ben Zakkai, "I ask thy protection."

"I am not cæsar," Vespasian replied.

"Thou art cæsar even now; for the cæsar in Rome is dead," the Rabbi said.

He had scarcely uttered the words, when a messenger entered the tent, bringing the news of Nero's death and of Vespasian's call to the throne.

"Thou art a Prophet, Rabbi," said Vespasian.

"The Lord our God hath given me knowledge. Thou art mighty, O cæsar, thou wilt take the tower. In the tower is a cask of honey, near the honey is a snake: kill the snake and save the cask of honey," said the Rabbi.[8]

Vespasian understood the metaphor.

"Nay, Rabbi," he said, "we destroy the tower, the snakes, and the cask with the honey. Ask for something else."

"Then, O cæsar, give me protection in the city of Yamnai; I am old, I am a lover of peace: permit me to spend my remaining years in study in the company of my few friends," the Rabbi said.

"Is that all?" cried Vespasian in wonder.

"One more request, cæsar: a friend of mine, Rabbi Zadok, is ill and worn from fasting, I pray thee, send thy physicians to heal him."

A Roman bearing such tidings would have asked gold, slaves, and honors, while this old Hebrew sought but study; as if study meant conquest or power! How could the Hebrews become a great nation if their distinguished men lacked ambition?

Perhaps these thoughts passed through the mind of Vespasian as he granted the Rabbi's request. He knew not that his word would undo the whole work of Roman conquest which he was engaged in. He thought to crush the Hebrew, his nationality, his Temple, his faith, while he gave Yamnai to Ben Zakkai, whose ambition seemed so small. From Yamnai went forth the law as well as from Zion; it spread over the world, and no power has ever been strong enough to stop its progress.

Ben Zakkai left Vespasian and went to Yamnai, where he soon gathered around him the noblest spirits of his time. He founded the great school known in the Talmud as "the school of Yamnai." He gave special attention to those of his disciples who he knew would continue the work after him, and began the reorganization of a new Sanhedrin. Unlike the old one in Jerusalem, its aim was the establishment of a spiritual government independent of place, rather than to change a fixed national authority from Jerusalem to Yamnai. Sadduceeism as a force was dead; its influence even remotely on the law-giving body of the nation was felt no more. The difficulties which later arose among the scholars was a contention against the power of Hillelism and the bold strides it made in its policy of universalism, rather than its sectarian doctrines. The men who fought them most bitterly were Ben Zakkai's own disciple, Eliezer ben Hyrkanos, and, later, Simon ben Yohai, both ambitious for leadership in the affairs of the Sanhedrin.

The destruction of the Temple, though he had foreseen the calamity, crushed the soul of Rabbi Yochanan. He and his disciples tore their garments and for seven days mourned in sackcloth and ashes. Then they went to Jerusalem to look on its ruin. The disciples threw themselves upon the sacred soil and lifted up their lamentations. Rabbi Yochanan ben Zakkai gazed at the ruins and then at his weeping friends. Tears blurred his vision; he was sorely stricken. But from the ruins and the mist and smoke he saw a new spiritual Temple rise, and its apex kissed the clouds which, lit by the wondrous light, cast upon the earth a glory beyond expression.

"My sons," said the master, "weep not, and dry your tears; the enemy hath destroyed the sanctuary of stone and mortar, but the true altar of the Lord, the place of forgiveness, is with us yet. Would you know where? Behold, in the homes of the poor, there is the altar; love, charity, mercy, and justice are the offerings, the sweet incense which pleases the Lord. Love ye one another, and ye shall find mercy and forgiveness." ⁹

"But, O Master," cried they, "the sanctuary of the Lord is destroyed, Israel has disappeared, and therefore the Lord's presence no longer abides with us."

"Say not so, my children," said the saint, "whithersoever the people of the Lord go, thither the holy presence goes with them."[10]

With over a hundred years on his head the venerable teacher turned away from the desolation of Jerusalem to build up again the spiritual organization of his people. Through the favor of Vespasian, who then ruled the Roman world, Ben Zakkai was able to open a college for his disciples in Yamnai. Other Rabbis gathered around to share the protection afforded him. He seized the opportunity to found a spiritual republic such as Hillel had outlined. With statesman-like skill, Ben Zakkai transferred the power hitherto held by the High Priests, recognized by Rome as the heads of the Jewish nation, into the hands of the Rabbis. The office of the Jewish Pontiff had disappeared with the destruction of the Temple. In its stead came the Patriarchate, which gradually increased in power and was favored even by Rome. Its organization was solidified by the master, Ben Zakkai, and thenceforth formed the only national government left to the Jewish people.

Ben Zakkai gathered around him the masters who had belonged to the Sanhedrin like himself. He filled up the numbers of the membership from the most learned of his disciples, and this national council, in fact, gained in power among the people with the fall of the Temple. Ben Zakkai was universally recognized as its natural head, both for his knowledge of the law and his commanding abilities. With self-sacrificing wisdom, however, he procured the election of the second Gamaliel, a descendant of Hillel, as president. He thought that the recognition of heredity and Davidic descent in the presidency of the national council would add an element of dignity and stability to the office which was needed in the troubled times. During the remnant of Ben Zakkai's life his authority, however, was deservedly paramount in the council of Israel.

The organization of the national council after the fall of Jerusalem was a vital measure in the life of the race. During the century that elapsed after the extinction of the national dynasty the minds of the Jewish people were mainly turned to the hope of a revived kingdom which should restore the glories of David and Solomon. For that reason they clung to Jerusalem and its Temple with a patriotic fervor which even the usurped tyranny of the High Priests of Phabi's house could not quench. When all these hopes were blighted and the spirit of resistance crushed by the swords of the Roman legionaries, Ben Zakkai recalled the people to the spiritual work which was the true essence of Judaism. The lesson that patience is better than strength, which he had preached in vain before, was now welcomed by every Hebrew, and it has become part of their nature in the long ages that have passed since. The sage was better than the soldier.

The religion of Israel is still a living force, while the material empire of Rome has crumbled in the dust. The Scriptures, the intellect, and the individuality of the race, which seemed to be doomed to extinction when Titus burned the Temple, survive to-day. They have penetrated like a leaven the moral and intellectual nature of every race within the old Roman empire and far beyond its limits. Christianity is, in truth, but Judaism developed to its fuller extent; for Judaism in its essence was the faith taught by Jesus of Nazareth. That Ben Zakkai understood this truth and worked with forethought and wisdom to save the truth contained in Judaism is his great glory. Hillel spoke prophetically when he styled Ben Zakkai "The father of wisdom for generations yet to come." " The great Rabbi had domestic as well as national sorrows. A dearly loved son was taken from him by death, and the soul of the father was filled with grief. His disciples came to offer what consolation they could. One recalled the sorrow that had been endured by Adam when he looked on the body of his murdered son. Another bade the sufferer consider the afflictions of Job.

"Children," answered Ben Zakkai, "how can my grief be lightened by thinking of the grief of other men?"

But Elazar ben Arakh spoke to him and said:

"A certain man had received the guardianship of a jewel of price, and he watched by day and night for its safe keeping. When the lord of the jewel came to take it back the man was happy, because he no longer could fear for the jewel. Even so, dear Master, thou shouldst rejoice when thou hast given thy son to God, who trusted thee with him, since thou hast given him in his innocence as thou didst first receive him."

And the master said to Elazar:

"Thou alone hast spoken wisely, and thy words have consoled my soul." [12]

Ben Zakkai had another son, Juda, who became a scholar worthy of his father.

When the master, after his long life, found his end draw near he was seized with great fear. His disciples, when they came to his bedside, were scandalized and asked:

"Master, thou art the light of Israel; why, then, dost thou tremble?"

"Were I going before a human judge to plead for life might I not justly tremble," the master answered; "yet a man can be swayed by words and favor, but the Judge before whom I must appear cannot be deceived. From His tribunal man must go the road of heaven or the road of hell. Can I tell which road I shall be sent?"

His disciples asked a last blessing, and he told them:

"May your fear of offending God be as great as your fear of man."

"What more?" they asked, and he said:

"If a man seeks to please God as eagerly as he seeks to please men, he will never sin." [13]

His death occurred a few years after the destruction of the Temple. The Talmud justly says of him: "With the death of Rabbi Yochanan ben Zakkai the light of wisdom was quenched." [14] None like him rose afterward in Israel.

CHAPTER IV

RABBI 'HANINAH BEN DOSA

TWO divisions of the Synagogue exist in the present day. The one looks with longing and prayer for a restored Jerusalem; the other desires assimilation with the nations of the world. The first is eager for a national theocracy on the very soil of Palestine; the other for a universal brotherhood of man. The so-called "Reform" wing of Jewry, the world over, looks with disdainful pity on those Jews who cling to tradition, believe in miracles, and with beating hearts and tear-filled eyes, pray daily for the coming of the Messiah, and look with confidence for the supernatural signs that are to herald it. They regard them as slaves to superstitions which entail sacrifices, agonies, tears, and self-denial. The origin of this division can be traced back as far as the first century of the present era in the life of the Jews of that day.

At that time Ben Zakkai and Ben Dosa already appeared as leaders of the two schools which are represented in the Jewish race in the nineteenth century. Both were attached to the faith and devoted to the maintenance of the law given to Moses, but they differed as to the best counsel for perpetuating it.

Ben Zakkai realized that Titus had closed the political career of Jewish nationality, and that, if that nationality were still to exist, it must struggle with intellectual weapons alone, with the all-conquering humanitarian principle. He would perpetuate Judaism by spreading its moral teachings throughout the heathen world, building a temple of souls in place of the ruined Temple of stone.

To the mind of his rival, Ben Dosa, Judaism could only be perfectly maintained in a Jewish state where the civil administration was carried out in strict conformity with the religious law, binding the individual conscience of every believing Jew. If such a state were impossible from external causes, then the law at least should be kept intact by the individual children of Israel. That could only be done by jealously excluding the heathen and his ways from all contact with the inner life of the faithful Jew.[1]

To Ben Zakkai the law was only a means, though a most potent one, for promoting the human welfare of his race. To Ben Dosa human life was only the means by which the supreme law of the universe could be fulfilled by man. In itself the fulfilment of the law was better than any human happiness, better than life itself.[2]

While Ben Zakkai would adapt its precepts to promote the interests of his people, in a worldly sense, Ben Dosa saw mysteries of another world and another life in every word of its text. He cared nothing for the material comforts of life or the splendor of high position, both of which Ben Zakkai keenly appreciated. Ben Dosa was an ascetic, who found his only joy in mystic contemplation, and lived in want. His asceticism awed the people. Ben Zakkai, who in his heart despised the mystic teacher, yet appreciated his influence with the people. Ben Dosa, on his side, felt little respect for the man of the world, who knew the law indeed as an intellectual study, but seemed to take no heed to conform his practice to its precepts.[3]

Ben Dosa was not the founder of the system of religious observance which bore the name of Practice, and called for a close and minute fulfilment of every point of the law as a strict duty. That theory dates back to Rabbi Simon the Just, the last member of the great synod, in the third century before Christ. He was, however, the true follower of Shammai, a fervent adherent to nationalism and its leader at a most critical time for the Jewish race. He was the immediate forerunner of Rabbi Akibah, and the great revolution attempted by Bar Kochba may be traced to the effects of his teaching. Without the silent persistence in working for political independence as a requisite for the theocratic government to which he looked as the true fulfilment of the Law of Moses, the hope of a Messiah might have died out of the hearts of Israel. Though that spirit has caused the Jew sorrow and tears and oceans of blood, yet without it, who can tell whether there would be to-day any memory of the Jew, or whether he would stand as an unimpeachable witness of the marvellous wisdom and mercy of divine providence? This spirit gave the Jew his particular individuality among the nations during the centuries gone by, and it shows itself whenever disorganization threatens his religious autonomy. It is the *perpetuum mobile* of the Jewish faith, a marvel in the eyes of men.

It had its dangers, however, in the days we now speak of and they were appreciated by the politic Ben Zakkai. If it were to grow unchecked, he felt, it was bound to result in a war of extermination against the Jewish race and an ossification of Judaism itself, which would hinder rather than help the maintenance of the Mosaic law. He felt, too, that it was useless to oppose it by external force. Religious ideas, forcibly repressed, break out after lapse of time with the accumulated power stored during their period of enforced inactivity. Such at least was the belief of Ben Zakkai. He tried to win over the mystic to his own policy by treating him with personal respect. He asked him to his house, sought his advice, and treated it with consideration externally. The Talmud gives a characteristic anecdote of this intercourse between the politician and the mystic.

"It came to pass that Rabbi 'Haninah ben Dosa went to Rabbi Yochanan ben Zakkai to discuss the Law with him, and while he was in his house the son of Ben Zakkai fell ill. Then Ben Zakkai said:

"'Haninah, my son, ask the mercy of Heaven that my son may live.'

"And 'Haninah bowed his head even between his knees and so he prayed to the Lord. And the Lord healed the son of Ben Zakkai.

"Then said Ben Zakkai:

"'Had I bowed my head between my knees a whole day Heaven would not have heeded me.'

"Then 'Haninah went his way, and Ben Zakkai's wife asked her husband:

"'Is 'Haninah, then, greater than thou art?'

"And Ben Zakkai answered:

"'No. He is like a servant before the king, but I am as a lord before the king.'" [4]

The pride of the ruler in Israel could not be better described.

The sayings recorded of Ben Dosa breathe a different spirit and show how widely divergent were his thoughts from those of the great politician.

"If a man fears sin more than he loves knowledge, his knowledge will abide with him, but the knowledge of him who loves it more than he fears sin will pass away."

"If a wise man's good works are greater than his wisdom, his wisdom will abide, but if a wise man's works are not equal to his wisdom, then his wisdom itself will decay."

"He who finds grace with man's conscience will find grace with the Most High, but he whose deeds are reprobated by just men will also be reprobated by the Most High." [5]

These maxims express the principle of Ben Dosa's national policy, and no argument could swerve him from his chosen path. Whatever plea the diplomatists set up to make him relent, his reply was always the same: "The Jews have brought their misfortune upon themselves by laxity in the observance of the law, hence nothing but the strictest adherence could restore them to the grace of God, and bring back their former happiness. Had they paid less attention to external affairs and more to that domestic theocracy established by the great lawgiver, there would have been no cause to practise diplomacy against the heathen and to protect the law against him. In sooth the law would have been as a strong walled fortress to the Jew, and he would not have needed to fear any but God."

Stern as Ben Dosa was with others, far more stern was he with himself. His life was pure and holy. His domestic happiness was perfect in spite of his awful poverty. His fame as a man of divine power travelled through all the land, and from the length and breadth thereof people came to him asking his intercession with Heaven for every ill of the body and soul. Even in matters which required human judgment rather than divine interposition, such as quarrels between neighbors, ordinary jealousies between peddlers, or where stray goats took a particular fancy to the cabbage in some pious widow's garden, they came to him; and as his simple word had the power of commanding obedience from beings natural and supernatural, he made every one happy. To him also came farmers whose crops promised poorly on account of tardy rain, and, being master of the highest mysteries, he commanded the elements and they obeyed (Taanith 24).

But none appreciated his worth more than his wife. She knew that temporal poverty with 'Haninah meant everlasting bliss with him in paradise. And so jealous was she that her beloved saint should have his undiminished share in the world to come that she refused earthly wealth, though she had it in her power to get as much as she desired. For she, too, was beloved of the Lord and He performed miracles in her favor. But of wealth she would have none. Though a wonderful woman, Mrs. 'Haninah was not without that housewifely pride which does not permit an inquisitive neighbor to pry into one's pots. And the good neighbor women, who may have thought that there was something wrong with the 'Haninahs after all, since he could assist everybody else and remained so very poor himself, were often eager to find out how the 'Haninahs lived; what they dined on; whether they had plenty of Sabbath loaves and fish and meat as was the custom and usage in Jewish households on the Sabbath. But 'Haninah's wife was as shrewd as she was holy, and on Friday afternoons she would make a great fire in the oven, and the neighbor women, seeing the volume of smoke issuing from the smoke-stack, would whisper to each other that 'Haninah's wife must be baking bread and roasting meat for the Sabbath. But there was nothing in the oven save the fire, which was a weak reflex of the holy fire that burned in the great soul of that pious and God-fearing woman. But the neighbor women were burning with a curiosity to peep in to find out. And as woman will have her way, though the way be sometime far from the heavenly, even so did one of them go by stealth into the kitchen while 'Haninah's wife was away and look into the oven. What she saw astounded her greatly; for the oven was filled with many loaves, just turning to a golden brown, and dishes of pastry and meats. "It is a miracle," the inquisitive woman said to the others, "a miracle, I tell you; for what I saw in that oven is fit for the khadi or the president of the Sanhedrin." And a miracle it was, indeed, wrought by the Lord for His beloved, so as not to bring them to shame before malicious and inquisitive eyes.[6]

In her younger days 'Haninah's wife may have had moments when her heart longed for the comforts which ordinary wealth affords. When the Temple in Jerusalem was as yet undefiled by heathen hands, and the thousands of men and women dressed in festive garb, carrying offerings of doves and spices, or holding high the slender palm and the aromatic citron, while singing joyful psalms as they went on their pilgrimage to the sanctuary of the Lord; when she beheld the youths and maidens radiant with happiness, then she may have had regrets, longings, desires. She may have wished to be, if but for a moment, rich, or at least relieved of oppressive poverty. It was during one such moment of depression that 'Haninah found her. He so loved her that his soul was smitten with sorrow at her sadness and he asked the cause thereof. Amidst tears and sobs she told him of the yearning of her heart and begged him to pray Heaven for wealth. 'Haninah turned pale; not that he feared the Lord's refusal, for the celestial voice had regretfully exclaimed that "the entire world is supported on account of ' Haninah, and he is satisfied with a measure of figs."[7] And the popular voice was fully on the side of Heaven.

'Haninah, they thought, ought to be, if not wealthy, at least comfortable. But 'Haninah knew that comforts in this world were merely an advance from the world to come, and that he would miss there what he would have enjoyed here. However, he could refuse his wife nothing, since what she asked was really very reasonable. He promised to pray for riches. When night came 'Haninah retired to his chamber to pray and his wife went to sleep.

And, sleeping, she dreamed. In her dream she had a vision of paradise. She saw the righteous of all Israel clothed in shining garments, crowned with jewelled crowns, seated upon chairs of gold at golden tripods and contemplating the shekhinah, the supreme glory of the Lord.

One seat was unoccupied and before it stood a tripod like the others, but wanting one of its supports. She asked for whom it was thus placed, and the angel, with a look of sadness, replied it was the place of 'Haninah ben Dosa. "But why, my Lord," she asked, "is the tripod thus maimed?" "Because he among the Just who receives part of his reward on earth forfeits that part in eternity." 'Haninah's wife awoke, and she went to tell the strange dream to her husband. She found him in his room, and beside him lay a bar of gold like the leg of one of the tripods which she had seen in her dream. He bade her take it and use it for her wants. But the woman thought of the angel's words and her heart was grieved.

"I will not touch it, my husband," she said, "and do you pray at once to Heaven to take back its gift, unless thou wouldst forfeit thy share in the world to come."

"But it was at thy asking that I prayed for gold," he rejoined.

"Nay, but I have seen awful things in a dream," she answered.

"Ah, then," said Ben Dosa, "thou knowest now that our glory would be less in paradise by as much as we had received here?"

"Yes, my beloved one, I have seen, and now pray the Lord to take back His gift."

So 'Haninah prayed again and the angel took away the golden bar, and 'Haninah and his wife were happy in their great poverty.[8]

Then 'Haninah made a pilgrimage to Jerusalem in gratitude for the favor shown him. As he went, the roads were full of cattle which pilgrims were bringing to offer in the Temple, and 'Haninah desired to make an offering, too, but he had not the means. As he walked sadly, he saw a block of marble in a desert place, and he thought with himself: "I have found an offering meet for the Temple." So he sought for tools, and cut and polished the rough stone till it was a perfect block; but he knew not how he would get it to Jerusalem. He asked some pilgrims to help him, but they would not unless he would pay them fifty pieces of silver. 'Haninah had only five, so the pilgrims left him. But five men came along, who were angels, and they agreed to carry the block for five pieces, if he would bear a part of the load. 'Haninah accepted thankfully, and they carried the offering to the Temple. The others bore it into the chamber where marble was stored, and 'Haninah followed with the money to pay them; but when he entered they had disappeared, and the guardians of the Temple told him that they were not porters but ministering angels who had brought his offering.[9]

So 'Haninah went back glad, and when he came to his house it was Friday. As he entered, he heard his daughter weeping. Her mother asked the reason of her tears, and the maiden told how by mistake she had filled the Sabbath lamp with vinegar instead of oil.

"Weep not," said 'Haninah as he entered, "for He who hath made oil to burn will also cause vinegar to burn."

And so it was. The lamp burned clear all night and all day until the stars on the Sabbath evening and the time of the prayer of separation had come.[10]

'Haninah felt that the liberal Hillelites cared not for his ways and would be glad to deride him, but he was undisturbed. He continued his task of purifying the life of the Jewish people on their own soil, and of asking aid from God rather than man in its execution. He taught the people that He who could work wonders in ordinary life might also, if He willed, restore the glory of Israel and the Temple. He regarded the men who trusted in heathen help as of the lighter wing of the faith. Ben Zakkai had asked Vespasian to send his physician to heal Rabbi Zadok when he escaped from Jerusalem; 'Haninah would never have asked such a favor. His confidence was wholly in supernatural aid. Men derided him as the "miracle-worker," but when sorrow befell these same mockers came to seek his aid. Among them was a second Gamaliel, president of the Sanhedrin. Gamaliel's son was sick unto death, and the doctors found their skill unavailing to cure him. Some of his friends urged Gamaliel to ask the help of Ben Dosa, and he did, though unwillingly. When Gamaliel's messengers brought the request 'Haninah went up to the loft of his cottage and remained there some time in prayer. When he came down 'his face was resplendent with superhuman light. He told the messengers that the boy was safe, and that even then he had asked for water. They asked him: "Art thou then a prophet?" And he said: "I am neither a prophet nor the son of a prophet, but when my prayer floweth smoothly, I know it is granted."

The messengers noted the time and went back to their master.

"'Haninah's prayer hath been in vain," said the latter; "for ere you reached his house my son sat up and asked for water."

But when the students told him what 'Haninah had said, Gamaliel was silent. He appreciated the power of 'Haninah's prayer."

In the estimation of the great men what lowered the value of 'Haninah's work was the ready exercise of his power in trivial matters. Being caught in a rain, he said: "All people rejoice at this rain, while I am drenched." And the rain suddenly ceased. Arrived at home he heard people say that more rain was needed to secure a good harvest. "Then," said he, "as I am under shelter there is nothing to keep heaven from giving rain to the earth." He had scarcely finished the word when the rain started again."[12] One day a widow came to him and tearfully told of a mishap in the building of her cottage. "The carpenter finds the cross-beams too short, and I am too poor to buy new ones," she cried. "What is thy name?" asked 'Haninah. "My name is Ikho," said the widow. "Ikho, the beams are long enough," said 'Haninah, and bade her go."[13] Full of faith, the woman told the carpenter to try the same beams again. The man shook his head, but did as requested, and to his inexpressible astonishment the beams projected an ell on either side.[14] On another occasion Rabbi 'Haninah again demonstrated his power in a manner equally marvellous. He had several goats, and these, with their natural inclination for mischief, invaded the neighboring vegetable gardens. But, being brought up in a saintly atmosphere, they nibbled a leaf here and there, but did no further damage. The owners of the gardens, however, would take no chances on goats, ever so pious, where flowering vegetables offered temptation, and told the Rabbi to keep his goats where they would be less dangerous to people's cabbage. However, the saint knew his goats; he knew that they would go against a pack of wild animals rather than steal a blade of grass not their master's.

"My goats have done no damage to your gardens," said he; "but if it be as you say, let bears come and kill them: if not, then let each goat come forth carrying a bear upon its horns." The words

86 JEWISH FORERUNNERS OF CHRISTIANITY

were scarcely uttered when 'Haninah's goats appeared, and, to the discomfiture of the neighbors, were bearing expiring bears upon their horns, thus making obvious their innocence.[15]

The opposition to 'Haninah was not always passive. Those men who later on played an important part in the affairs of the intellectual commonwealth and who worked for progress and a better policy toward the victorious enemy, Rome; those leaders of thought, disciples of the sagacious Ben Zakkai, saw in 'Haninah and his adherents a hindrance to overcome which they bent every energy; and but for the sincere piety and simplicity of 'Haninah, there might have been enacted a tragedy as shocking as that on Calvary. The Rabbis were as yet in the throes of fear which the great national calamity had produced. Rome needed but the slightest pretext to swoop down upon them and annihilate the last vestige saved from the ruins of Jerusalem, and such a pretext could readily be found in the actions of such men as 'Haninah. If endowed with some ambition it would have required but the turn of a straw to raise a rebellion, and this the Rabbis were determined to prevent. Hence they not infrequently asked him "catch questions" somewhat similar to those the pseudo-Pharisees asked Jesus. Moreover, the word had gone forth that with the destruction of the Temple prophecy had ceased, a warning intended to subdue ambitious aspirants to messianic distinction or prophetic authority.[16] The "men of miracles," therefore, had to be on their guard against those implacable protestants of the old synagogue; for at the least agitation of the masses they would have been the first to be delivered into the ever Moloch hands of Rome. It is equally noteworthy that the men who were sacrificed by those in power were always those of a sect with whom the latter had much sympathy, since they professed the same faith and were in the eyes of the Romans nothing more nor less than Hebrews. This diplomatic cruelty was practised in every case where a person's existence and political faith were a menace to the peace of the majority. And as surely as Rome knew no difference between Jew and Jew, so surely was a man's fate sealed whom the scholars saw fit to accuse. The men of miracles were the more dangerous because of their great popularity, a popularity seldom attained by the scholars, who repelled by their pride. No humble man dared approach a famous scholar, whereas the "saint" lent a willing ear and ready help to the lowliest and the most ignorant of his people.

It was precisely this which aroused suspicion and upon which the scholars frowned as they found no biblical or politico-national ground for decisive action. During the second century they found such grounds, but they were then swayed by the resistless power of a master mind, a mind trained in the cunning of the schools and aflame with the unquenchable fire of patriotism. Men like Rabbi 'Haninah, therefore, were watched and their every action scrutinized. Whatever he did by means of prayer they could afford to let pass, but woe to him if he claimed a more direct power! These threats are often clothed in the garb of a story; but to one acquainted with the spirit of the Talmud and the history and the conditions of those times it is as clear as the light of day. However, vigilance and cunning were not altogether on the side of the scholars; the "men of miracles" knew their delicate position and spoke accordingly. These thoughts are best illustrated in the following story:

The daughter of Rabbi Nehuniah, the grave-digger, fell into a deep cavern beneath a grave.

They came and told Rabbi 'Haninah of it.

"Peace!" said he, and the people went away, satisfied that the maiden would come out unharmed.

An hour passed, yet the maiden did not appear and the anxious people again went to the Rabbi.

"Peace!" he said, and remained quiet. But after the third hour the people, believing that the Rabbi's power had not been exerted sufficiently to rescue the maiden, came again and clamored for relief.

"She hath this moment left the cavern," said Rabbi 'Haninah.

A few moments later a great noise was heard, and soon the people came to the Rabbi's house with the rescued maiden.

"My daughter," said the saint, "who took thee from the cavern?"

"I saw a he-goat which was led by an old man, and I followed them out of the cavern," she replied, to the astonishment of all the people.

And they [the scholars] asked him:

"Art thou, then, a prophet?"

"I am neither a prophet nor the son of a prophet,"

he replied, " but I felt it was impossible that a grave dug by a pious man like Rabbi Nehuniah should prove disastrous to his daughter." [17]

It was a clever reply and the scholars were forced to leave the "man of miracles" to pursue his own works, trusting that his piety, which was sincere, would keep him from causing practical mischief.

Soon, however, matters of graver importance engrossed the attention of the Rabbis. Christianity began to assert itself; traditional differences among the scholars threatened Sanhedric disruption; two intellectual giants, disciples of the great Rabbi Yochanan ben Zakkai, came upon the scene and mustered their forces for supremacy in the religious life of the Hebrews. Great was that battle, loud the clash of opinion, and the stream of mental activity was, for a time at least, turned in a different direction. But it was only for a time. Even amidst the noises of academic disputations, the weapons were forged to drive the arch-enemy, Rome, from the country. And the men who prepared the way were not mystics, who, like 'Haninah ben Dosa, hid their political convictions behind the garb of piety and the performance of miracles. It is true their thoughts, words, and actions were exceedingly guarded, but there is not the least doubt about their aims. And the man who afterwards carried these ideas into fearful effect sat at the feet of these intellectual giants; he drank in every one of their words, and silently but thoroughly prepared the way for the greatest and last battle against the Roman yoke. In Rabbi Akibah the stern doctrines of Rabbi Eliezer and the nationalistic spirit of Rabbi 'Haninah ben Dosa found an ardent supporter. Eagerly, therefore, did he listen to the great disputes which were carried on between the matchless Rabbi Josua ben Hananiah and the great Rabbi Eliezer ben Hyrkanos. The former had taken Ben Zakkai's diplomacy as his sole guide in life, while the latter, who had retained all the learning of his master, was more inclined toward the national policy of 'Haninah ben Dosa; but, vastly more blunt and outspoken in his ideas than 'Haninah, he failed of his purpose and caused himself many years of sorrow.

CHAPTER V

RABBI ELIEZER BEN HYRKANOS

TRADITION in Judaism is like a colored thread running all through the woof of a cloth. One can hardly say where it begins, yet it is never broken. So it is with the teachings of the great masters in Israel. They appear in successive generations, but each stands as the pupil of some earlier teacher whose lessons he has received, and which in turn he transmits to his own disciples, amplified by his own experiences and thoughts.

At the time when writing was rare, it was by word of mouth mainly that the wisdom of one generation was transmitted to those that came after it. It was then a primary object with every great thinker to gather around him a school of disciples to whom as intellectual children he might leave the inheritance of the thoughts that were formed in his own mind.

Ben Zakkai showed a special care in the choice of such disciples from his numerous scholars. One he prized for his quick intelligence and ready wit, another for his marvellous powers of memory, and another for his lofty soul, pure heart, and burning eloquence.

It was for the last-named quality that he specially

favored Elazar ben Arakh. He chose him as his chief assistant in his school, and in his heart he desired him for his own successor. He did not wish, however, to impose him on his pupils merely by the power of his magisterial authority. He desired that the merit which he recognized in Elazar should be also acknowledged by his fellow-students, and for that end he was wont to hold exercises of intellectual powers among them by submitting questions for public discussion. One may serve as an example.

"My children," said the master, "let each of you say what virtue is the most important for man that he may walk the straight path during his life."

"A good eye," said Eliezer ben Hyrkanos. "An eye that desireth nothing which belongeth to others is the chief virtue."

"A worthy associate," said Josua ben Hananiah. "A worthy associate keepeth man from evil ways."

"A good neighbor," said Yosay. "A good neighbor promoteth peace, and peace bringeth happiness."

"Prescience," said Simon. "When one can foresee the consequences of an action he is sure to make no mistake in life."

"A good heart," said Elazar.

And the master, weighing the words of each, said: "The answer of Elazar is the best; for he who hath a good heart possesseth the noblest of all virtues; he is sure to pursue the right path in life; for he is sure to have all the other virtues you enumerated."

This preference established Elazar's position in the school, but in order to raise him to the dignity of Rabbi it was necessary to show the other disciples that Elazar was their superior not only in ethical teaching, but also in philosophical lore, in the mysticism which is contained in the study of the *merkabah*, the vision of Ezekiel, and kindred subjects, —the metaphysics of that day.

The Talmud thus tells how it was done:

"One day Rabbi Yochanan ben Zakkai was riding on the highway, and Elazar ben Arakh was behind with others, and Elazar said: 'Rabbi, repeat to me a passage from the *merkabah*.' And Rabbi Yochanan replied: 'I told thee the *merkabah* is not repeated aloud, but each one reasons upon it alone, according to his individual understanding.' 'Then permit me to discourse upon it,' said Elazar. 'Do so,' replied Rabbi Yochanan.

"They dismounted among the trees and Ben Arakh began to elucidate the *merkabah*. And lo! a fire came from heaven enveloping Rabbi Yochanan, Elazar, and the trees; and there was heard celestial music among the trees, and voices of angels that praised God for that such wisdom was given unto mortals. And when the great Ben Arakh ceased, Rabbi Yochanan rose, kissed his forehead, and said:

"'Praised be the Lord of Israel, who hath given our father Abraham a son who can penetrate and make clear the workings of the *merkabah*. There are some who preach fair but do not act fairly; thou [Ben Arakh] art fair in speech and fair in action. Hail unto thee, Father Abraham, that Elazar ben Arakh is of thy seed.'"[1]

It is to misunderstand the spirit of the Talmud to

suppose that this strange tale was to be taken in a literal sense. It would be childish to think that any supernatural interposition was needed to justify the selection of Elazar to the office for which he was so well qualified, and the talmudic writers were not childish in any sense. The Oriental mind is attached to imagery, and loves to speak in parables. The Hebrews of the time we speak of had, moreover, good reasons to conceal as far as possible their national and religious practices from the notice of the jealous Roman officials who regarded every Jew as a disguised rebel against the empire. The tale of the miraculous fire, if carried to Roman ears, would only be laughed at, but to the Jewish expert its meaning was easy of comprehension. It told in figurative language how Elazar had been duly invested with authority to teach the Law by the recognized master in Israel. The "highway" of discussion is the preliminary examination of his qualifications before the other disciples, figured by the trees. Elazar's knowledge of the practical application of the law, the *halakhah*, had been already known, as well as the soundness of his moral teachings. The master had to test him further in the more recondite doctrines of metaphysics. His eloquence and his insight are recognized by the fire, that is, by the enthusiasm which seizes his audience when he speaks. The praise of the master and the kiss bestowed on the disciple conveyed the tidings of his elevation to the rabbinical dignity to every Hebrew skilled in the law.

Ben Zakkai, though by the favor of Vespasian he

conducted his studies undisturbed, was careful not to let the Roman masters of Palestine know that he was training up teachers and masters in Israel, and forging weapons for an intellectual and moral struggle with the oppressor. The story of Elazar's election was then told to the faithful in Israel under the figure of this narrative.

Elazar needed no further credentials to command the respect of the people. His own character was enough. Generous and lovable, he was also powerful as a disputant and recognized as such.

"Know how to answer an epicurean," was a favorite maxim of his.

By "epicurean," apparently, are meant the followers of the sect of gnostics, a spurious Christian creed which combined the worst immoralities of Greek paganism with a few fragments of Christ's doctrines. Epicurus, the master of the Greek school of thought, which held pleasure to be the highest good, was to the Jewish mind typical of unrestrained sensuality. Hence the name was generally applied to scoffers at the rigid rules of the Mosaic law.

On the death of his master, Ben Zakkai, Elazar took up his abode in Emmaus, a town in the mountains of Palestine famous for the medicinal virtues of its hot springs. He intended to establish a school there and at the same time to restore his health, which had been seriously affected. He never carried out his project. He seemed to sink into a lethargy in his new abode. He wrote little or nothing, and in a few years he passed out of sight. The talmudic authors in two or three places [2] state that the great

Rabbi "forgot his learning." It is not impossible that there is a hidden meaning to these statements. In the mountain village Elazar had probably met with Christians, and been cured of his ailments among them. His acceptance of the faith in Christ would readily be described as "forgetting the Law" by talmudic imagination.

Ben Arakh was the admitted head of the college of students formed by Ben Zakkai. Eliezer ben Hyrkanos was next to him in reputation as a scholar. His memory was prodigious and he retained without apparent effort the contents of a library on its tablets. Indeed, so well stored was he with the maxims and decisions of the famous teachers of all Jewish schools that men often taxed him with betraying the cause of the Hillelites, to whom he properly belonged, by decisions made in the spirit of Shammaiism.[3] Eliezer was utterly indifferent to popular favor, and was stubborn in his own views. If the Sanhedrin decided, as it sometimes did, contrary to what Eliezer believed to be the genuine tradition of the law, he would not yield. Opinions, he held, should be weighed, not merely counted. So far did he carry his tenacity that he was finally laid under sentence of excommunication by the majority in the Sanhedrin. Gamaliel, its president and brother-in-law to Ben Hyrkanos, was obliged to pronounce the sentence.[4]

Eliezer's stubbornness was inherited from his father, a noble of the highest race by birth,[5] but by choice a farmer with no taste for books or learning. Eliezer alone among his brothers desired to become a scholar. The story of his choice is told in characteristic figurative style.

As Eliezer was ploughing one day a keen longing for learning came on him. He stopped his horse, sat down, and wept. His father came to ask the cause of his behavior.

"Why dost thou weep?" he asked. "Dost thou dislike the field thou art ploughing? If so, change places with another. Or dost thou dislike the whole task?"

Eliezer continued to weep, and the father rather hotly asked again the reason for such behavior.

"I desire to study the law," replied Eliezer at last.

"Thou art over old to begin now," said the old man. "At twenty-eight years it is time to marry. Thou mayest later send thy children to school, but it is too late for thee."

Eliezer made no answer and his father was mystified. His son began to pine away and for two weeks he could hardly eat or sleep. Then, while in the field, he again sat down and wept bitterly. An old man came by and asked:

"Why dost thou weep, son of Hyrkanos?"

"Because I long to study the law," Eliezer replied.

"Then go to Jerusalem, to Yochanan ben Zakkai, if thou wouldst study it," said the old man, who was no other than the prophet Elijah himself, and who then vanished from sight.

Eliezer arose and walked to Jerusalem. He found the college of the famous master and addressed him in a voice broken with sobs. The astonished Rabbi asked the reason of his grief.

"Because I desire to study the law," was the answer.

"Whose son art thou?" asked Rabbi Yochanan; but Eliezer was silent.

"Canst thou read the prayers?" was the next question, and Eliezer confessed he could not.

That a grown man who could not even read his prayers should want to be a student amused the Rabbi, who jocosely offered to teach him the prayers. Eliezer only wept afresh at the evident sarcasm of this answer.

"Why weepest thou now?" asked the master.

"It is the law I would study," Eliezer persisted.

Ben Zakkai was struck with the singular earnestness of the appeal and gently said:

"Son, I will teach thee myself two lessons in the law each week; they will be decisions which thou must commit to memory."

He then drew the new-comer apart from the others and gave him some comments on points of the law. Eliezer listened with rapture and drank in every word of the master. The latter finally concluded, and, telling the novice to return in a week for examination, sent him away. On the Rabbi's friendly suggestion, two residents of the city, the priest Yosay and Josua ben Hananiah, the teacher, offered a home and food to the new disciple. He went to the priest's house, was entertained hospitably, and then retired to repeat to himself the lesson he had received, no word of which escaped his singularly retentive memory. He repeated it over and over during the week with such anxiety that he would not even take time to eat. At the fixed time he came to Ben Zakkai.

The master received him with a smile. He fully expected a troublesome hour in going over the first lesson of an ignorant man, but was astounded when the novice recited his lesson word for word and commented on it with the sagacity of a master mind.

"This man's mind is like a cemented cistern, which lets no drop of water filter away," exclaimed Ben Zakkai in delight. He bent down to embrace his pupil, but the latter's breath, owing to his long fast, had an odor too strong for the Rabbi's endurance. Involuntarily he thrust Eliezer's head from him and the latter again burst into passionate tears.

"Son," exclaimed Rabbi Yochanan with a laugh, "if thy learning rises to heaven as forcibly as thy breath reaches my nostrils thou wilt be great among the greatest doctors of the law. Whose child art thou?"

"The son of Hyrkanos," said Eliezer this time.

"Verily, thou art sprung from a famous house and thou didst not tell me so. This very day thou must eat in my house," exclaimed Ben Zakkai.

"I have already eaten at the house of my host," said the haughty scholar, who felt insulted and scarcely cared to accept the proffered hospitality.

"Where dost thou stay?" asked the master, who doubted the statement after his experience.

"I live with Rabbi Yosay the priest, and with Rabbi Josua ben Hananiah."

Ben Zakkai sent to inquire whether Eliezer had dined that day. He learned he had eaten nothing for eight days. Ben Zakkai then insisted upon Eliezer's dining with him, and thenceforth his position as one of the disciples was fixed in the school.

His brothers were glad that Eliezer had incurred his father's displeasure by leaving home. They disliked him because the father showed him preference, and as they beheld the rage of Hyrkanos they heaped abuse upon Eliezer, and urged their father to go to Jerusalem and publicly disinherit the disobedient son. The old man, who knew not the hearts of his sons, vowed that he would disinherit Eliezer. But as day followed day, and month month, his heart was sad, and he stayed at home; he could not find it in his heart to cut off his beloved son Eliezer. Thus years passed by, in toil and in bitterness; for the eager student seemed to have forgotten his kindred altogether.

One day Hyrkanos heard that Eliezer was a student at Ben Zakkai's academy. The intelligence affected him like a stroke of lightning. The old anger which had been dormant awoke.

"A student!" he said. "A student of the law, which saith, 'Honor thy father'! A disobedient son is he and naught else."

Forthwith he journeyed to Jerusalem. It happened that Ben Zakkai gave a feast to which all the great men in Jerusalem were bidden. Hyrkanos, whose family was one of the noblest in Israel, went to Ben Zakkai's house. There he met the foremost nobles of Palestine, Ben Sisith Hacknass and Nakdimon ben Gorion, who could have given to every inhabitant of Jerusalem three hundred measures of flour and still have retained enough to feed the entire country for ten years,[6] and Calba Sebuah, the owner of immense gold-mines.[7]

It was not easy to get into the hall. Hundreds had been bidden, and others had come without that formality, with all who belonged to the academy besides, and innumerable attendants.

Hyrkanos at length made his way into the great hall and asked for his son Eliezer.

"Which Eliezer seekest thou?" some students asked.

"Which Eliezer!" cried the old noble. "I seek the son of Hyrkanos, that disobedient——"

He stopped; for at that moment the students made way for a distinguished-looking man. Even the angry Hyrkanos was awed at the majesty which shone from his face.

"Who is he?" Hyrkanos asked in a whisper.

"That is the great disciple, Rabbi Eliezer ben Hyrkanos," they answered.

A mist rose before Hyrkanos's eyes; he could hardly believe his senses.

"Who did you say this man is?" he asked again.

"Dost thou not know him?" they cried, "of whom 't is said that if all the laws and ordinances were lost he could write them from memory; he of whom the master hath said that his mind is like a cemented cistern which lets no drop of water filter away, our great Rabbi Eliezer ben Hyrkanos?"

A revulsion of feeling took place in the father's

heart. Anger gave way to pride and love; tears fell from his eyes. He mastered himself and, seeing his son take his seat near Ben Zakkai, he sent word to the latter, saying:

"Hyrkanos, the father of Eliezer, is here, unknown to him."

Ben Zakkai at once ordered that the old noble be seated by his side. He looked at Eliezer and said to him:

"Say something."

"I am like a cistern, which can give just as much water as was put into it; even so, O master, can I but repeat what I learned from thee," Eliezer replied.

"Nay, thou art a living spring, which giveth water without measure. Thou canst discourse more law than was given on Mount Sinai. But lest my presence be a hindrance to thy discourse, I will leave the room," said the master, and went out.

Rabbi Eliezer began. As he spoke light seemed to shine from his face like that of Moses. All the people stood in rapt attention at the marvellous speech which came from the mouth of Eliezer. But Rabbi Yochanan ben Zakkai came from behind and kissed his head and said:

"Glory be to thee, Father Abraham, and to you, Fathers Isaac and Jacob, that this one is descended from your seed!"

When Hyrkanos saw what the master did, and heard his words, he cried:

"Verily, glory should be mine; for he is descended from me."

But when Eliezer recognized his father, he feared.

"Father," said he, "be seated elsewhere; I shall be unable to continue."

The happy father did not want him to continue.

"My son, my beloved son," he cried, "come to me."

In a moment Eliezer was by his father's side, begging forgiveness.

"Dear son," said Hyrkanos, "I came to disinherit thee; but now I bid thee come home, thou shalt have all."

"I seek not earthly treasure, father," said Eliezer, "I strive for spiritual wealth, and here indeed have I found what I sought, and here shall I remain."*

He continued his studies in Jerusalem. He was one of the disciples who carried their master through the Death Gate into the Roman camp,* and when Ben Zakkai founded his school in Yamnai, Eliezer assisted him in teaching the law. After the master's death, Eliezer went to Lydda in Southern Judea, and there opened a school. Soon his auditors became so numerous that he hired a ruined circus, and there taught the multitude the Word of God and the sayings of the great men in Israel.

It is probable that the veneration accorded him by the crowd made him arrogant. In virtue of his unfailing memory he claimed the obedience of the Sanhedrin to his decisions.

That body, however, declined to accept Ben Hyrkanos's decisions as supreme in the law. The majority of the day, it held, had that supremacy, and to oppose the will of the majority was treason.

Eliezer opposed it, however, in the full assurance that right was on his own side. He was specially severe on the president, Gamaliel, though the latter was married to his sister.[10]

Rabbi Josua was the champion of the majority rule against Eliezer. He was presiding Judge under Gamaliel. A question was submitted to Eliezer's decision which had already been ruled on in the Sanhedrin. Eliezer laid down the law in a directly contrary sense. He was cited before the tribunal as a teacher of false laws. There he maintained his former decision and claimed that tradition was the infallible tribunal at which the law could be properly interpreted.

The trial is told in the Talmud in figurative language, which, however, gives the substantial facts clearly enough. On that day, it says,[11] Rabbi Eliezer answered every question, but the council would not accept his answers as the true meaning of the law.

"If the law be as I say, let that fruit tree bear witness," said Rabbi Eliezer.

Whereupon the tree near the school was torn from its place and cast away a hundred yards.

"The testimony of the fruit tree is not enough," the Rabbis replied.

"If the law be as I say, yonder brook shall bear witness," said Rabbi Eliezer.

And lo, the water in the brook flowed backwards.

"The testimony of the brook is insufficient," they said.

"If the law be as I say, the walls of this house shall bear witness," Rabbi Eliezer cried.

Thereupon the walls bent inward as if to fall. But Rabbi Josua called to them, saying:

"When sages dispute about the law, how dare you interfere?"

And the walls did not fall, because of the presence of Rabbi Josua, neither did they straighten, because of the presence of Rabbi Eliezer, and they are yet standing so.

And again the voice of Rabbi Eliezer was heard:

"If the law be as I say, let the host of heaven bear witness."

Whereupon a voice from heaven spoke:

"What would you with Rabbi Eliezer, since the law is ever as he sayeth?"

At this Rabbi Josua arose and said:

"We heed not the celestial voice in matters of the law; the law is not in heaven."

This Rabbi Jeremiah explains to mean that though God had given the law on Mount Sinai, he had also given to man to interpret the law, and in the law it is written that the majority shall decide.

A knowledge of the affairs, both religious and political, of that day is required, as well as a clear comprehension of the spirit of the Talmud, to understand the peculiar form of expression employed by the Rabbis. Only then can the full gravity of that famous trial be appreciated. Then the "testimony" is both material and relevant, and because of the historical truth underlying it we recognize in that trial a critical moment in the history of the Jewish religion. I venture to say that that trial has had its effect upon Judaism and the Jews during all the centuries that have passed since that memorable day; that it has settled many vexed questions, and has made clear the way pursued by the leaders in Israel for all time. This hyperbolical account of the famous trial is not a mere fancy of the Rabbis interlarded with superstitions, as has been claimed by some writers on talmudical subjects. There is real pathos in Rabbi Eliezer's plea, and there is force in the exceptions taken by these Rabbis of the majority. Eliezer pleads for tradition,—strict adherence to the law as transmitted from master to master. He held that no man nor body of men had the right to change aught in the body of the law under any conditions. The other Rabbis of the Sanhedrin, particularly Josua, opposed this idea, and held, with Ben Zakkai and Hillel, that the end of the law is the welfare of humanity, and that all in it is subordinate to this principle; that there is a wide difference between religion itself and the customs which in time gather around it, customs which die or become obsolete when the necessity or the expediency for their observance ceases.

Eliezer failed to understand his master. Maybe Ben Zakkai knew that Eliezer did not understand him, that he did not penetrate his policy and the motives which prompted his utterances; maybe the master knew that Eliezer was but a receptacle of learning, without discrimination, and Ben Zakkai, therefore, ironically called Eliezer "a cemented cistern which lets no drop of water filter away." Eliezer's was not a pliant mind. He knew all the lore and law of his people, and his obedience to the law equalled his knowledge; to make the law subservient to circumstances was repugnant to his nature. The religious conditions of that day strengthened his preconceived ideas. Christianity with its excrescence, gnosticism, had sprung into existence on precisely the principles advocated by Eliezer's opponents, namely, that altered conditions made altered laws. Eliezer's quarrel with the Sanhedrists recalls Hillel's dispute with the Bethyrahs.[12] Did Eliezer entertain aspirations for the presidency? Did he hope that the Sanhedrin, seeing that he was the only one who knew every tradition, would give him Gamaliel's place? It is hardly possible that he did not know the character of Hillel's successors, who would have given up anything rather than the presidency. Though this feature of the controversy may have interest from a local political point the chief interest and value must be sought in the religious considerations that prompted Eliezer's stand against the other Rabbis. His reference to the bread-fruit tree points to Christianity, which, though it had its origin in tradition, refused to abide by it.[13]

The Sanhedric Rabbis have no regard for Eliezer's argument. The reference to Christianity they think a point ill taken. There was nothing in Christianity; its roots were too shallow in the national and religious soil; it could be uprooted and cast away a hundred, nay, four hundred, yards.

"Hold you so lightly," cried Eliezer, "the traditions of our masters? Would you arrogate unto yourselves authority to add to or to abridge the law? I tell you, there is no authority that at any time could lawfully do this. We must abide by tradition, which runneth like a murmuring brook through the meadows of Hebraic law and lore. Our masters taught and builded the spiritual kingdom on tradition. I have received it from Ben Zakkai, and he received it from Hillel, and he from Shemaiah and Abtalion, and they received it from the Great Synod, and they again from the prophets, and so on, up to Moses, the lawgiver himself, who received the oral law from God on Sinai." By slighting tradition, you sever the present from the past, you cause the waters of the brook to recede and flow backwards. Taken from its glorious tradition Judaism cannot survive."

At this plea many of the Sanhedrists are affected. They become thoughtful, retrospective. In sooth, "the brook flows backwards." They contemplate this grand source of Judaism, they follow the turns and windings of the brook, they hear its murmuring, they see the checkered scenes, they behold the great vistas strewn with the dead, the martyred men and women of their race, who gave up life for their glorious heritage; they behold Egypt, Syria, Babylon; they see Moses, Ezra, Nehemiah, Cyrus; they see gloom and glory, thrones and tears, joy and sorrow, sanctity and defilement, Temple and ruins; they see all that as they mentally travel along the edge of the brook; they behold and reflect, and their hearts turn to Eliezer.

But there are in that body of men some whose reflections have brought them to far different conclusions. What they have seen convinces them that the law was always suited to prevalent conditions. It is true, the surroundings of the brook may be grander near its source; there are dells and glens and fair fields, but the brook itself is narrow at its starting-point. Thence removed by distance, the brook grows shallow and wide. Barren fields, ruined cities, desolate homes, and blighted hopes line its path. An oppressor has forced the Jew to worship the ever-living God of Israel secretly; the Sanhedrin must devise means so to administer the law as to offend neither God nor cæsar. Since there is no higher human authority, a majority of its own body must decide what is right and what is wrong, and from its decision there shall be no appeal. Innovations? yea, even innovations and total abrogation of certain laws shall be undertaken, if such a procedure be deemed necessary.

Eliezer saw countless dangers in innovations. He whose rigorous adherence to religious discipline had prompted him to apply even the strict measures of the Shammaiites, so that he was thought to be one of them,[16] could see no reason for changing aught in the religious principles simply because the times required it. To him it seemed an undermining of ancient authority, aye, even of the very school that opposed him. They were shaking an established system, thereby giving tacit licence to future scholars for vandalism. He could not believe that his brother-in-law, the president of the Sanhedrin, could so far forget what he owed to Ben Zakkai as to oppose his decisions for which Eliezer now pleaded. He could scarcely believe that Akibah, his favorite disciple, whose soul was aflame with the idea of restoring the independence of the commonwealth, could oppose him. How could the proud Gamaliel, who boasted Davidic descent, attack the foundation upon which rested the glory of his patriarchate? Nothing would suit Rome better than a weakening in traditional belief. You think of policy against Rome, said Eliezer, while she thinks only of your destruction. Your strength can come only by an unswerving adherence to the law. With it there is power, without it weakness; with it realization of thy hope, Akibah, and thy ambition, House of David: without it there is blight, eternal bondage, and ignominy. And you two, Gamaliel and Akibah, you who are the walls of the school, will you not testify to the truth of my words, give evidence as to the justice of my cause?

And the "walls" yielded, and bent forward. How could they withstand that plea? How could they sit silent, when he had laid bare their innermost thoughts? How remain calm in the face of those facts? How could they leave the great master to shame and sorrow? Akibah in particular was touched; he knew what Eliezer said was the truth. He recognized the force of his master's words; he felt their prophetic import, and who knows but that at that moment his mind conceived the plan of the revolution, which later cost Rome more blood and gold than the campaign of Titus? It was he who first yielded to his master's plea. Gamaliel, the president, too, was moved. It was a moment pregnant with danger of division and disruption.

The pleader was not only the president's brother-in-law, but his superior in learning, the disciple and friend of Ben Zakkai. He wavered. But his throat was dry, his tongue cleaved to his palate. He could not utter a sound. The feeling of the Sanhedrin was intense, the silence oppressive. It needed but a word to give the assembly a powerful momentum in favor of Eliezer, to acknowledge him their master, perhaps their president. But at that moment the fate of the Sanhedrin and of Eliezer was decided by his former companion and colleague, the intrepid Rabbi Josua. He saw the weakness of Gamaliel; he knew the bent of Akibah's mind. In a measure he sympathized with them. But he knew also that it was impossible to accept inflexible tradition or the maxims of Eliezer. He saw that it would disrupt the Sanhedrin; that it would lose its power of independent action; that it would remain servile to the will of one man—a great man, surely—but one man only. And this last Sanhedrin, the faint reflection of that older one which had given character and grandeur to Judaism, should bequeath to coming generations the great principle of popular rule by representative power, the direction of which should forever be in the hands of the majority. He felt keenly when he saw the faltering "walls," Gamaliel and Akibah, and it is his scathing sarcasm which dooms them to silence for the time being. Nothing hurt Gamaliel like being told that he did not belong to the learned, and had no sympathy with them.[16] The pliant Akibah felt less hurt at insults, but he heard them often enough.[17] Seeing the proceedings in this light, one feels keenly the force of Josua's words:

"When sages are doing battle in the law, why do you mix in? Why show your weakness so?" he cries. "This is not a question of individual opinion, but of national solidarity, and we can only grow in strength when we sustain the majority." The "walls," cowed by Josua's remarks, were silent. They loved Eliezer and would gladly have sided with him, but they feared to oppose the blacksmith, whose arguments were made with an intellectual force like that with which he wielded the sledge-hammer."[18]

But Eliezer was a great master; he had gone into that contest to establish a rule for himself and his school. He was fighting for a lofty object. He would not be ruled by incompetents. On his side was the matchless authority of tradition, the heaven-given. He knew it. In the storehouse of his mind there were treasures heaped upon treasures, and the people knew that he spoke by authority. They flocked to hear his discourses; they hung upon his words; they believed him; they preferred his word, sanctified by the magic phrase, "so have I heard it," to the decisions of the Sanhedrin. He appealed now to those who were bent upon his ruin.

"The voice of the people is as the voice of heaven," he cried; "the people know that I was ordained by the great master, Ben Zakkai; let the people decide whether my authority shall stand or no."

This appeal brought Josua upon his feet. His

keen intellect saw the seriousness of the situation. Eliezer's words were something more than a plea,—they threatened the very existence of the Sanhedrin. None knew as well as he what power Rabbi Eliezer's word had with the masses. He was of the gallant band that had stood around their master, Ben Zakkai, whom the multitude adored, and of its survivors none enjoyed the people's confidence as Eliezer. Heroic measures were needed to curb Eliezer's power.

"The people are guided by the decisions of this Sanhedrin," cried Josua; "to it has been given the right of judgment. The law does not abide in heaven, it has been given to man on Sinai. There it was ordained that the majority should rule,[19] and if a voice from heaven spake otherwise we should not heed it. I repeat, the majority rules, and he is a traitor who speaks to the contrary—excommunication shall fall upon him."

The word was spoken. Every man in the room trembled. Gamaliel was silent. As president of the Sanhedrin he had to act, and rather than jeopardize his own position he sacrificed his brother-in-law.

Eliezer hated him unto death, and though Gamaliel later excused himself, on the plea of preventing a quarrel in Israel,[20] Eliezer never forgave him. He was less wroth with Rabbi Akibah, for whom he had small respect, and whom he considered "one of the contemptible people "[21]; but Gamaliel's vacillation filled him with bitterness. He was heedless of Rabbi Josua's warning. He defied the Sanhedrin and left it, still maintaining his right against their decisions. His punishment was swift and severe. He was excommunicated. His decisions were annulled, and the objects he had declared clean were taken to the public square and burned.[22]

To conciliate Rabbi Josua and the Sanhedrin, and to save himself a severe discipline, Akibah volunteered his services as messenger to bear the evil tidings to Eliezer.

"If an improper person were to take the message," said the diplomatic Rabbi Akibah, "he would destroy the world." [23]

Thereupon he put on a black mantle, covered his head with a black cloth, and sat down upon the ground, four yards' distance from Eliezer's house.

When Eliezer saw him dressed in black, he asked:

"Why art thou dressed in black, and why sittest thou at a distance?"

"It would seem, O Rabbi, that thy colleagues are separating themselves from thee," Akibah said gently.

Eliezer understood. He tore his garments, took off his sandals, and sat himself on the ground. His tears fell fast; he did not think they would resort to such a measure.

When it was known that Rabbi Eliezer had been excommunicated by the Sanhedrin, sorrow showed itself on all sides. Even women discussed the punishment of the great Rabbi and neglected their housework; or, as the Talmud puts it, "the dough spoiled in their hands." [24]

Sad were the days of his life then. Excluded

from all intercourse even with his disciples, gloomy thoughts darkened his mind; what was his great learning, his life, good for now? He thought of ending his misery by self-destruction. But in those dark moments light came to him from the past. His soul gained strength from the reflection of the life and hardships of his master, Ben Zakkai, who in ruin and despair held to the Word of God as the only means of salvation. And then the soul of Rabbi Eliezer grew strong again; his faith returned. Suicide, he saw, was the coward's means of shirking supreme effort and responsibility. And in this spirit he wrote a decision against suicide, which (referring to Genesis ix., 5), he says, is as criminal as murder.[25] His faith in God's mercy became as a rock. A great joy entered his heart. He felt kindly towards all Israel, even to those who had wrought his ruin. Love of his fellow-man and faith in God were the two lights which illumined his soul. "The honor of thy fellow-man shall be dear to thee as thine own," he says.[26] "He, who, having bread in his basket, asketh, What shall I eat to-morrow? belongeth to those who have little faith in God's providence," is another maxim of his. This sentiment, though thoroughly Jewish, even rabbinical, was in all probability learned by him from the apostles, with some of whom he was in fraternal intercourse after his excommunication."[27]

The fact that Rabbi Eliezer was excommunicated had no effect upon the people of Lydda. The harsh decree of the Sanhedrin against their beloved Rabbi incensed them to such a degree that many refused to abide by the Sanhedric decisions. A split in the ranks of the remnant of Israel seemed imminent. Eliezer saw that such an unfortunate movement would not only cause the law of God to suffer, but that Rome, finding a pretext for interference, would stamp out the last vestige of Jewish life on Palestinian soil. Believing that the people needed an authority for their guidance, and that, despite its faults, the Sanhedrin was the only authority by whose mandates the people could live in peace, Rabbi Eliezer gave up his school in Lydda and moved to Cæsarea. There he was in close intercourse with James, the disciple of Jesus,"' and others who confessed Him of Nazareth as the promised Messiah. The Christian body stood just then in very bad repute with Rome. Christians were put to death when arrested, and suspicion of one's being a Christian was sufficient to cause his arrest. Eliezer was a man of distinction, whose associates were easily noted. Rome watched the movements and doings of the great men among the Hebrews. Perhaps, too, some Jews themselves, disliking Eliezer's relationship with the Christians, informed the Roman authorities. Be this as it may, Rabbi Eliezer was arrested and charged with being a Christian.

There was no evidence to prove the charge, but the Roman judges had a simple way of finding the adherents of that "rebel," over whose crucified form they had mockingly written the word "INRI," the initials of the words, "Iesus Nazarae, Rex Iudæorum" (Jesus of Nazareth, King of the Jews). The adherents of that man recognized no judge other than Him; they took punishment and death with the same meekness and resignation as He whom they adored, rejoicing at the privilege of being crucified as was their Messiah.

It was different with the Jews who, after their conquest by Rome, accepted, outwardly at least, the Roman sovereignty. The Roman judges knew that an orthodox Jew would bend before a Roman rather than be thought a Christian.

The judge before whom Eliezer was taken knew of the Rabbi's great learning and scarcely believed him guilty of the charge.

"Can it be that thou, a scholar, dost adhere to such folly?" he said.

The question brought a train of thought into the mind of Eliezer. The judge called Christianity folly. It is a wonderful folly which centres in human love, in mercy, in kindness, in charity, in self-denial. That is a strange folly which lifts up the fallen, gives hope to the despairing, and promises salvation to all. That is a gracious folly which bids forgive a brother man seven times seven times, though he had offended as often. That is a divine folly which seeks its glory in meekness, its reward in bestowing human happiness, its hope in heaven.

Where was Josua in the hour of distress? Where was the man who, though a scholastic opponent, had been his friend for so many years,—the friend with whom he had shared the trials of the siege in Jerusalem; with whom he had shared sufferings and sorrows, and the dangers in rescuing their beloved master from the besieged city; with whom he had travelled over land and sea to the city of Rome to plead with the emperor Trajan to revoke the edicts against the Jews?[29] Eliezer was bitter against Akibah who, after the excommunication, never came near him. It hurt him to think that in the disregard of his scholastic authority, against which the ban was directed, he had forgotten their friendly relations of former days.

Here, on the other hand, were James and his fellow-believers in Jesus as the Messiah, men whose association was not reminiscent of past grandeur and sorrow, of scholastic fellowship and youthful friendship; with whom he had no learned disputes that left in his soul either the pleasure of the conqueror or the regret of the vanquished; nothing but simple faith, nothing but brotherly love, nothing but the grace born of meekness and piety. And these strange men, these despised Christians, had come to him like elder brothers; they had soothed his turbulent soul and healed his wounded heart; they had surrounded him with love and devotion without asking on his part, and without price on theirs. He loved them for that, and as the thought passed through his mind the spirit in him grew keen for self-sacrifice.

His eye fell upon the judge, whose face was mild and whose speech had a certain amount of reverence. This reverence was due to the learned Jew, who, despite all the political disabilities imposed on him, had to be humored. The Romans knew the influence the learned among the Jews wielded among the masses. If Eliezer confessed himself a Christian, he would be outside the pale of that regard for Rome. A Christian could have no influence with the Jews, be his learning ever so great. Eliezer knew that such was the judgment of the Romans. The thought, too, came to him of a possible reconciliation with his former friends; he saw himself reinstated in his former position, again shining as the light in Israel, the disciple of the great Ben Zakkai. What was James to him? What were all the Christians?

"I trust in the justice of the judge," he said.

The word was spoken. By it Eliezer denied the Nazarene and proclaimed his disregard for the Christians. It was so understood by the judge, who said:

"It is evident from thy speech that thou art no Christian, since thou wouldst abide by my judgment." [80]

Eliezer was dismissed, but the incident had its effect upon his mind. Having thus openly renounced Christianity, James and the other Christians shunned him. Soon loneliness, wounded pride, and remorse were the only reward of his vacillation. His body soon succumbed to his mental suffering,—Rabbi Eliezer became sick unto death.

The Rabbis in Yamnai, hearing of his illness, sent Akibah and others to visit him. The sight of his former disciple greatly affected the sick man. After all, thought he, old friends were the best, they could always be relied on at the last moment. Gently he reproached Akibah for his neglect: the latter as gently told Eliezer that the main reason why the

Rabbis had kept away was because of the report of his apostasy. When Eliezer heard this he was quite overcome. Then after all they had not been his enemies, but friends bewailing his error. He made an open confession and again recanted Christianity.[31] But when the visiting Rabbis asked his opinion whether *Peloni*, by which they meant Jesus,[32] had a share in the bliss of Paradise,[33] he evaded the question; he could not bring himself to speak ill of one whose teachings seemed to him sublime; and to speak well of Him was, in the present state of recantation, equally impossible. Therefore he started a discussion about Sanhedric decisions, and soon the combative spirit overpowered all other sentiments, even that of physical pain. He was again the aggressive Titan who once defied the entire Sanhedrin. He seemed to grow in strength, his voice gathered volume and power as he hurled his sharp sentences against those who opposed the authority of what he had conceived to be the right form of interpretation in accordance with tradition. He put the entire force of his fast-fading life into his assertions. What the others had declared to be unclean he pronounced clean, and with the word "clean" on his lips he sank down and died.

A great light had gone out in Israel; forgotten were all disputes of former days; forgotten was the bitterness which these quarrels had engendered. Rabbi Josua bent down and kissed the face of the dear dead friend and companion, and at once removed the ban. Then the Rabbis carried the body to Lydda, Eliezer's former place of activity. There

Rabbi Akibah delivered a touching eulogy over the remains of his master, and amidst groans and lamentations, the foremost man in Israel was laid to his last rest.[34]

Rabbi Josua, more than any other, felt that with the death of Eliezer ben Hyrkanos much valuable learning was lost; that his mind had indeed been as a "cemented cistern which lets no drop of water filter away." Josua felt that they had buried a book of wisdom,[35] and though the death of Eliezer removed a dangerous opponent to his activity, Josua yet loved the man, who always fought fair, though often fierce and vicious as a lion. And when, after a time, some Sanhedrists sought to repeal certain laws and decisions enacted by Rabbi Eliezer, Josua, who was then Acting Patriarch, cried:

"It is not meet to fight a dead lion."[36]

Thus it came to pass that he who fought Eliezer bitterest when alive became his defender and, maybe, the conserver of the literary works which bear Eliezer's name. Their quarrels, it must be remembered, were not for self-aggrandizement, but for the perpetuation of Judaism; and any harshness that sprang out of them was directed against the means rather than against the aim. After the death of Eliezer, the activity of the schools became marked for its decided national aspect, which the circumspect Josua could not check, but which his wonderful sagacity could conceal and protect from without.

CHAPTER VI

RABBI JOSUA BEN HANANIAH

RABBI JOSUA BEN HANANIAH, the third disciple of Ben Zakkai, differed from Eliezer as day from night. Eliezer's obstinacy brought him under the judgment of the Sanhedrin,—Josua's subtlety made him its master. He supported the authority of the majority in principle, and in practice he managed the majority. Gamaliel, the president, was but a figure-head when Josua attended the sessions. The shrewd and calm Josua, as presiding judge of the Sanhedric court, easily manipulated matters to his own benefit, and appeared as the injured party, to whom an apology was due.[1] His master mind commanded respect from the populace and Sanhedrin alike, and even from a Roman emperor. Ben Zakkai characterized him in a pithy sentence: "He is like a three-ply cord, which doth not break."[2]

He was from birth intended for the sacred profession.[3] Being of the tribe of Levi, he early became a member of the Temple choir, and thence a pupil of Ben Zakkai. Music and Hebrew were not his only studies. He applied himself to Latin and Greek, to mathematics, geography, physics, and astronomy. In the latter science he computed the appearance of a comet for the year 89 A.C.⁴ His familiarity with Greek was extensive. A relative of Hadrian, Aquila, who translated the Pentateuch into that language, submitted his work for criticism to Josua and Eliezer. Josua expressed himself in terms of praise.⁵ This diplomacy served the Rabbi later with Hadrian. Josua was in temper a modern Bohemian, careless of his personal appearance, but of sparkling wit and biting sarcasm. Subtle in argument, liberal in religion, he was full of resources for moulding public opinion. In his day there was none like him as statesman, orator, or diplomat. His life was not without romance, yet affections of the heart had not sufficient power to influence the mental balance of Josua. When quite young he fell in love with the daughter of a priest. The engagement was made public and the young scholar was happy. One day he met with an accident which confined him to his bed for some time. Meanwhile the father found what seemed a better match, and broke the engagement with Josua.

The lovers met once more and the girl told a tearful tale of a father's tyranny to which she was forced to submit. Josua felt much hurt. The priest was but one of the licensed paupers, of whom there were thousands in Jerusalem, and whose descent from Aaron, the first High Priest, was largely supported by the evidence of their own assertions, while Josua was already a rising scholar, who it was surmised would later play a great part in the commonwealth. Josua was conscious of his own worth, and when his colleagues sought to console him, he remarked with sarcasm :

"I suppose an alliance with me was not honor enough for the High Priest Aaron." [6]

It does not appear that Josua ever married. He sought diversion in study, manual labor (he became a smith and a needle-maker), and in travel, which broadened his views and later on made him a mighty power among the ever-discontented Hebrews.

As a student he won the highest fame. He was made president of the Court of Appeals, the highest office of the Sanhedrin after that of president. He was not one to let passion interfere with political designs, and, his policy being popular power, he was ready to sacrifice all sentiment to that aim. It was he who cut off Eliezer's authority in the Sanhedrin; because in his course he foresaw danger to the solidarity of that institution; and he it was who defeated the president of the Sanhedrin, when that official opposed him in the assembly. Josua disliked a one-man power. His spirit was democratic, and he suffered no law to pass which tended to increase the religious burden of the people, unless the law was directed to prevent immorality.

"You cannot hinder lewdness, but you can check it by care," was his sententious remark.'

In the matter of ceremonialism, in long prayers, in countless observances which Gamaliel tried to add, he stood for the people and against the Rabbis.

"Let them observe the laws they have," he said; "don't increase them. Busy men and laborers have no time for minute and useless observances. If you pour water into a cask full of oil, the oil is bound to flow over and get lost. Make no law which the congregation as a body cannot observe."[8]

Gamaliel, the president, would have dealt with Josua, if he could, as the latter dealt with Eliezer. But he found himself against a majority which he could not move. The majority was with the intrepid and witty debater. Unable to conquer Josua, he sought to humiliate him. It was not permissible to advise any one against the expressed instruction of the president unless openly debated and voted on. In other words, the president's command or decision in any question was operative as law until the Sanhedrin had voted against it. In simpler affairs such procedure was not taken, and the president's decision not only had all the force of a law, but became immediately operative. Josua disliked this arbitrary power and at every opportunity worked against it. Gamaliel knew of Josua's opposition, but was unable to confront him. At length the day came; the president was determined to silence Josua for good. Gamaliel had decided that evening prayers were obligatory, the decision being based on biblical authority. This decision created much hardship for the busy men, who if they failed in that devotion became amenable to the law. Rabbi Akibah,[9] who thought the time opportune to avenge his master Eliezer, Gamaliel, and his own wrongs upon Josua, and get him into contempt with the Sanhedrin, asked him if he thought evening prayers obligatory.

"I hold evening prayers to be a matter of individual conscience," said Josua; "if a man feels like praying let him do so."

This was all Akibah wanted. He went to Gamaliel and informed him that Josua was speaking against his decision. Gamaliel saw a chance to punish Josua if the latter would publicly repeat what he had said privately. Accordingly he instructed his informant to ask him the same question in the Sanhedrin, and ordered Josua to be present. When, the session had opened, Akibah asked whether evening prayers were obligatory.

"They are," said the president. "Does any one object to this decision?" he continued, looking at Josua.

The latter recognized that Gamaliel had planned a deliberate attack on him.

"No voice is raised against thy decision," he said.

"I am told that thou didst declare evening prayer a matter of individual conscience. Stand up; there is a witness against thee," the president said, pointing at Akibah.

"A living witness is here to testify against me," Josua quietly replied, "and I acknowledge that I have uttered such an opinion."

Gamaliel was not satisfied with this confession. Turning from Josua with a contemptuous shrug, he began his discourse for the day without bidding Josua to sit down, which he could not do without the president's permission. Josua stood without protest.

The Sanhedrin, considering Gamaliel's action an

affront to the president of the court as severe as undeserved, rose in a body and commanded Gamaliel to stop his discourse and step down. He was declared unfit longer to occupy his exalted office, and a wealthy and learned young man, Elazar ben Azariah, was thereupon elected in Gamaliel's place. Not until he had humbly asked Josua's pardon, which the latter readily granted, did the Sanhedrin reinstate Gamaliel in the presidential chair.

Thus did Rabbi Josua's diplomatic silence defeat a man who thought himself in the height of his power; whereas if Josua had lost control of himself even by but a word, he might have been subjected to severe discipline, if not to excommunication.

Gamaliel was a man who needed but a hint to see the error of his ways. He felt that he was dealing not with an individual, but with a power. A man who, without fortune, could make the council of the nation subservient to his will, deserved admiration. No sooner did Gamaliel recognize this than anger fled his soul. He recognized that it was Josua who really had put supreme power in the hands of the majority. But for his subtle intellect, another, perhaps the stubborn Eliezer ben Hyrkanos, with his Shammaittic tendencies to inflexible law, might have occupied the presidential chair. Gamaliel one day went to Josua's house, which was not much better than a hovel, being a smith's shop and living-room. When the wealthy Gamaliel saw its black walls, he could not suppress a shudder.

"By the walls one would know that thou art a smith," he said.

Josua's independence was dear to him, and though he ate his bread by the sweat of his brow he never complained.

"Woe to the generation whose leader thou art:" he answered bitterly. "Thou hast no conception how hard poor scholars have to work to earn a living."

"Pardon me, I did thee an injustice," said Gamaliel.

Josua was silent.

"Pardon me in honor of my father," pleaded Gamaliel.

Thereupon Josua stretched forth his hand, which the other grasped and pressed with emotion. The two went to the session arm in arm, and the people were so touched at the sight, that they elected Gamaliel joint-president with Elazar ben Azariah.[10]

Josua travelled extensively through Palestine, and was several times in Rome and in Alexandria. His first trip to Rome was in company with Eliezer.[11] The manners of the people in the Eternal City made a deep impression upon him. He recognized that his people's political salvation depended upon submission, at least in appearance, to Rome's rule. On his return he warned the turbulent Hebrews not to ask too much of Rome; she had given them some privileges,—let them be contented. The commonwealth was lost before because the people had been inconsiderate and hasty. They never had made preparations for war; their finances were mismanaged; they sought no outside alliances as the Romans did. A people so poorly directed could not withstand the power of a great nation. These ideas he embodied in his discourses, cloaked in parables or in supposed experiences. One story he told thus:

"In my life, no one ever put me down but a woman, a girl, and a boy. You ask how I was put down by the woman? I came to an inn, where the landlady, a very pious woman, gave me a meal of beans and bread. I ate the beans, leaving nothing in the dish. The second day, she again gave me beans and bread, and again I ate all and left nothing in the dish. On the third day, she brought me the same dish again; but as she had put too much salt into the beans I could not eat them. And so I ate but the bread. Whereupon she said:

"'Rabbi, why dost thou not eat the beans?'

"'I have dined once already,' said I.

"'Then,' said she, 'why didst thou eat the bread? Is it because thou didst leave nothing in the dish yesterday nor the day before, that thou wouldst leave all to-day? Let me remind thee of the old saying, that a man, eating, should always leave something in the dish.'

"Would you know how I was vanquished by a little girl? Once, while travelling, my way led through a field. I had not gone far when a girl met me.

"'Rabbi,' said the girl, 'dost know that thou art trespassing on a private field?'

"'I am walking on a well-worn path,' I replied.

"'Aye, evil-doers such as thou have worn this path in our fair field,' she said.

"And wouldst thou know how I was worsted by a little boy? One day, near a city, I came upon a crossroad. At the roadside sat a boy.

"'Which way leadeth to the city?' I asked him.

"'This one here is short and long, and the other is long and short,' he said.

"I took the one which was 'short and long,' and soon came within sight of the city. But, alas! I found that my way had led to private gardens which were surrounded by high hedges and I was forced to return.

"'My son,' said I, to the boy, 'didst thou not tell me that this road was short?'

"'I did,' said he, 'but, Rabbi, I told thee also that it was long.'

"I kissed the head of that boy and said, 'Hail unto Israel! It is a sage people from the highest to the lowest.'" [12]

Valuable as was his judgment in religious matters, it was even greater in dealing with the projects of the revolutionary party. His spies were everywhere—he knew everything. At the court of Domitian or Nerva in Rome, he was in favor, and though these emperors taxed the Hebrews mercilessly, they granted Josua personally many favors, among them a reduction of the *fiscus judæus*, or the "Jew Tax." He was held in esteem by Domitian's daughter, who invited him to her table despite his careless dress and ugly visage.

"Rabbi," said she one day, "how is it that so great a mind as thine dwelleth in so homely a body?"

"Pray, tell me, princess, in what kind of vessels doth thy father keep his best wines?"

"In wooden casks," said she.

"The best wine in wooden casks!" Josua exclaimed; "I thought he kept them in golden casks."

"The wine would spoil in golden casks," said the princess.

"Behold, princess," Josua rejoined, "as old wine is better kept in wooden than in golden casks, even so is wisdom often given to the homely, who are less liable to spoil it by earthly vanity." [13]

He was on equally good terms with emperor Trajan, whom he induced to recall the cruel Quietus from Palestine, to forgive the Hebrews, and to set free the two revolutionary leaders, Pappus and Julianus. The Hebrews were so happy at this edict that they proclaimed an annual "Trajan Day." [14]

Josua also gained the good graces of Hadrian. He was then vice-president of the Sanhedrin, almost a prince, and the foremost intellect of his time. He saw that the people could not be kept down much longer. Neither Trajan nor Hadrian had kept faith with the Jews. Hadrian had promised to rebuild the Temple, but he made no attempt to keep his promise. The Hebrews rose in arms in the Valley of Rimmon. Josua hastened to caution his people. The times were not ripe for revolution. Rome was on guard, her legions were massed around Palestine like birds of prey. On the military highway he met his trusted agent, Ben Zoma, but the latter did not salute him. Josua asked him what was the impending danger. Ben Zoma told him that the country swarmed with Romans; that Roman eyes were then watching them. He bade

Josua hasten with the flight of an eagle to warn the people.

The Talmud tells this in the form of a parable.

Rabbi Josua met Ben Zoma, and the latter did not salute.

"Whence and whither, Ben Zoma?" asked Rabbi Josua.

"I have thought of the history of creation and I have found that it is not the width of a hand 'tween the upper waters and the lower as it is written (Genesis i., 2), 'And the Spirit of the Lord hovered above the waters.' (There is no system, nor preparation in the camp of Israel,—all is chaos, while the Romans are well organized, ready to strike.) And as is written (Deuteronomy xxxii., 11), 'As the eagle fluttereth above the nest.'"

This story the Talmud further states, that Ben Zoma's remarks refer to a band of warriors who pass through a hollow way: on one side is fire, which, if it touch, will burn them, and on the other side is a bank of snow, which will stiffen their limbs. If the Hebrews fight the Romans now, they will meet with defeat, because the Romans are like a burning fire; but in view of their sad condition, inactivity will lead to stagnation. To give no clue to any Roman who might seek to interpret Ben Zoma's words, Rabbi Josua cried out to his followers:

"Ben Zoma is beside himself; he hath lost his reason."[1b]

Whether Ben Zoma was killed by the Romans, or, fearing an uprising, went to lead a hermit life in one of the caves in the mountains is not known.

The Talmud only says that a few days after this message to Rabbi Josua "Ben Zoma was called away from this life." [16]

Josua hastened to Rimmon and there addressed the assembled Hebrews. An eloquent speech it was, and full of meaning to those who knew the orator. He ended with a parable:

"A lion [Rome] had swallowed a bone which stuck in his throat; he promised great reward to any one who would extract it. A Nile stork came and with his long beak took the bone from the lion's throat. When the stork asked for the promised reward, the lion said:

"'Go hence and tell the people that thou hast been in the mouth of a lion and hast come away unharmed.'

"We should be satisfied to have escaped from Roman kindness with our lives." [17]

The news that Josua had prevented an uprising of the Hebrews was brought to Hadrian, and remembering what his relative, Aquila, had written about the Hebrew sage, he showed him great favor. But Hadrian's edicts against the poor Hebrews continued to be very cruel. The Jews dared hope for no more favor from him. Instead of restoring the Temple, he began to lay ruthless hands on their faith. He forbade the study of the law and the practice of circumcision. Sorrowfully the people came to Josua and begged his intercession with the tyrant, who was then in the city of Alexandria, and Josua went to see Hadrian.

He was received with great consideration, but it

was long before he could bring the emperor to favor his petition.

Hadrian wished to test the wisdom of the Hebrew sage.

"Thy people are rebels and barbarians," said Hadrian; "let them abandon their obsolete laws of Moses and obey mine. I am greater than Moses, since I can enforce obedience and he can not, and by the testimony of your own Scriptures it is shown that 'a live dog is better than a dead lion.'" [18]

The emperor's logic seemed irrefragable; he was lord of life and death of the people, he could enforce obedience. But obedience from fear of violence is one thing and obedience from love and reverence of the law is another. But he who has no power over the minds and hearts of those he rules may not hope to receive implicit obedience at all times nor in all places.

"Canst thou forbid the kindling of fire for three days, O mighty emperor?" said Josua.

"I can," Hadrian replied, and forthwith he commanded that for three days no fire be made in the city.

But that very afternoon smoke issued from one of the chimneys of Hadrian's own palace. On investigation it was found that one of the generals had fallen ill and ordered a fire.

"Behold," said Rabbi Josua, "thy command for three days has been disobeyed here even now, but the command of Moses not to kindle a fire on the Sabbath is obeyed to this day, thousands of years after his death."

This gave Hadrian food for thought. The Hebrews must have some high qualities to obey implicitly their teacher's laws for reverence alone, while Romans had to be held to the obedience of the law by an iron hand. A man who could win the love of such a people might build a commonwealth to outlast the ages.

"Great indeed is the lamb [Israel] which still liveth though surrounded by seventy wolves," he said, following the trend of his thoughts.

"Not the lamb is great, but God who protects it," said Rabbi Josua.[19]

In this thoughtful manner the Rabbi at length succeeded in having the edicts annulled, and the Hebrews breathed easier for a while.

In the conversations which took place between the learned emperor and the Jewish sage many references were made to the existing conditions of the Jewish race. Josua endeavored to conciliate Hadrian's opinions towards his people by his wit. Some Jewish bandits had taken refuge in the Parthian dominions and thence ravaged the Roman borders with impunity. Hadrian had a dislike of war, and especially of any repetition of Trajan's Asiatic campaigns, and preferred to endure the banditti of the deserts as a lesser evil. One day in company with Josua he said:

"I could set a table in the centre of the world and be host to the immortal gods; aye, even to thy God."

"Thou forgettest the Parthians, O cæsar," said the Rabbi.[20]

Hadrian looked keenly at the speaker.

"What of the Parthians?" said he.

"They are lions," the Rabbi replied.

"A hunter kills lions," the emperor rejoined.

"But not those lions; if they were let loose Rome would tremble," said the Rabbi.

"I have legions," said Hadrian.

"They would be swept away as by a whirlwind," was the Rabbi's rejoinder.

"I'll call back Severus and the veterans from Britannia," said the emperor.

"An uncertain force to rely on; they have to cross the seas, and may never see land again," the Rabbi persisted.

"Why dost thou say all this?" asked the emperor.

The Rabbi was silent.

"Speak," commanded Hadrian.

"I was thinking how weak even a powerful king may be when he faces the elements of nature; and yet these are but the servants of God."

"I believe not in thy God; He hath no form; He is not tangible; He hath no power; He hath no servants other than the Hebrews whom Rome hath crushed."

"Say not so, O cæsar; our God is the creator of heaven and earth, and the least of His servants is more powerful than all mortals."

"But I cannot see Him; nor canst thou show Him to me."

"No, I cannot show Him to thee; for no mortal can see Him and live; but I can show thee His works and His servants and by their greatness judge then of the magnitude of the Lord God of Israel. Look into the sun."

"I cannot; it hurts the eye," said Hadrian.

"And thou wouldst look at the Lord, whose servant is the sun?" was the Rabbi's reply.[21]

Rabbi Josua was one of the few who were given the opportunity to speak with royal personages on the questions of that day, and he invariably gained their respect. Hadrian, writing to his wife, speaks in deferential terms of Rabbi Josua, the vice-patriarch of the Hebrews.[22] The relations between Josua and the Roman emperor are told with Oriental fancy in the Talmud.[23] It narrates how one day Hadrian asked:

"What is the duration of a snake's pregnancy?"[24]

"Seven years," replied Josua.

"The wise men of the Roman Academy have found that snakes bring forth after three years," rejoined the emperor.

"It was because the pregnancy had begun four years before the Roman wise men observed it," was the retort, the meaning of which is clear enough in reference to the Jewish troubles.[25]

"But the men of the Roman Academy are indeed wise," urged Hadrian.

"We of Judah are wiser," as proudly said Josua.

"Then go to Rome," commanded the cæsar, "and if thou art wiser conquer them in discussion and bring them to me here."

"How many members are in the Academy?" queried the Rabbi.

"Sixty."

"Then give me a ship with sixty cabins and as many chairs in each cabin."

The remarkable ship was, of course, furnished, and in it Josua sailed to Rome. There a difficulty awaited him. The Academy was a secret society of the most rigorous kind, and even to point out its place of meeting was forbidden to the uninitiated. Josua finally discovered the butcher who carried daily supplies to the immured sages. He found the butcher cutting up a sheep and asked him:

"Hast thou a head?"

"I have," replied the butcher.

"Is thy head for sale, and for how much?"

"It is for sale for half a *sus*."

The Rabbi handed over the half-*sus*, and the butcher tendered the sheep's head.

"It is not that I have bought and paid for," said the crafty Rabbi; "it is thy own head. Now if thou wouldst keep it thou must show me the entrance to the Academy of the Wise."

"But the guards will slay me if I point it out to thee," said the alarmed butcher.

"If thou dost not show it to me, thou must surrender thy head," was the reply.

However Josua was good enough to spend his wisdom in a solution of this dilemma.

"You need only take a bundle on your shoulder and lay it down for a moment at the entrance and pass on," he said.

The butcher agreed and Josua soon stood at the Academy gate.

The finding the entrance was only the first difficulty of many. The Roman Academy of the talmudic legend was like one of the Arabian fairy palaces. A separate guard stood outside the entrance and inside the main gates without communication between them. A patrol passed at stated times to see that no visitor left by the entrance, as the outer guards were forbidden to let any out though he might pass them unquestioned going in. The Rabbi was refused admittance at the inner portal, and death would be his doom when the patrol should arrive. He was equal to the occasion. The entrance was covered with fine sand which showed whether any one had passed it to the patrol. Josua had turned his sandals backwards when he passed the outward guard and when repulsed from the gate he walked away with his footgear in its natural position. The patrol arrived while he was hiding within the entrance, and at once decided that two people had passed out, so they immediately executed the guards in the style so common in Oriental legend. Josua, when the patrol had left, walked boldly into the Academy itself.[28]

The Roman sages of the Talmud had a primitive test for outside visitors. The salutation must be addressed in proper form or the head of the rash uninitiated one would be promptly removed. The sages sat in peculiar order. The juniors had the highest seats, to give the impression that they were highest in rank and entitled to the first salute. Josua was not to be so easily fooled. He simply said, "Peace to all here assembled," and so escaped the risk of mistaking the precedence due.

They recognized his right to retain his head on this, and the spokesman asked who the stranger was and what he wanted.

"I am a sage from Judea, and I come to learn wisdom of the sages of Rome," answered Josua.

"We will ask thee some questions to test thy title to be called a sage."

"I am willing to be tested," said Josua, "but it is only just that there should be reward for wisdom. If you puzzle me, my head is at your disposal, if you fail to puzzle me, you shall all come to my ship to dine there."

They agreed that the proposal was fair, and the contest of wits began.

"If a man has been rejected by one woman what will be his thoughts when he woos a woman of higher rank?" was the first question proposed.

Josua took a hook and tapped the wall of the chamber near the ground, where it was formed of solid marble. He could find no crevice to insert the point. He went above the wainscot to the wall of smaller blocks and found a joint to thrust it in easily. Thereupon he said:

"The man who did not succeed with one woman thinks he may succeed even with one of higher birth, as she may be intended for him by fate."

"Will a man, who trusted another without witness and had to use force to get back his money, lend again?" was the second query.

"A grass seller went to the meadow and cut a bundle of rush grass too large to lift upon his shoulders. He went and cut more grass and added it to the bundle and then waited till a man came and assisted him. Such is the creditor who, failing to properly secure his money with the first debtor, will be more careful with the second, but he will continue to lend money, if that is his business."

"Tell us lies," was the next order, and Josua gave his fancy rein.

"We had a mule, which gave birth to a little mule; around its neck we found a document on which was written: 'So and So owes our house one hundred thousand pieces of silver.'"[27]

"Can a mule give birth?" they said.

"You asked me to tell you lies."

"When salt putrefies, how can it be cured?" he was asked.

"By the afterbirth of a mule."

"But is it possible for a mule to have an afterbirth?"

"As possible as for salt to putrefy."

"Build a house in the air."

"Place enough brick and mortar there and I will build the house."

"Who can place brick and mortar in the air?"

"It is easier than to build a house there."

"Where is the centre of the universe?"

"Straight up here where I am pointing my finger."

"How canst thou prove it?"

"If you don't believe me, take lines and measure the universe."

"On yonder meadow is a cistern: bring it hither."

"Make ropes of bran, and I will haul it hither."

"That is impossible."

"So is that which you demand."

"Here are broken millstones: sew them together."

"Here is a piece of the millstone: twist it into thread and I will do it."

"But that is impossible."

"Not any more than your request."

"With what wouldst thou mow a field where knives grow?"

"With the horns of asses."

"Have asses horns?"

"Do knives grow on a field?"

"Here are two eggs,—which is from a white hen and which from a black one?" they asked him.

"Here are two pieces of cheese,—which is from the milk of a black goat and which is from that of a white one?" he asked in return.

"How doth the ghost leave, when a chicken dieth in its unbroken shell?" they continued.

"The same way it entered," he replied.

"Show us an object which hath not the value of the damage it can do?"

"Bring hither a bastion."

"We could not get it into the building," they said.

"Take axes and break down the walls, and you will have an object which hath not the value of the damage it will do," he answered.

The Roman sages gave up the task of puzzling the sharp-witted sage from Judea, and promised to visit his ship, but not in a body. Josua had each visitor shown into one of his sixty cabins and when all were on board he hoisted sail and carried the Roman sages to Alexandria, where he presented them to Hadrian. The latter, on hearing of the facts, made them over to Josua's disposition as unworthy of imperial protection after such an intellectual defeat. Josua, according to the legend, set them to the job of filling a bottomless cask with water, at which they toiled till their shoulders fell off and they all died.[28]

The sense of superior wisdom entertained by the Jewish people in all their disasters is illustrated well by this strange tale, where Oriental and Western wits are represented as clashing in battle.

Josua's knowledge of human nature in practical life is illustrated by another anecdote.

A suspicious-looking individual begged a night's lodging in his house. The Rabbi fed him, as hospitality required, and located him for the night in the attic of his house, where some valuables were stored. Though a strict observer of hospitality to strangers, Josua had a favorite maxim, "Think every man a thief till he is proved honest; but meantime treat him as civilly as the president of the Sanhedrin." He doubted his unknown guest, and when the household was at rest he quietly removed the ladder which led to the attic and then retired.

The tramp visitor rose in the night and packed as much as he could carry of Josua's household goods; but on stepping through the door he fell and broke his legs. He was found in this condition by the Rabbi, who told him that he was a greater fool than knave.[29]

His sense of wit made him tell stories even at his own expense.

"Once," he told, "I met a child who carried a covered platter.

" 'What is in the platter?' I inquired.

" 'If my mother had wanted everybody to know, she would not have covered it,' said the child and walked on."[30]

"Another time," said he, "I rode up to a well and, seeing a maiden with a jar of water, begged her for a drink.

" 'Drink thou, Rabbi, and thine ass also,' said the maiden.

"When I had drank enough, I said to her:

" 'Thou hast done like Rebekah at the well.'

" 'Aye, Rabbi,' said she, 'but thou hast not done as Eliezer, who gave Rebekah costly presents.' "[31]

Josua was mystic as well as wit. The Talmud tells of him many wonders. He could deal with wizards in their line as readily as with politicians.

One day, while taking a bath in the city of Tiberias, a sorcerer, thinking to have some merriment at the Rabbi's expense, cast a spell upon him, and as he tried to leave the bathtub his limbs were paralyzed. He guessed who had caused the trouble, and spoke a few words, when lo, the sorcerer was rooted to the spot where he stood. Then a joke suggested itself to the Rabbi. He withdrew the spell from the sorcerer's right hand and left foot, and as he stood near the door, made him strike each newcomer and kick every one who went out of the bath. The master of the bath tried to eject the troublesome guest; but neither he nor all his assistants could move the spellbound man from the spot.

"Release me, O Rabbi!" cried the sorcerer.

"Not until thou hast released me," the Rabbi answered.

Having released each other, the sorcerer entered into conversation with Rabbi Josua. He boasted of the marvellous feats he had performed, and his repute as the greatest of sorcerers.

"In good sooth," said the Rabbi, "I believe all thy great feats were probably such petty tricks as those exhibited a while ago."

"I can accomplish as great miracles as Moses," cried the sorcerer angrily.

Rabbi Josua expressed his desire to witness some of these wonders. Whereupon the sorcerer said:

"Come to the seaside, and thou shalt see."

They went to the seaside; there the magician spoke a few words, and the waters receded, and the deep was laid bare.

"Thou art indeed a sorcerer," said the Rabbi, "but canst thou go down into the deep like Moses?"

"Aye, and more," replied the sorcerer, and he walked upon the dry bed of the ocean. But Rabbi Josua commanded the spirit of the sea, and the great waters engulfed the sorcerer and drowned him.[32]

Once Rabbi Josua and Rabbi Eliezer, travelling together, came to a town where some Hebrews dwelt. One of these they visited and were received with friendliness. While at meat the Rabbis noticed that each dish was taken into a small chamber off the dining-room, and then brought to the table and placed before them. The travellers asked their host the reason.

"It is done," said he, "in honor of my aged father, who hath vowed not to leave his room until one or more of the sages in Israel shall have entered this house."

"Tell thy father," said Rabbi Josua, "that sages in Israel are sitting at thy table."

The host went to his father's room and soon returned with the aged man.

"Rabbis," cried the old man, "my house is blessed from this day forth, and joy hath come into my heart at beholding you. I shut myself up through grief that my son hath no issue. I prayed long; but the Lord heard not my prayer, and then I vowed not to leave the four walls of my chamber till the Lord sent holy men to my house, and these would I ask to pray for my son, so that the curse of childlessness be removed."

When Rabbi Josua heard the man's words, he knew that it was the malice of Satan which had afflicted this pious house. He asked for some flax-seed, which he mixed and spoke some cabalistic sentences. Then he said:

"Thy son hath been bewitched by an old woman in the neighborhood; summon her."

The witch was summoned, and acknowledged that she had put a spell on the old man's son by means of a twisted hair.

"Give me the twisted hair," said the Rabbi.

"I cannot; I threw it into the sea," the witch replied.

Josua commanded the spirit of the sea to bring him the twisted hair, and, having it, he prayed to the Lord to grant issue to this pious family. The Lord heard the Rabbi's prayer, and the old man lived to see a grandson born unto him who afterwards became a famous Rabbi.[33]

Once, while on a visit to Hadrian, the emperor's daughter asked Rabbi Josua if it was true that the God of the Hebrews was a cabinetmaker, as the psalmist says (Psalm civ., 3).

"Everything that King David says is true," replied the Rabbi.

"In that case I wish he would make me a spindle," merrily exclaimed the princess.

"Thy wish, O princess, shall be fulfilled," the Rabbi seriously replied.

Hardly had he finished the sentence when her body was covered with ulcers. She was pronounced a leper, and was taken to the lepers' asylum outside of the city. There she was given a spindle with which to while away the time.

Shortly afterwards, Rabbi Josua, passing by the asylum, saw the princess at the spindle.

"How dost thou like the spindle, which our Lord hath given thee?" he asked.

"I do not like it at all. I wish He would take it back," the poor princess cried.

"Our God never takes back His gifts," said the Rabbi, and went on. Soon after, however, he healed her, and the princess never again demanded anything in jest from the God of the Hebrews.[34]

Josua's expressions indicate his lovable disposition, his liberal mind, and utter disregard for the cares of life so far as he was personally concerned.

148 JEWISH FORERUNNERS OF CHRISTIANITY

Long before the wealthy Gamaliel had accorded him the pension which freed him from the necessity of daily toil,[35] Josua used to say:

"The Giver of Life gives also wherewith to live."[36]

It is worth while to quote a few more of the recorded sayings of this master in Israel, who by a rare exception enjoyed the respect and good-will of his own people and the Gentiles alike. They breathe a mild and sententious wisdom not bounded by the limits of Judaism or nationality.

"If a needy man ask alms of thee in the morning, give to him. If he ask again at evening then give again."[37]

"Alms benefit the giver more than the receiver."[38]

"The student who lets his knowledge pass from his mind is like a woman who bears children only to bury them. The student who ceases to study is like the sower who neglects to reap."[39]

"The Sabbath observance should be twofold: part for divine service, part for lawful recreation of body and mind."[40]

"It is well for a man not to touch a woman lasciviously, but he that will not touch a drowning woman lest he be tempted is a pious fool."[41]

This is a sarcasm on the fanatical scrupulousness taught by some Jews of his day, notably a certain class of Pharisees.

"The just of all nations shall share in the bliss of the future life," is a remarkable expression of Josua's spirit of liberality.[42]

His relations with the Christians of his time are

not directly mentioned in the Talmud, but the tenor of his life leaves every reason to believe that, like Eliezer, Josua was familiar with them and the teachings of Christ. He was by nature reticent and guarded in his public utterances, but the whole course of his policy indicates that he did not share the expectation of a messianic restorer of the kingdom of Israel, so prevalent among his countrymen at the time. He kept aloof from the national conspiracies which resulted in the rising of Bar Kochba, and did not go near the Academy." He freely warned his people of their folly and danger. Though he enjoyed the favor of Hadrian, the Roman emperor, when the project of rebuilding the Jewish Temple was agitated he never seems to have urged the proposed restoration. The Talmud has no hint of any such action of his in any of its numerous references to Josua. His mind had a broader grasp than the limits of Palestine. He looked forward to the spread of the moral and religious principles of the law among the outside nations as the development of the Jewish race. With that object he urged the maintenance of peace on his people, and he gave his most earnest efforts to the task of conciliating the good-will of the learned and powerful among the Romans to Judaic law and wisdom.

Though he discouraged the wild outburst of national spirit which after his death ended in the final rebellion of Bar Kochba, his patriotism was recognized by even the fanatical revolutionists. All the Jewish factions trusted implicitly in his honesty of purpose and freely used his influence with the

Roman rulers to obtain protection from oppression at home. He never used that influence for merely personal profit or betrayed the confidence of his countrymen by sacrificing their real interests to those of their foreign masters. Hence the respect with which all the talmudic writers speak of Josua even when they did not agree with his sentiments towards the Christians. "Who knows what evil the Christians may yet bring on us," is the cry of a talmudic writer."

Josua kept the even tenor of his way, unmoved by the outbursts of fierce patriotism. "Forbearance is better than daring," was a favorite maxim of his in those troubled times. He sympathized with the teachings of the Nazarene, and his influence was used for the protection of Christians as well as his other countrymen. In the Talmud we find evidence of a remarkable friendly intercourse between some of the Rabbis of the Sanhedrin and the followers of Christ, which seems to have been due to the influence of Josua. The public discussion of the fulfilment of the messianic prophecies, which had been common and bitter at a former period, gradually ceased when his influence became predominant in Palestine. A large body, even of those Jews who refused to accept Jesus as the promised Messiah, considered the difference between themselves and the Christians on that point not a vital one. There was little of the fierce hatred which developed in later ages. Even a hundred years later Jews and Christians mingled on friendly terms in Palestine. Rabbi Judah the Prince entertained a Christian guest at his table.

"Wilt thou say grace according to Jewish fashion?"

he asked him, "or wilt thou receive forty shekels?" The Christian readily agreed to say grace as a compliment to his host.[46]

Josua lived to an advanced age. He saw the burial of his friends Eliezer and Gamaliel II. the president of the Sanhedrin, before he was gathered to his fathers. At his death, though he had kept aloof from the society of the Rabbis of the nationalist school,[46] it was felt that a light was extinguished in Israel. As the Talmud pithily puts it, "Wise counsel died with Josua."[47] Scarcely was he in the grave when the great rebellion broke out which, after temporary success, ruined the national existence of his people. Of that movement the guiding spirit was one not of Jewish blood,—the famous Akibah.

CHAPTER VII

RABBI AKIBAH

IN the last desperate struggle of the Jewish people to establish an independent national existence, the central figure is Rabbi Akibah. He it was that called from obscurity the military leader, Bar Kochba, who for a time was hailed as the very Messiah. In him the political wisdom of Ben Zakkai was blended with the mysticism of Ben Dosa, and with a patriotic ardor all his own. He was great among the greatest doctors of the law, as well as a political leader who swayed the popular masses by the power of his word, and led them on through a two-years struggle with the might of the Roman empire such as has hardly a parallel in history.

In spite of his fervid Jewish patriotism, the famous Rabbi was not of Jewish race. Elazar ben Azariah, the assistant president of the Sanhedrin, spoke of this in a eulogy which he pronounced on him.

"The sages of Israel are but garlic peelings to me except this bald head, Akibah ben Joseph, whose father was a proselyte of righteousness."[1]

The pride of race so deeprooted in the Jewish people makes this testimony to the abilities of Akibah very remarkable in the mouth of Elazar.

His foreign origin was not the only difficulty which Akibah had to struggle with in his path to the eminence he at last attained. He began life as a herder of cattle, an unlettered peasant who, as he said of himself, "would bite a scholar like a snake if he met one." [2] He was forty years old before he conceived the thought of any higher career in life. His inspiration came in a romantic way. Rachel, the daughter of his employer, Calba Sebuah, fell in love with the handsome herdsman. Her father's wealth placed him among the foremost of his nation. The Talmud says, in its usual florid style, that he could feed all Palestine for ten years from his stores. His daughter's attachment to her father's servant made her urge him to enter the schools of the law as the easiest road to success in life.

An incident determined the mind of Akibah to a life of study. The legend makes him tell it. "My becoming a learned man began thus," he said. "One day I found a corpse in the fields. I took it up and carried it to the burying-ground, where I interred it. Some days later I met the great Rabbis Ben Hyrkanos and Josua. I told them what I had done for the body. They told me that in carrying that body I had broken the law as grievously as if I had shed human blood, since it is of precept that wherever a body is found deserted there it should be interred. I said to myself, if I had sinned so grievously through ignorance when I thought to do good, how much more grievously must I have sinned at other times when I had no good intentions. And from that moment I resolved to be a student of the law." [3]

Rachel, however, was the active cause of Akibah's new career. She engaged to wed him if he would promise to enter the school of Eliezer, who had been, like Akibah, unlettered till advanced in life, but was then a master in Israel. Her father had other designs in view for his daughter, and he drove her from his house when he learned of this engagement.[4] Rachel then married Akibah legally and shared his cabin and bed of straw.[5] Even food was often lacking to the couple, and Rachel cut off her hair on one occasion to buy bread for their support.[6] Akibah appreciated his wife's devotion and cried out in transport, "I will yet buy thee a golden city for this when I am wealthy, as I shall be."[7]

He finally entered the school of Eliezer as she had asked him to do.[8] Rachel accepted the separation gladly for the sake of the future greatness which she anticipated with prophetic eye for her loved husband.

Akibah's experience in the school which he entered at so advanced an age was no easy one. Eliezer was a stern master, and he sometimes sneered at the task which Akibah had undertaken.

"Thou wouldst be a famous man," he told him once, "and thou mayest, but as yet thou hast not shown brains to make a cowherd."

"No, not even a good shepherd," answered the disciple humbly, and his answer mollified the master's severity.[9]

He retained a remarkable modesty regarding himself long after he had became famous in the Sanhedrin. Eliezer, in his pride of intellect, once said:

"Were all men writers, with the ocean for ink, all reeds pens, and all heaven and earth for parchment, they could not write out all that I know of the law, yet I only know of the law as much as a man might take of water from the ocean on a needle-point."

"I cannot say so much of myself," Akibah modestly replied, "I have gained but such knowledge of the law as one gains of a Paradise-apple when he inhales its perfume, or of a lamp when he lights a candle from its blaze."[10]

His abilities, however, soon attracted notice among his fellow-students in Eliezer's school. He was recognized as a master and followed by disciples while yet a student. One day, when the hall was crowded with debaters, Akibah could not enter for the throng. A strictly legal question was raised and debated, but though the master Eliezer presided, the students would not hear a decision in Akibah's absence. "Legal lore is without," was the general cry, and Eliezer had to pass to another subject, this time of Holy Writ. "Scripture lore, too, is without," was proclaimed, and, on a third point being proposed, all united in bringing Akibah in with triumph and seating him beside Eliezer."[11]

The admiration thus shown for Akibah's talent was well deserved. His powers of analysis explained the whole mass of Scripture lore with a fulness and clearness beyond that of the most famous masters. He classified the traditions of the past, drew laws from them, and found new hidden meanings in every phrase. In Eastern hyperbole the rabbinical writers tell that when Moses entered heaven he saw the

Lord crowning the letters of the Hebrew alphabet, and when he reverently asked for whom this work was being done,[12] the Lord replied:

"Hereafter a man will exist by name Akibah the son of Joseph, who will draw countless laws from every dot of these letters."[13]

Another and more fanciful legend tells how the first father, Adam, was shown by the Lord all the coming generations of man and the leaders among them. When Akibah was shown to him, Adam rejoiced to see one so learned, but he grieved for the sore death that was to befall him.[14] Such legends show the high estimate placed on the mental powers of Akibah by his contemporaries. The lore of ages of Judaism found in him its best exponent in the judgment of his fellows.

When Akibah found himself thus honored by his associates in Eliezer's school, he thought of his faithful wife and determined to visit her. With the development of his intellectual powers he could appreciate more justly the sacrifice she had made for him when only a hired shepherd, and he resolved to repay it abundantly. He was already himself a lecturer whom crowds of the most ardent young men followed, as later the French students of Brittany followed Abelard. He invited them to accompany him on an excursion into the country, to the village where Rachel dwelt in obscurity. A crowd of disciples[15] followed his steps, eager to profit by the lessons he gave them on the way, and to show him honor. When he drew near the hamlet where his wife dwelt, Akibah bade his followers stop while he went on alone to his wife's humble dwelling.

Rachel's lot had been a specially hard one since her husband's departure for Jerusalem. Her father had offered to receive her back to his home if she would forever renounce her coarse peasant husband, but the faithful Rachel refused that condition. She continued to live in the cabin where Akibah had left her, supporting herself by daily toil among the peasant women of the village. She mixed but little in their daily gossip, and many regarded her reserve as pride. They delighted to insult the high-born lady who had been reduced to their own poor condition. They called her "a living widow," and taunted her with what they called her desertion by her husband. Rachel bore it all in her strong faith in Akibah's future eminence, and when from time to time news reached her of the fame he was winning in the distant city, she forgot every suffering for joy. She had not heard of his approach to her dwelling, when he came with his disciples.

It was dusk when Akibah approached the cottage of his wife. When he entered its inclosure he paused for a while. Then a harsh voice from within grated on his ear. It was a neighbor's, who had come to pay a visit to Rachel in no friendly spirit.

"Thou art proud, Rachel, and thinkest thyself better than the rest of us villagers," said the visitor as Akibah listened.

"Not their better," was the reply, "but I am the wife of Akibah, and my lord is a master in Israel."

"Akibah's wife!" said a man's voice ironically;

"Akibah's wife, cursed by her father; Akibah's wife, a beggar."

"I am rich beyond measure in my husband's love," said Rachel. "His glory is mine."

"Love and glory indeed! Thy husband hath abandoned thee; thou art only a living widow; he hath been years away,—where is his love?" came the female voice.

"I fear not. My husband hath been away for years to study the divine Law. He will come when the time is fit. Who am I to hinder his studies? Let him study; even if twelve years more are needed to finish his work let him stay twelve years. Love is strong: it lasteth. It endureth forever," was Rachel's answer.[16]

Akibah was about to enter and confound the malevolent neighbors, but a consideration entered his mind. "If I go in," he said, "I shall not be able to part again from my wife for any motive; yet my work is not done. I am but a scholar yet. When I become of the Sanhedrin of Israel I shall return never more to separate from her. Till then I shall remember thy words, O wife; for, verily, great is thy merit, and it shall be made greater by the knowledge I shall acquire. Back I go, then, to further work and study that I may be worthy of thee, Rachel."

With this apostrophe Akibah stole away from the cottage, went back to his waiting disciples, and returned with them to the Academy. His mind was made up for a wider range of studies than those of his master Eliezer. In the national ferment then prevalent, new schools, both political and religious, had sprung up in Judea. The traditional school of Hillel was still in possession of the Sanhedrin and recognized as the orthodox learning. There were other masters, however, men of a new learning, who without rejecting the received doctrines added to them new studies and methods of interpretation. Politics were also involved in the scholastic questions of the time. The older Rabbis, who dominated the great colleges, were afraid of any resistance to the Roman power, of which they had so terrible an experience in the days of Titus. The younger generation of students chafed under the foreign rule and hoped that they would yet be strong enough to restore the independence of Israel by armed force. The messianic leader, it was expected by many, would soon arise to crush the legions and restore both the Temple and the throne of David. Mysticism was mingled to a large extent with the patriotic aspirations for self-government and possibly a world-wide Jewish empire.

The student element of this patriotic party gathered itself around a famous doctor then in Jerusalem, Nahum of Gamsu." He was distinguished as a scholar. He had introduced a new system of interpretation which met with high approval from the learned and drew crowds to his lectures. None were admitted but such as were already familiar with the received interpretations of the law. Nahum's teaching was for advanced scholars. He discussed recent decisions according to a system devised by his own ingenuity, which found new meanings in the sacred text by certain rules of interpretation. Indeed, he was a mystic of the school of Ben Dosa,[18] as well as a scholar, and moreover he was devoted to the plans of the party among the nation then plotting an insurrection against the Roman rule. His teaching was mainly directed to strengthening the patriotism of his scholars and nerving their minds for a struggle of life and death in behalf of the independence of his native land. A fatalist in belief, his favorite maxim was, "Gam zu letobah" (This, too, is for the best).[19] With this remark he faced every misfortune stoically, and he endeavored to instil the same spirit into the young men who followed his lectures. He hated Rome with a mighty hate. The submissive course of the Rabbis of Hillel's school was repugnant to his nature. He would have no intercourse with the heathen, he would not admit Roman customs nor dress to use in Judea, nor would he court the favor of Roman governors by flattery. He was a Hebrew of the Hebrews, and he was ready to give his life for his people. He impressed upon his disciples the importance of maintaining the spirit of union among themselves as a means of preventing the fall of the House of Israel. He bade them avoid everything Roman. Rome, he said, has blinded your eyes that you should not see your true interests; she has cut off your hands that you may not defend yourselves, and your feet so that you can seek no alliances abroad among her foes; but so long as dissension does not reign among yourselves she cannot crush you.

A legend **ex**presses this teaching of Nahum. According to the Talmud the famous master himself was blind, crippled, and without hands, and moreover his body was covered with ulcers, a punishment for the tardy attention he accorded a man he found starving on the highway, and who died ere the Rabbi reached him. Nahum looked upon the disease that soon after robbed him of sight and the use of his limbs as a retribution sent by heaven to punish him for his guilt.[20] He lived in a hut whose walls threatened hourly to collapse and which was overrun with insects so that the feet of his bedstead stood in pails of water to keep the ants from devouring the invalid. His pupils at last got his consent to remove him to a better dwelling.

"My children," said he, "remove everything first; the house will stand while I am in it."

The disciples obeyed, and hardly had they carried the bed-ridden Nahum out when the house fell with a crash. They then saw that it was his sanctity alone that kept the walls standing. In like manner the known rottenness of the temporal government of the Jews was checked by the spirit of patriotism kept alive by Nahum in his people. They might be blind, crippled, and without hands for defence, but a higher power still kept their tottering national government intact as by a miracle.

To Nahum's school Akibah joined himself after his visit to Rachel's cottage. He seemed to have then definitely conceived the plan of combining all the forces, moral, intellectual, and material, of his countrymen for a new struggle against the Roman power. To that end he would make himself equally at home in every school of Jewish thought. The mystic Nahum became his master after the prudent Eliezer. He afterwards frequented the schools of other famous Rabbis, of Josua, of Gamaliel II., and in all his learning was fully recognized."

He pushed his studies outside the Jewish law and traditions. He studied the doctrines of the Gnostics, the rites of the heathen nations, and their ways of life. Soon his name became famous as a prodigy of learning through Palestine. He now fulfilled his promise and returned to his wife Rachel to have her share the benefits of the exalted position he had gained. The crowd that gathered around the popular hero in the village was so dense that Rachel could not get through it when she tried. A man was pushing her back when Akibah saw him and stayed his hand.

"Lay not a hand on her," he said, "for all that I am and all that you are through me is due to this woman." [22]

Another joy was in store for the former shepherd. Calba Sebuah, Rachel's father, in his first anger at her marriage, had made a solemn vow never to receive the low-born husband into his house. He had later repented of his promise, and especially when his daughter refused to return to him unless in company with her chosen partner. But a vow must be kept if once made, unless dispensed by the authority of the religious teachers of Judah. Calba resolved to seek this dispensation, and when word came to him that a great, even one of the greatest, doctors of the law had arrived at his village Calba went to seek him." He was admitted, told his case and asked the aid of the Rabbi.

"Didst thou vow against Akibah?" asked he calmly.

"Yes, Master, even against the man who married my child against my will; but he is gone and I desire my child's welfare."

"Knowest thou what hath become of Abikah?"

"I do not; but a father's anger passeth. I forgive even him," was the answer.

"Forgiveness is a great merit. Mercy to others is God's command. Thou shalt find reward because thou hast shown mercy. Know, now, that I am he against whom thy wrath was kindled and thy vow made; I am Abikah."

The father fell down and kissed the master's feet.

"Forgive me thou," he said; "forgive a father whose pride was greater than his love for his child."

Akibah raised the old man and assured him that he was forgiven.

"Whatever the Merciful doth is for the best," he repeated, and the reconciliation was complete.

Calba took Akibah and his daughter to his home. He shared his vast possessions with them. He had lands and money and richly laden ships, and of all he gave a half to the master in Israel who had wedded his child."

The wealth of Calba Sebuah insured the position of Akibah in the Jewish commonwealth as it still existed under the Roman rule. Then as now wealth played a greater part in political success than mere learning or personal merit. The son-in-law of Calba was called to a seat in the national council under the presidency of the second Gamaliel. The policy of the Roman emperors left the subject nations a large amount of self-government, especially in the Eastern provinces. Though the authority of the Roman governors was supreme in Palestine, the Jewish people continued to be ruled by their own law and its recognized exponents in the matters of daily life. As a member of the Sanhedrin the former shepherd was now a ruler and judge as well as a public teacher. He showed himself equally capable in those practical functions as he had in the debates of the schools. He struck out a course of action for himself as a judge, based rather on broad general principles than on the technicalities which were prevalent in the Jewish courts of his day. A celebrated Rabbi, Tarphon, was frequently in collision with Akibah's decisions, and some curious instances are told in the Talmud. On one occasion a man had promised to marry one of five sisters, but could not make up his mind as to which. Each of the five demanded the dower which by Jewish law should be paid for breach of promise of marriage. The rival judges gave opinions on the case.[15] Rabbi Tarphon decided that the recreant suitor should formally release all the prospective brides from engagement and leave the dower to be divided between them. Akibah required him to pay the full dower to each.[16]

Another time a man was brought before him who had sent his wife away but refused to pay her more than half of the dower he had settled on her at marriage. He claimed that his whole living was only equal to that amount, and that by another law she was only entitled to half his possessions. Akibah settled the claim shortly.

"Thou must pay to the full what thou didst promise, though thou hadst to sell the hair of thy head to pay."

The husband decided to hold on to both wife and property, and divorce was stopped.⁷⁷

Though the law as laid down provided a definite fine (four hundred *sus*) for personal insults offered, it had become customary in the rabbinical courts to grade the fine according to the rank of the parties. Akibah held that in the administration of justice all children of Abraham should be held equal, and that penalties for personal offences should not depend on rank or wealth.

A decision recorded of Akibah's is worth recalling as an illustration of the customs of the time in Palestine. A man had a quarrel with a woman, and in it he pulled off the veil which covered her head. By the law this was an insult of the grossest kind, and punishable with a fine of four hundred pence (*sus*). Five insults were thus classified as equal, namely, to pull a man's hair or ear, to tear off his coat, or spit in his face.⁹⁸ Akibah heard the complaint and gave judgment for the legal damages. The defendant pleaded for time, and then concocted a scheme to evade judgment. He employed a man to drop a jar of oil near the woman as she passed in the street. The bait took, and she lifted the veil from her head to anoint her hair with the oil. A witness immediately reported the occurrence and charged her with infamy on the ground that a woman was forbidden to unveil herself in public. As in other Eastern countries this was held an act of gross indecency, and the defendant used it as an argument that she must be a person of bad character and not entitled to the damages already adjudged her. Akibah refused this conclusion and renewed his decision emphatically.[29]

Akibah's maxims fill a large space in the Talmud legend. They are terse and lofty in tone, and in keeping with the tenor of his life.

"Levity and jesting lead to lewdness." [30]

"Strictly attend to the exact words in Holy Writ. They are safeguards of the law."

"Charity is the safeguard of riches."

"Silence is the safeguard of wisdom."

"Pledges of temperance are the guard of temperance."

"Great is man's privilege that he has been made in God's image, but greater is the privilege to know this."

"Israel is blessed in that he is the Lord's child, but more blessed in his knowledge that he is such."

"Israel is honored by possession of the Jewel of the law; but more honored in being allowed to know the value of that Jewel."

" The Lord knoweth all, yet man's will is free to act."

"The world is ruled with love, yet that love is according to man's work and good-will.[31]

"Everything man hath is but a loan."

"Wealth passeth away."

"A net is spread over all that liveth," that is, man is held by invisible bonds of fate.[32]

This axiom is in accordance with the fatalism so marked in other utterances of Akibah. His summary of human life and its many temptations and trials is in true Oriental style.

"The market is open; good and evil are spread before man. The merchant offers credit — so sin offers temptation. The account book is open and the hand writes down the debts, but the collectors follow day by day, and they take payment whether the debtor will or not, for the collectors fail not in their work—so sin writes its account on body and soul. After debauch cometh suffering and pain. Merciless devils torture the sinner. He has enjoyed his sin, he must pay for his enjoyment. The last verdict is that of Truth, and everything must appear when God comes to judge."[33]

That a shepherd of foreign race should have become a ruler and judge in the Jewish commonwealth by sheer mental power was a remarkable fact, but it did not satisfy the ambition of Akibah. When his master Eliezer said that Akibah wished to be world-famous he unconsciously divined the secret aspirations of the shepherd student. Akibah was not content with being a foremost man among his own people. He aspired to absolute rule, and to an authority equal or superior to that of the Roman emperor himself. Though the Hebrews had bent to the power of Rome they still thirsted for independence. In their hearts they believed themselves superior to their heathen masters. As the depositaries of the divine revelation, the chosen people of the Almighty, they thought themselves by natural right the first among mankind. They chafed under the haughty rule of the foreigner. Akibah shared the popular feeling in this respect. What was more, he believed it possible to win national independence even from the mighty Empire. He shared the belief in the superiority of the Jewish race, but his belief was of a material kind. That Jewish intellect was more subtle; that Jewish patriotism was stronger than Roman; that Jewish valor could overcome the disciplined Roman legions, if well directed, were all beliefs with Akibah. He devoted himself to organize the Jewish nation for a new struggle with the same persevering energy he had shown in winning his way from the plough to the Sanhedrin at middle life. He would restore not only the independence of his people, but would found a Jewish empire. His conception of the future of his race was an empire such as, five centuries later, was actually realized by an Arab camel-driver. Akibah may in many respects be compared to Mohammed, though the result of his enterprise was so different for his people and himself. He, as well as Mohammed, was influenced by his Jewish mother, and the man he afterwards brought forth to lead his people against the Romans was of Jewish blood only on his mother's side. Mohammed proclaimed himself the Prophet of Allah: even so Akibah assumed but the dignity of forerunner of the Messiah he would give to his people for the realization of his dreams of empire.

His entrance in the Sanhedrin was, then, only a step to a mightier task. He gave himself up to it entirely. He fanned the religious fervor of his nation as a powerful stimulus to the political struggle he planned. He encouraged the national discontent with Roman rule by constant secret lessons. He strengthened the influence of the Sanhedrin as a means of preserving unity in the nation. For that end he sacrificed his former master, Eliezer, when the latter refused on principle to accept the vote of the majority as the supreme law. He carried the decree of excommunication to Eliezer personally, and thus endeavored to secure the good-will of the fallen teacher. He also succeeded in impressing his colleagues in the Sanhedrin with a fear of his influence and ability, which kept the majority from any direct condemnation of his revolutionary projects even if they did not approve them openly.

He built up his reputation among the doctors as a means of influencing the people. He was the first to reduce to system the mass of legal decisions which formed the "oral law" of the Rabbis.[34] He arranged and methodized the *Agadah*, that important part of Hebrew literature of which the style is reflected in the writings of Paul of Tarsus. He was almost another Ezra in reforming the law.[35]

His attention was even given to the hidden sciences of magic and kindred subjects in favor among his countrymen. The students of the Cabalah believed they could find the secrets of nature in the mystic construction of the *Tetragrammaton*, and many students lost their reason or their belief in the mazes of the study of magic. Akibah seems to have dipped into them as a part of his task of swaying the populace against Rome. The Talmud figuratively tells that four men were boldest in their exploration of the mystic *pardes* or paradise.[36] Ben Azzai looked in and then died; Ben Zoma looked and straightway became mad; Acher looked and he destroyed the planets (became an atheist); Akibah looked and went away in peace.[37] This seems to refer to some actual occurrence in the life of one or all of the four men named, but Akibah's record is the most important as a testimony to public belief in his regard.

It was not to study, however, that Akibah devoted himself mainly. His political projects called for active work, and the wealth of his father-in-law was used freely in the propaganda of the Jewish revolution. He travelled through many lands, and everywhere enlisted adherents and collected abundant funds through the Jews of those and other lands. In Palestine he supported numerous poor scholars who became his devoted agents. Foremost among his assistants were the great Rabbi Mair and the stern Simon ben Yohai. The mild Josua opposed the projects of Akibah and during his life prevented the outbreak of the rebellion,[38] but the propaganda went on through the tireless energy of Akibah.

That it needed no common energy to rouse the men of Judea to another struggle with Rome is shown by the Talmud narrative.[39] It runs thus:

"Rabbi Akibah once came to a town [40] and asked hospitality. He was refused churlishly and had to sleep in the fields outside. Now Akibah, when he travelled, always had with him a lantern and a cock, so that he might read in the inns by the lantern-light, and be awakened for his early prayers by the cry of the cock. When in the field this night he lighted his lantern, tethered his mule, placed the cock in another place, and lay down to rest. While he slept the wind blew down the lantern, a lynx killed the bird, and later a lion came and killed the mule. The Rabbi woke in the morning and saw the wreck. 'Whatever the Merciful hath done is for the best,' was his only comment.[41]

"Now during the night a band of marauding soldiers came through the town and plundered it. The Rabbi came there on the morrow and saw death and ruin all around. The few survivors lamented their fate bitterly.

"'I told you,' said Akibah, 'whatever the Merciful doth is for the best. Yesterday you would not receive me nor listen to my words: you thought I slandered the Romans, and that they were friends who would secure you peace and protection. You see now what Roman friendship is and the folly of your belief. Safety can only come to the people when it rises in its strength against the enemy of the Lord.'"[42]

This story describes what must have been a common experience of the reception given to Akibah during the years of his propaganda of revolution among the Jewish community of Palestine.

Akibah did not confine his efforts to his native land. With the wealth of Calba at his disposal he began a series of travels through Asia Minor, Babylonia, Arabia, and Africa, to incite the scattered branches of the Jewish race in his propaganda, and to secure allies among other races against the common Roman foe. Though Akibah exerted himself to stir up the enthusiasm of his people by appeals to their religious feelings, he had no scruple in uniting in alliance with the outside heathen for political ends. Neither did he refuse to adopt such of the customs of other races as he deemed better than those of Judea. When Jewish zealots of the strict observance blamed his alliance with the heathen Persians, he replied:

"The sun and moon are God's creatures. If man be unwise enough to worship them, it is to God he will answer. God will not destroy nature's works to keep man from sinning by their abuse."

His teaching, "If a man's belief be right and one despise him for it, he offends God, who knoweth what belief is right," is certainly unlike what one would expect from a strict adherent of the Jewish law.[43] He himself certainly did not despise the heathens nor even their worship. When at times Jews came to tell him of prodigies and cures wrought by idols, he only answered that the supposed cures were merely accidental, and spoke little against idolatry itself.[44] He recommended three customs of the Medes, whom he had visited on his travels, to his own countrymen. One was to sit on seats at table instead of on the ground; another, to kiss only on the hand instead of on the lips, and a third, that of holding all political meetings in the fields, as walls have ears.[45]

A nobler teaching was that which he gave to some Jews of his time who held that the truth and honesty required by the Mosaic Law were only binding in intercourse with their own countrymen.

"It is equally wrong to deceive a heathen as to deceive a Jew."[46] He also laid down that 'Love thy neighbour as thyself,' is the root and completion of the Law."

Akibah's liberality in ethics, however, did not extend to the Roman rulers. His work against them was indefatigable, and carried out in a manner not unlike that of the Young Italy of Mazzini in our own time. His propaganda began under the reign of Trajan. That emperor's Eastern campaigns filled Asia, and especially Syria, with the soldiers of Rome and made the work of preparation for a Jewish insurrection all the more hard. Still it went on and with marvellous secrecy. An outbreak prematurely made in the year 115 by the leaders known as Julianus and Pappus was put down with such ease that the rulers of Rome regarded the allegiance of the Jews to the Empire as secure. On one occasion an army of Jews gathered in the valley of Rimmon to begin a rebellion. Rabbi Josua came to dissuade them from what he deemed madness. It had been rumored that the Roman government proposed to rebuild the Temple on another site, which in the mind of every true Jew would be a sacrilege. Josua told them to be glad no worse evil was threatened. A stork that has had its head in the mouth of a lion should be more glad to tell the story than anxious to avenge the insult, was his sharp remark which did for the time avert the insurrection."[47]

The accession of Hadrian and his abandonment of Trajan's late conquests gave promise of better times to the Jews under Roman dominion. Hadrian showed favor to some Rabbis; he pardoned Julianus and Pappus, and he began to rebuild Jerusalem as a Roman city under the name of Ælia Capitolina. He even spoke of restoring the Temple for a while, and the partisans of Rome were full of joy at the success which seemed to have attended their policy of submission. Not so Akibah, who never desisted from his revolutionary schemes, though he veiled them so carefully as to deceive the watchful Hadrian. The latter thought he had secured peace by his treaty with the Parthians. He had medals struck with the inscription "Tellus Stabilita" (the world is settled), and he began a personal tour of his vast dominions at the moment when Judea was preparing to rise again in arms. Hadrian, when in Palestine in 130, saw nothing to indicate the vast plot devised by Akibah. Rufus, the governor of Judea, conversed with the revolutionary leader in friendly terms, and questioned him on points of the Jewish law. He could not understand why the Jews, though poor themselves, should be ready to aid the unfortunate among themselves. The heathen maxim was that no mercy should be shown to those whom the gods have cursed, and on this principle the Romans treated the poor and suffering with barbarous cruelty.

"Think you not it an offence against your God to relieve such as He hath doomed to suffering?" asked Rufus.

"No," replied Akibah. "If a king had justly deprived his son of food for a time by way of punishment, and if another found the prince dying of hunger and fed him, think you his father would be angry with the helper of his son? Even so will God deal with those who minister to their suffering fellow-men; for all men, however sinful, are children of God." [48]

The interest taken by the Roman governor in Jewish laws was shared by his wife. She became acquainted with Akibah at her husband's house and joined in the intercourse that took place between them. She was captivated by the personal beauty which marked Akibah's features and which years before had won him the hand of the daughter of Calba Shebuah. Akibah himself was smitten with the charms of the high-born Roman lady. The Talmud says that when he first saw her he wept and then laughed. He wept that so fair a being should be in heathen darkness; he laughed because he foresaw that she would become a proselyte and his own wife.[49] The wife of Rufus studied the doctrines of Judaism and finally professed herself a believer.[50] She left her husband's house and joined her aged lover, who formally married her.

It may be imagined what was the wrath of the Roman noble at the injury thus done him, alike in family and personal honor. Akibah was searched for diligently, but was hidden by his political friends.

The time for revolution was at hand when Akibah carried off the wife of Rufus. The suspicion of the authorities had been aroused, and some severe measures were adopted to cow the spirit of rebellion among the Jews. The sacred site of the Temple was ordered to be ploughed up and sown as a sign that it should never be built again. Rabbi Ishmael, a close friend and colleague of Akibah, who was held in the highest regard by the people, was arrested and executed without trial.[61] He and Akibah enjoyed the common title of "Fathers of Wisdom."[62] Akibah felt the death of Ishmael keenly. He spoke in impassioned language at his funeral and stirred up the hearts of the people against Rome. Within a brief time Israel was in arms against the legions of the Roman empire again.

It did not begin, however, till the provident Akibah had found a leader fit to lead the Hebrews to battle with the legions of Rome. He was, with all his ability, no soldier himself, and it needed a soldier, above all, to realize his dream of material empire. Akibah did not venture to put himself forward, like Mohammed in later years, as a Heaven-sent prophet. He chose rather to act the part of a precursor, as John the Baptist had been to another in past time. Akibah was famed far and wide for his holiness and extraordinary powers, so that it was easy for him to make the people believe that he was the incorporation of the prophet Elijah, who according to prophecy was to precede the coming of the Messiah. The expectation of a Messiah to be sent by the Almighty to change the condition of the human race was general among the Jews of the time. Many looked for him as an invincible leader who would go forth in the power of the supreme Lord to make Israel the earthly ruler of the human race. Akibah used this faith to forward the political object to which he had devoted his life, and to precipitate the rebellion which destroyed the separate national existence of the Jewish race. A false Elijah preceded a false Messiah.

During his propaganda among the Jewish people, Akibah had met a young man in whom his keen judgment recognized a great though unknown military genius. This unknown was said to come from the town of Cozibah, but his origin was hid in obscurity. He was without family, and strange tales were told of his origin.[63] A popular legend made him the natural son of the Roman Emperor Hadrian himself. It was said that his birth was the result of an intrigue between Hadrian when in Syria in early life and the wife of a prince of Hebrew race, but a Moor in complexion.[64] Be this as it may, Akibah, when the Jewish people were excited to madness by the execution of Ishmael, presented this young man to them as the one destined by Heaven to work their deliverance. When his name and origin were asked, Akibah replied that his name was Bar Kochba, the son of the star, the "star" that should come forth from Jacob according to prophecy, the true Messiah come to crush the enemies of the Lord and of His people.[65]

The people accepted the words of Akibah and rose in arms under this new leader. His success for a time was remarkable. He captured fifty towns; he defied the Roman armies. The Romans were discouraged by the feats of this unknown warrior, and a superstitious awe grew around his name among them. They dared not meet him in battle. They shut themselves up in their fortifications and even wished to abandon Judea as the provinces beyond the Euphrates had been given up by Hadrian a few years earlier.[56]

Hadrian called his best general, Julius Severus, from Britain with a veteran army to suppress the Jewish rebellion. Bar Kochba was no match for these foes. Severus drove the insurgents from post after post and finally shut up their leader with the flower of his forces in the fortified city of Bethar. There he held out against all attacks for two years, until a Samaritan betrayed to the Romans an underground passage to the heart of the city. The Hebrews were surprised and slaughtered after a desperate struggle. Bar Kochba's body, it is said, was found crushed in the coils of a serpent after the battle. The revolution was quenched in Jewish blood. He so audaciously proclaimed as the son of the star had proved a false guide, and had led Israel not to glory, but to temporal ruin. The indignant populace heaped execration on his memory. The title Bar Kochba was changed by the people to another derived from his supposed place of birth, and at the same time descriptive of his character. He was called Bar Kozibah, or son of lies.[57]

Rabbi Akibah was not involved in the destruction which fell on the Jewish host in Bethar. He escaped to Lydda when the stronghold of Jewish resistance was captured. He does not seem to have lost credit as a teacher even after the fall of him whom he had proclaimed the Messiah. At Lydda, in company with his old opponent, Rabbi Tarphon, he held a council of doctors of the law to decide what course should be followed by the Jewish people in the days of tribulation which had fallen on them. The Roman authorities, exasperated at the stubborn defence of Bethar, had refused all toleration to the professors of Judaism. To practise the rites of the Law of Moses, to teach it publicly, and even to meet in any numbers were forbidden to the Jews of Palestine under pain of death. The council at Lydda adopted the advice of Akibah, and proclaimed that it was lawful to dissemble the profession of faith outwardly under these circumstances, though the believers were urged to retain the faith in their hearts and teach it to their children in secret. The old saying of Abtalion, "and ye shall live by the laws, but ye shall not die by them,"[58] was revived and adopted. This decision was very different from that of the Maccabees under the persecution of Antiochus, but it was in accordance with the tenor of policy of Akibah's life.

After the council he hid among the friends who still remained faithful to him and for some time baffled the pursuit of the Romans. Though the effect of the great Rabbi's policy and teaching had been so disastrous, he yet retained the respect of the people to a remarkable extent. In the ruin that had fallen on their nation, zealous Jews still sought for instruction in the law and looked to Akibah as their most trusted teacher.

The Talmud tells the story of his closing days in a way which leaves no doubt of this fact. Simon, a former pupil of Akibah, and son of a man high in office under the Roman government, it is told, was so anxious to continue his studies that he sought out Akibah in his concealment and urged him to renew the work of training doctors of the law. The Rabbi pleaded the danger under the existing laws.

"My son," the Talmud makes him say, "as the cow is more ready to give milk to her calf than the calf is to draw that milk, so am I more anxious to teach than thou art to learn. But see the danger."

"Ignorance is a greater danger," replied Simon. "Rome can only kill the body: ignorance kills the soul. Rome kills only for time: ignorance kills for eternity." [59]

As this plea had no effect, the enthusiastic youth threatened to reveal Akibah's abode to his father and let him deliver him to the Romans unless he would consent to instruct him in the proscribed religion. Akibah yielded at last and again gathered pupils around him. He was warned of the danger of his course by friends, amongst whom were the celebrated Rabbi Yosai ben Kisma and Pappus, but his fatalistic philosophy came to his aid and he continued to teach regardless of the advice he had already given at Lydda. Pappus, who found him surrounded by pupils, asked:

"Rabbi, dost thou not know that if thou teach the Law thou wilt lose thy life?"

"Even so," answered Akibah, "the fox once asked the little fishes to leave the water, where they were in danger of being devoured by larger fish, and live with him on land, and the fishes told him it was safer to take risks in their element than sure death for want of it. Thus may I say to thee, Pappus, that if death threaten me when teaching God's Word, the tree of life, the true living waters, it will surely come on me if I neglect to teach. Neglect of the law brings everlasting death; Rome can only kill the body." [60]

His career after that was short as a teacher, but before its close he ordained Simon as Rabbi and desired to ordain Mair, another pupil, but the latter declined on the ground that he was not married. Simon, protected by his father's position under the Roman governor, carried on the work of teaching after Akibah's death and transmitted the traditions of the Rabbis to future ages.

The Roman governor finally discovered Akibah's hiding-place, and made him prisoner. The contempt which the former felt for the rebel against the empire was intensified by the hatred he had towards the man who had drawn away his own wife from his household. He doomed the captive to death by torture. Akibah knew that there was no hope of pity from the exasperated Rufus. He called his fatalistic theories to his aid and faced the Roman fires with the stoical courage of an Indian warrior at the stake.

His skin was seared slowly with hot iron combs, while he continued to pray and thank Heaven for the privilege of dying in such a cause. The executioners then pierced various parts of his flesh with pointed rods. Akibah looked on his disciples, who had been brought there by command of Rufus, and smiled. The exasperated Roman asked harshly why he smiled under pain.

"One whose wish is gratified must be happy," Akibah is quoted as saying. "My chief wish was ever to give myself to God. Hitherto I could only give my works, now that I can give Him my life itself, why should I not rejoice?" [61]

Rufus ordered the executioners to finish the victim's life, and Akibah expired with the cry, "Hear, O, Israel, the Lord our God, the Lord is one," on his lips. [62] The stoicism with which he met his death, and the patriotic fervor of his character, have made of Akibah a national hero among subsequent generations. With him the separate political existence of the Jewish people came to an end, and patriotic sympathy has enshrined his memory in the hearts of the Jews. The calamities that befell his nation through his policy are forgotten in the case of Akibah as in that of Hannibal. His political projects were a failure. He failed to grasp the mission of the Jewish race under the divine dispensation. It was to be the messenger bearing revealed truth to the other children of man. Akibah conceived it as holding revelation for its own benefit, and in virtue of it as lording it over all other nations from the heights of Mount Moriah.

As a teacher of religion and morals it is hard to find praise for one who proclaimed a false Messiah to his people to attain a political end, and who counselled outward denial of religious belief when its profession involved serious danger. Nevertheless, as a scholar, a judge, an organizer, and patriotic Jew, Akibah holds a foremost rank among the recognized masters in Israel.

"A man's sayings are his true monument," is a rabbinical proverb.[63] We shall add a few of Akibah's to the story of his life.

"It is sin when one is scorned to say that others ought to be scorned, or when one is abused that others should be abused likewise."[64]

"Labor is honorable to man."[65]

"If thou needest, do any work and excuse not thyself if perchance thou art a priest or a noble."[66]

"If life is equally at stake, first save thyself, then look for thy neighbor's life," is a saying quite in keeping with Akibah's own practice.[67]

"They err who say, I will sin now and repent after. The Day of Atonement brings no forgiveness to the insincere," is an axiom of a different nature.[68]

"As a golden vase when flawed may be melted to a new vessel, so the sinner may repent and become a new man," embodies his theory on sin and its forgiveness.[69]

On family life his precepts are equally clear, terse, and beautiful.

"God is with the married who are faithful to one another."[70]

"He who keeps his daughter long unmarried is as though he showed her the way to incontinence."[71]

"He who receiveth alms when he needs them not, will need them before he dieth."[72]

Other of Akibah's maxims have been already given, so these will suffice as characteristic of the great Rabbi.

Akibah was old at his death. The Talmud, with Eastern exaggeration, says, a hundred and twenty years, but this means little more than he died full of years and works.[73]

A son and a daughter survived him. The son, Josua, was himself a distinguished doctor of the law. Akibah's daughter was married to Ben Azzai, but as he desired to devote his life to study she voluntarily separated from him. The talmudic writers said of her, "The lamb followeth its mother," that is, she did for Ben Azzai what her mother, Rachel, did for Akibah.[74]

CHAPTER VIII

RABBI MAIR

THE years immediately after the rebellion of Bar Kochba were the darkest in Jewish history. Hadrian prohibited, under pain of death, all public exercise of Jewish religion or even the teaching of its doctrines. The teachers were, many of them, executed and the lately flourishing schools were destroyed. With the death of Akibah and Ishmael, the "Wells of Wisdom were dried up," in the language of their contemporaries.[1] But the national spirit survived even this test. Hadrian died, and his successor, Antoninus Pius, the best of the Roman cæsars, relaxed the edicts of persecution. The schools were opened again, though most of the great Rabbis had perished.

A prominent figure in the new generation of Rabbis was Mair.[2] His character is enigmatical. The Talmud does not tell of his origin or history except in disjointed sentences. It even hints that he was a descendant of Nero, who, according to a wild legend, had escaped death at the time of his deposition, and became a proselyte to Judaism subsequently.[3] The chief interest of this surmise is that it indicates that in features and character Mair showed traces of a non-Jewish origin. His sayings and doctrines, too, have a certain Greek flavor which suggests the same conclusion. In his lectures he compared Hebrew and Greek words in a manner which showed his familiar acquaintance with both. His methods were rather those of a Greek sophist than an Oriental. The Rabbis describe his many-sided versatility in astonishment. It was said that when he discussed a question he would bring such strong reasons for both sides that it was impossible to know his own judgment.[5] He was especially fond of parables, and "Great Speaker of Parables" was his title of honor in the Jewish schools. Yet the few specimens of his skill that survive have a Greek cast in their imagery. We give one of the three preserved in the Talmud, out of three hundred with the authorship of which he is credited, to illustrate this point. Mair was elucidating the saying of Ezekiel, "The fathers have eaten sour grapes and the teeth of their children are on edge." This is his illustration:

"A lion caught a fox and was about to devour him, when the fox exclaimed that his carcase would be but a mouthful, and that if the lion spared him he would guide him to a man who would furnish a more ample meal. The lion consented. The fox led to a hunter who had dug a pitfall and was lying quietly beyond it. The lion felt some awe about attacking a human being.

" 'The Lord may hear that man's prayer,' he remarked nervously.

" 'Don't fear,' said the fox. 'It is wrong to kill

one made in God's image, but, too, it is written, that God will visit the sins of the fathers on their children. Thy son or his son will have to pay the penalty of thy sin, not thou.'

"The lion took courage and sprang at the man, but only to fall helpless in the pit.

"'Thou art justly punished,' cried the fox, calmly looking down.

"'Didst thou not tell,' growled the lion, 'that it is the sons that pay for their fathers' sins?'

"'I did, indeed,' said the fox, 'and don't forget that thy father and grandfather have sinned before thee and it is for their sins thou dost suffer now.'"[6]

Mair supported himself by various kinds of literary work.[7] He wrote the sacred scrolls for the synagogues, and letters for the people. He also wrote verses for public feasts.[8] He spent his earnings freely, and supported several needy students; but his own family were but scanty sharers in his liberality. He justified himself in his mocking fashion.

"If my children turn out good the Lord will provide for them. David says in the Psalms, 'I was young and I am old, yet I have not seen the righteous forsaken nor his seed needing bread.' If my children are not good, they deserve nothing, and it would be helping the enemies of the Lord if I left them wealth."[9]

It is little wonder that Mair was credited with finding reasons for any course after this specimen. The serious Rabbis told with indignation how Mair could give a hundred and fifty reasons to prove an object legally clean and as many more to show it utterly unclean.[10] His was the spirit of Lucian under the garb of a Rabbi. The other Rabbis looked askance at the erratic flights of their brilliant colleague. Mair had refused ordination at the hands of Akibah, but after his marriage he asked it from Rabbi Judah ben Baba.[11] Judah and the father of Mair's wife were among the Rabbis who lost their lives during the persecution of Hadrian. There is no evidence that Mair took any active part in the rebellion, and the tenor of his character makes it unlikely. Some sneers recorded in the Talmud [12] would imply that he was not popular with the Rabbis of the patriot faction. However, none contested his intellectual ability, or cared to enter the arena of debate with the clever sophist.[13] He was called to the Sanhedrin when that body was again assembled under the presidency of Simon, the son of the second, Gamaliel. He was made *Haham* or reader, the third office in that body, his friend Rabbi Nathan being presiding judge. With the president these three formed a committee which was practically supreme in the Council. Simon, amid the misfortunes of his people, retained an exaggerated idea of the importance of his office. He had neither the learning nor the generous temper of his father, and his jealous maintenance of his official dignity excited many quarrels in the Sanhedrin.

Custom required the members of the Sanhedrin to rise and remain standing when the president, the judge, or the reader entered the Assembly. They did not resume their seats till motioned to do so by the president after the three superiors were seated.[14]

Simon, in the absence of Mair and Nathan, issued an order that the Assembly should only rise as a body on his own entrance. At the entrance of the judge only the first row of members were to rise, and on the entrance of the reader the second row. Rabbis Nathan and Mair were indignant at this change and revenged themselves at a subsequent meeting by proposing a number of difficult questions. Their object was to puzzle Simon and possibly show his unfitness for the office he held; but it failed. Simon had got information of the scheme, and not only worsted his assailants in debate, but obtained their deposition from office on the ground of conspiracy against himself.

Mair was not the man to yield on such a point. In the session he plied the president with so many questions that the latter was bewildered and offered to reinstate the judge and reader if they would apologize for their conduct. Nathan consented: Mair refused. He was threatened with excommunication.

"I shall submit readily," he said, "if the president will explain when and how excommunication may justly be incurred." [16]

The excommunication was not attempted. This episode gives a noteworthy idea of the workings of the venerable Assembly seventeen hundred years ago.

Mair had a large fund of intellectual pride, and his dislike was intense for those who scorned studies and gave themselves up to sensual pleasures. This class was a large one in Palestine at the time, and receives frequent reprobation through the Talmud.[16] The materialists scoffed at the pains taken by the scholars to store their minds with decisions and rules of the law. Their favorite theory was that the true way of fulfilling the law was to enrich the people," a maxim not unknown in our own days. The austere among the Rabbis lavished condemnation on these doctrines and their maintainers.

"One might as well give his daughter to a lion in marriage as to a Man of Earth," was one maxim.

"He who leaves a Man of Earth in his house asleep and returns to find him awake may be sure that pollution has been abroad in that house," was another saying.[18]

Mair was strict even to harshness in speaking of this class of men. Study, for him, was the first duty and privilege of man.

"Learn the ways of the Lord with thy whole heart and with thy whole soul. Watch at the gate of the law. Keep the law in thy heart. Let the fear of the Lord be ever before thine eyes and keep thy tongue from evil words. Cleanse and make pure thyself that thou mayest stand without sin or guilt before the Lord, and He will be with thee wherever thou art."[19]

It must be owned that there is a tincture of the pride of intellect in Mair's strictures on the Men of Earth,—the unlettered. In later days, when domestic sorrow had touched himself, his utterances took a milder form and breathed a more charitable spirit. A parable told by him after the death of his sons may illustrate this change:

"A king had a twin brother like to himself in face. This brother left his home and became a robber who wasted the country. The king, who knew not that the robber was his brother, ordered his soldiers to capture and hang him. It was done, and the robber's body was hung on high as a warning to all who might be tempted to follow unrighteousness.

"Now the common people, who knew the face of the king, but did not know the robber, thought the body was that of the king. They said to one another, 'The king is hanged! the king is hanged!' Then the king heard, and he bade his servants take down the body of his brother and bury it from the sight of men. Even so God finds no glory in the shame of His erring children, nor can Israel have honor in the disgrace of his twin brother." [20]

The family life of Rabbi Mair is told in great detail by the rabbinical writers. It throws much light on the social conditions of life in Palestine in the Roman days and on the position then held by woman in society among the Jews. Beruriah, his wife, was the child of a distinguished Rabbi who was one of the ten Rabbis slain by Hadrian. [21]

She was to Mair what Rachel was to Akibah, and more; for she exercised a marked influence in the formation of his character. She was clever as well as fair, and her charity to all was boundless. Her husband's fiery temper she gradually modified by gentleness, while she was ever ready to sacrifice her own desires to his advancement, and to stimulate his mind by gentle suggestion. When Mair quoted in hot wrath the text from the Psalm which says, "Let sinners perish from the land," Beruriah corrected his zeal.

"It is written," she said, " 'Let sin (*'hataim*)

perish, not sinners' (*'hoteim*). Rather let us pray that the sinners may be converted from their ways and then sin and sinners shall pass away." [22]

Beruriah frequently showed her own skill in controversy with unbelievers.[23] She advised as to the best methods of study, and her judgment on points of the law were often ratified by the authority of the Rabbis themselves.[24] Her wit was as quick as her husband's. She discussed philosophy with him as well as the law, and few cared to enter on a contest with the witty Beruriah. Once a famous Rabbi, Yosai of Galilee, met her on the road and asked in pompous style:

"What is the road that people dwelling around here take to go to Lydda?"

"Man of Galilee," answered Beruriah, "don't you know the saying, 'Speak not more than necessary to a woman'? You could have asked, What is the road to Lydda?"

Poor Yosai slunk away discomfited at this palpable hit.[25]

A great domestic misfortune which befell Beruriah brought out the nobler side of her character in a very touching way. Her two sons, beautiful boys, were accidentally drowned in a cistern while playing. It was a Sabbath Day and the father was teaching in the school. Beruriah in her grief would not interrupt his duties. She covered the bodies of her children with a sheet on the bed and awaited Mair's return till sunset. His first inquiry was where the children were. His wife told him they had gone out to the College, and then brought the golden goblet of the feast day, filled it with wine, and asked him to repeat the grace for the close of the Sabbath Day. Mair complied, and intoned the blessing with a cheerful heart. He then asked again where the children were.

"They are in the house, not far away," was the wife's answer. "Eat, dear, the Sabbath meal must not wait."

Rabbi Mair sat down and made his Sabbath meal. He repeated the grace at the end with joy, for he felt thoroughly blessed in his wife and children at that moment. Beruriah then spoke.

"Master," said she, "may I ask thee a question?"

"Ask," he said cheerfully.

"Some time ago one gave me a treasure which he now asks back. Shall I return it?"

"Dost thou ask such a question?" sharply answered Mair.

"But," Beruriah urged, "I have grown to love this treasure, and I am loath to part with it."

"Things entrusted to us are sacred," said the Rabbi. "They must be returned when demanded. Hesitate not, lest thou sin against the Lord."

"Must I not repine against him who gave the treasure?" she asked.

"Certainly not," replied the Rabbi.

"Come, then, my lord, and I will show the treasure to thee."

She led him to the room and, removing the sheet from the bodies of her children, said:

"See the treasure that He who gave hath demanded back."

Mair was stricken speechless at the sight. His frame shook for some moments with convulsions. Then tears came and he cried aloud:

"My sons, my sons, I was your father and your teacher, but you are now my masters in the law."

Then Beruriah's tears broke out and she, too, wept. But after a brief space she took her husband's hand and whispered:

"Remember, my beloved, that the treasure must be returned."

Mair grew strong from her resolution. He arose and said:

"The Lord hath given them to us, the Lord hath taken them away; blessed be the name of the Lord."

Again and again he repeated the words and he grew composed, at least outwardly, but his soul was sad and his heart bleeding for many days."[26]

A tale of the rescue of his sister-in-law, though embellished with legend, may have a foundation in fact. After the defeat of Bar Kochba, the sister of Beruriah, a beautiful girl, was carried away to slavery. It was learned after many days that she had been carried to Rome and sold to the keeper of a house of ill-fame. Beruriah urged her husband to attempt her rescue. Mair at first demurred. He feared the task and in his pride he dreaded the disgrace that would attach to himself if he should bring a fallen woman to his house. Beruriah maintained her faith in her sister's constancy, and pledged her word that she would forfeit life rather than virtue. Mair yielded.

"If she remain pure," he said, "it is by miracle, and a miracle may be wrought for her deliverance."

He journeyed to Rome, according to the legend, dressed as a wealthy Roman, and found the house where the girl was kept.

"Thou hast in this house a comely Hebrew maiden, I am told," he said to the owner, giving him at the same time several pieces of gold.

"I have, my lord," the man replied. "She is very beautiful, but no man hath as yet gained her favor."

"Let me see her," said Mair, scarcely able to conceal his joy.

The man led the Rabbi into the room where the maiden was kept, and left them.

Rabbi Mair beheld the beautiful and weeping daughter of Palestine, seated upon a low divan, her head turned toward the window, gazing upon the blue horizon, far beyond the green meadows and hills, in longing for the land of her fathers and those she loved.

He approached her. When she saw him, she quickly arose and asked his errand. He told her that he had come to rescue her. Misfortune had made her incredulous; she was afraid of men under any guise. But when he told her who he was she fell upon her knees and thanked God.

Rabbi Mair then told the keeper that he desired to take away the maiden, offering him a large sum of money. But the keeper hesitated.

"When this is found out it will cost my head," he said.

"Fear not," said the Rabbi, "when danger threatens thee, say, ' Mair's God, help me! ' and thou shalt be safe."

Still the man hesitated.

"Convince me that what thou sayest is the truth," he said.

"Behold," said the Rabbi, and he approached a number of savage watch-dogs at the gate. He uttered a mystic word, and the dogs cringed at his feet.

Convinced that the Rabbi spoke truth, the man let the maiden go for the price offered. When the two had departed he felt afraid and raised an alarm, saying that a Hebrew had come and abducted the maiden, and he gave a detailed description of the pseudo-Roman.

Rabbi Mair had meanwhile taken the maiden to a safe hiding-place, and then made his escape from the city alone. The Talmud tells that the keeper was given an opportunity to test the cabalistic formula of Rabbi Mair, with safety to his life.

Watch was set for the Jewish abductor on the roads. A party of the watchers were eating in an inn some miles from the city, when a dignified Roman entered and sat down to eat. The guards thought he resembled the description given them of the unknown. One of them said, it must be he. Another, that no Jew could carry himself so proudly. As a test they resolved to ask him to eat.

"Good sir," said their leader, "pray join us in this dish of swine's flesh, for it is good."

"I am not hungry," said the supposed Roman,

"but I cannot refuse your kind invitation, so I will taste your fare, though I care not to dine."

He dipped a finger in the gravy, conveyed another finger to his lips, and, saluting, left in haste. The soldiers were deceived and believed he could not be the man they sought. No Hebrew would even taste the flesh of swine."

The Talmud has other stories illustrating the Rabbi's ready wit, and one or two may be given as examples.

While travelling, Rabbi Mair came to an inn. It had a bad reputation, as the host was held to be leagued with robbers, but there was no other resting-place near. When Mair took out his purse to pay for his lodging, he noticed the look of greed that came over the host's face.

"My friend Ki Tobh (for it is good) will soon come here after me," he quietly remarked, and then went to his room.

He rose at dawn and, as he was leaving, the host met him and asked:

"Hath thy friend come?"

"He hath," replied Mair.

"Where is he?"

"There," said the Rabbi, pointing to the sun.

"What dost thou mean?" asked the puzzled innkeeper.

"That I saw thine intention last night," was the reply. "Night is for deeds of darkness and sin such as were in thy mind; but daylight is the traveller's friend. Ki Tobh is its name by Holy Writ; for 'The Lord saw light that it was good, and He called it day.' Had not I told thee I expected a friend thou wouldst have slain me as thou and thine evil comrades have slain many other travellers who sought thy shelter."[28] And Rabbi Mair went on his way.

Advice for travellers was a favorite subject of Mair's. He left numerous wise maxims on this subject.

"When thou art at Rome do as the Romans do," was one.[29]

"Travellers should go in threes," was another, with the gloss, "A lone traveller is like to be murdered; two are likely to quarrel; but three together will always make their way in peace."[30]

The nicknames so commonly applied in the East he considered valuable indications of character. If they had reference to anything connected with good in Scripture lore, the bearers were sure of Mair's confidence; if to evil, he distrusted as strongly. "The voice of the people is the voice of God," was his apology for this theory, which was not generally shared by other Rabbis.

Once, the Talmud tells, Rabbi Mair, Rabbi Juda, and Rabbi Yosai travelled together. They came late to a certain town where a man offered them hospitality for the night. Now this man was known as Ki Dor. As it chances, these two words are at the beginning of a sentence in Holy Writ speaking of a perverse generation. Juda and Yosai paid no particular attention to the man's name. They accepted his offer and gave him their purses for safe keeping, but Rabbi Mair would not enter the house.

"I trust not that man," he said, "for evil is attached to his name." [31]

So he went away and buried his money in a graveyard, and then he went and ate and slept. While he slept he dreamed that he was warned to remove his money from its hiding-place. He interpreted his dream that his friends were in danger of loss, and in the morning he went to them and told his dream and its meaning. Juda and Yosai laughed and told him sunset dreams were idle, as a sly hint that his late supper was accountable for the supposed warning.[32] So Rabbi Mair went about his business as a public writer; but he watched Ki Dor all day.[33]

Rabbi Juda and Rabbi Yosai rested a day in Ki Dor's house, but when they were leaving and asked the return of their money, Ki Dor denied having had any money of them. They sought Rabbi Mair and told him, and Mair asked:

"Why did you not heed my warning concerning his name?"

"Why didst thou not tell us plainly?" they said.

"I had only suspicion myself, so I could not speak as one certain," was Mair's answer.

As they spoke they were before a wine shop, and lo, Ki Dor came up. The Rabbis seized him and pulled him into the house. And Ki Dor was afeared; for he thought they meant to kill him. But they bade him sit down and drink wine with them, and they made as if they had all been drunken, and had forgotten their money completely. Then Ki Dor felt glad; he had robbed the great Rabbis of their money, and now he was drinking at their cost besides.

He loved wine and would drink much when others paid for it. So he now drank till his head sank on the table. Now Ki Dor was not only a thief, but he was a sloven in his ways. His beard was smeared with the remains of the dinner he had eaten when he met the Rabbis, and they noted that his food had been lentils. So while Mair watched the drunken man, Judah and Josai went to Ki Dor's house and told his wife that her husband had sent them for the money he had given her the night before.

"What word or token hath he sent?" she asked.

"The token is that he had lentils for his meal," was the answer, and the woman believed them and gave the stolen money back. They went in haste away.

When Ki Dor awoke he went home and looked for the money in vain. He questioned his wife and she told him how two men had brought the token from him and carried off the money. Then Ki Dor was so wroth that he slew his wife.

The moral drawn by the Talmud from this tale is an admirable example of the spirit of hair-splitting prevalent in the rabbinical schools. "Therefore," it sagely rules, "no one should leave table without washing face and hands after eating." [34] It would be hard to find a more characteristic example of the spirit which would "tithe mint and cummin and aniseed," and leave unnoticed the weighty things of the law,—mercy and justice and truth.

These tales show that in private life relations of intimacy existed between Mair and his brother Rabbis of other schools. Other statements indicate that his public work as teacher of the law was troubled sorely by the jealousies prevailing among the students of his time. The party feelings of the revolutionary movement were still bitter after the death of Bar Kochba, and Mair as a moderate in politics was subjected to unworthy persecution by some of his own disciples. An attempt was made to blast his character. A woman one day was hired to enter his school while his disciples were gathered together.

"Rabbi," she said, "one of you here has seduced me under promise. I demand my right." [35]

The law of the Rabbis on seduction is worth recording. If a man were found alone in a room with an unmarried woman it was regarded as legal evidence of seduction. Such constituted marriage in the eyes of the law if demanded by the woman. On the other hand, if a man was found alone in a room with the wife of another, it was legal evidence of adultery against them. It brought the woman's reputation into doubt and warranted her husband to divorce her without compensation.[36]

The manner in which the woman's claim was put forward was evidently aimed to compromise the master, who was included with his disciples in the term "one of you." Mair rose up and calmly gave her a legal bill of divorce. All his disciples followed the master's example, and the deceit of the complainant was made manifest. Mair's character remained untouched by evil tongues.

The hostility against him, however, found a more dastardly means of attack on his honor. It resembles closely the plot told in *Cymbeline*, for which, indeed, it may have furnished the hint. One day the school disputed and the debate was whether man was naturally more moral than woman or not. The champions of female morality declared that their master's wife was the superior morally of any man living. An insolent student maintained that any woman was ready to yield if approached on her weak side.

"Dost thou speak of Beruriah?" asked Mair quickly.

"Even of thy Beruriah," answered the student with insolence.

"Try thy skill," said Mair indignantly, and he left the room in hot wrath."

The audacious libertine caught at the chance rashly given him by Mair's word. He went straight to the house where Beruriah was engaged in her daily tasks among her maids and female pupils whom she instructed in the law. She knew the visitor as a member of her husband's college; she greeted him kindly and asked the purpose of his call.

"I have a message to thee from thy husband, my master," he said.

"Speak it," said Beruriah.

"Nay, learned lady, it is for thy private ear alone; so, pray, send out thy maids."

With all her knowledge Beruriah forgot the warning of the law and sent out the maidens. The visitor then told her, saying, "Thy husband hath given thee to me."

The indignant wife bade him begone and went to call for help, but the mocking libertine restrained her.

"It is too late now to save thy character," he said. "Thou and I are alone in this room. Thy name as a faithful wife is ruined. Be mine and I will take thee away from this place."

Beruriah again spurned his offer and the would-be seducer left. He revenged himself by boasting of his success which seemed proved by the private interview so treacherously obtained.

Both husband and wife felt acutely the weight of the disgrace which had fallen on them. Beruriah, like the Roman Lucretia, took her own life in despair. Rabbi Mair closed his school and left his native land forever.

He travelled through many lands seeking peace or, at least, distraction of thought for his harassed soul. Babylonia, Cappadocia, the Ægean coast were visited in succession by the sad-hearted traveller.[38]

"Look not to the cask, but to what is in it; for there be new casks which hold rare old wine, and others that are old and yet have not even new wine within," was his bitter remark as he left his native land.[39]

He finally settled in Sardes in Asia Minor, where he resumed his profession as a teacher. Large crowds came to his lectures.[40] Gradually he recovered his peace of mind, and the trials he had suffered softened his original harshness. His later sayings are full of mild and humble wisdom, very different from the pride of earlier days.

"Who is truly rich, but he who is content with his fortune."[41]

"Repentance is great, for when one man repents all human nature is forgiven."[42]

"Humble thyself before every man."[43]

This last precept he urged on his disciples earnestly and acted on it in his own later practice.

"Man comes into the world with closed hands, as though claiming ownership of everything, but he leaves with hands open and limp, as though to show he takes naught with him. Yet if man has sought the best couse in life, his reward awaits him beyond the grave. There he finds the table set for the happy feast that lasts through eternity."[44]

In Mair's school at Sardes one of his most devoted auditors was a married woman who missed no lecture. On one occasion a long discourse made her late in preparing the dinner for her husband.

The latter threatened to divorce her on this ground, which was recognized as a valid one by rabbinical law, unless she would spit at the Rabbi who had been responsible for her neglect of home. The story was carried to his ears, and when the woman next came to the school he insisted on her carrying out the husband's vindictive wish. He knew too well the meaning of a family disruption to let others incur it for the sake of his own dignity.[45]

Mair was not the only distinguished master in Israel who had to suffer in repute at the hands of his own people during these disastrous times for the Jews. His first teacher, Elisha ben Abuiah, with whom Mair kept a close intimacy during life, was a

still more conspicuous mark for jealousy. He was
a man of distinction in the schools. According to
the Talmud, Elisha ben Abuiah was taken into the
Academy of Rabbi Yochanan ben Zakkai at a very
early age and enrolled as one of the great master's
disciples.[46] Under the guidance of Ben Zakkai he
soon developed into a great scholar. He devoted
himself to the study of Greek and Latin, in both of
which he became proficient. He specially liked the
Greek language and he always carried a copy of
Homer with him.[47] He loved Greek songs and sang
them in the Academy, much to the annoyance of the
zealots.[48] He was wont to compare the literature
of his people with that of the Greeks. This soon
brought him to the consideration of other subjects.
He contrasted the artistic culture of Greece with the,
hard and dull life and works of his own people. He
compared the hopeless political position of Palestine
with the ever-growing power and splendor of Rome.
He lost sympathy with the Hebrew students who
crowded dingy schoolrooms to discuss petty points
of law. His heart longed for the glorious cities of
Greece; he desired to sit at the feet of the philosophers in its academies and to walk in the colonnades
of its museums.

Though the Rabbis of the Nationalist party could
condone, if they did not share, Elisha's enthusiasm
for Grecian language and culture, it exposed his life
to serious danger from the blind fury of the populace when the revolutionary plot of Akibah was developed. The organized "dagger men"—Siccarees
—of the party of action called for unhesitating

adhesion to the Jewish revolution from the learned and unlearned alike. Lukewarmness in that cause was avenged by assassination. The only safety for those who, like Elisha, saw the hopelessness of the attempt and were unwilling to prevaricate lay in flight from Palestine or in joining actively with the Roman authorities. He chose the latter and he was thenceforth branded as a traitor. It is said that he took part in persecuting the rebels afterwards, but the few particulars given of this charge may have been but an exaggeration of those whom he had quitted.

The mystic entrance into *Pardes* of the four Rabbis, Akibah, Ben Azzai, Ben Zoma, and Elisha, —the fate which ensued for each has already been mentioned—[49] may have a political meaning. It may refer to a council held to prepare the revolution projected by Akibah, and the failure of his colleagues to co-operate successfully with him. The death of Ben Azzai at the hands of the Siccarees was a not unlikely event if his fidelity were doubted. The "cutting of the plants of *Pardes*" by Elisha may be typical of his absolute withdrawal from the council of the Jewish revolution. Certain it is his name was branded as that of a traitor and apostate. The Talmud refuses even to call him by his own name. He is usually Acher (Another), the changeling, the renegade, not Elisha, the Rabbi and master in Israel. Under this name he was held up to execration by the Rabbis of the revolutionary party. His fate was sealed in their minds for eternity. The dictum of the zealots in his case was, "Repentance can win pardon for all but Acher." [50]

The same spirit prevailed after the fall of Bethar had crushed the life of the rebellion of Bar Kochba. The Rabbis accused Acher of aiding the Roman officials in the suppression of the Jewish religious practices and pointing out the stratagems employed for evading the penal laws. They charged him with openly breaking the ceremonial law, and with leading the young away from their religion and the study of the Sacred Writings.[51] He was said to break intentionally the law of the Sabbath, the worst offence a conscientious Jew could commit.[52]

While Acher was thus publicly hated, Rabbi Mair never ceased to maintain close intercourse with him. When reproached for his intimacy with an apostate, he justified himself by the intellectual worth of his friend and protested his own fidelity to Judaism.

"I eat the kernel and throw away the husk," was his pithy description of his intercourse with his former master.

Even the most hostile of Elisha's critics recognized the force of this remark, and in the Talmud the sayings of Elisha ben Abuiah are treasured as a valued part of the intellectual glories of Israel.

It is told of Mair that one day as he was delivering the Sabbath discourse in the school it was told him that Acher was riding by. Rabbi Mair abruptly ceased his sermon, went out to greet his friend, and accompanied him along the road to gather knowledge from his lips. The more zealous Rabbis condemned this act of Mair, but one said:

"A man like Acher is as a nut which hath fallen into filth, but yet may be eaten when its husk is separated from it. The sage may sin, yet the wisdom he hath gained is none the less divine." [63]

Acher appears to have definitely renounced the practice of Judaism, and his friend tried unsuccessfully to bring him back to the fold. He visited him on his death-bed, and Acher listened to his words with pleasure, but there is no sign of his having sought reconciliation. Later Rabbis said of him that, "he died in error and would not be punished, because he had learned the law, nor would he enter Paradise, because he had sinned." [64]

This has a curious resemblance to the subsequent teachings of Mohammed. It is more than probable that Elisha had embraced Christianity. Mair's temper would readily condone such a change in his friend, however it might be resented by the zealous nationalists of the Sanhedrin.

When Rabbi Mair left his native land after the death of his wife, the jealousy of his enemies, which had been kept in check while he occupied a seat in the Sanhedrin, broke out. His friendship for Elisha was made a charge against him, as if he, too, had become "Another." Simon ben Gamaliel, the President, did not forget the humiliations he had received from the wit of Rabbi Mair, and he avenged himself by refusing to allow him the title of Rabbi. When necessity forced him to quote any of Mair's former decisions he always suppressed his name, and prefaced them with the remark, "Others say." The allusion to "Acher," the hated "Other one," was palpable, and the object was to brand the illustrious exile with a charge which he dared not make in set terms.

Mair, with all his Grecian tastes and wit, was a thorough Hebrew in love for his land and people. When death came to him in Sardes, his dying injunction was:

"Bury me on the shore, that the sea which washes the land of my fathers may also touch my bones." [55]

With his death, as often happens, a revulsion came in the minds of the people towards the illustrious dead. The Rabbis who had assailed him while living bewailed his death as the fall of a "Mighty one in Israel."

"With Mair died the race of makers of parables" was their verdict on him.[56]

His words were recorded and handed down for the instruction of future generations. Even Acher's memory shared in the popular favor.

"When Rabbi Mair died the smoke that was rising from the grave of Acher passed away," is the quaint expression with which the Talmud records this fact.[57]

The sayings of Acher under his own name were embodied in Jewish literature in the work of *Chapters of the Fathers*.[58] His name, though not coupled with the title Rabbi, was reverenced as that of a sage who was one of the intellectual glories of his people. His honorable poverty, too, was remembered, and when in after years his daughter came to ask of Rabbi Juda the prince a pension for her support, as was wont for the children of Rabbis, he granted it in memory of his learning.[59] The words of Acher, the branded Jew of his time, have furnished themes for preachers of the Synagogue during the subsequent ages. When Rabbi Juda compiled the Mishnah, he gave place in its pages to the sayings of both Mair and Elisha, as two of the foremost lights of Israel.

It was a notable instance of the passing nature of the cause of Jewish independence which had clouded the lives of both. Intellectual work was recognized as too precious a part of the national inheritance to be thrown away, however hated in life the workers might have been. The truth of the axiom formulated by Rabbi Mair was recognized by all, and with it this chapter may fittingly close:

"He who studies the law for its own sake," he says, "merits much, and the world owes him much. He is called a dear friend: dear to God and dear to mankind. He rejoiceth God and His creatures. Study clotheth him with meekness and the fear of God; it showeth the way to justice, to piety, righteousness, and faith; it removeth from sin, and bringeth to high station. The world is benefited by his counsel, wisdom, understanding, and strength. . . . It bestoweth empire, dominion, and reason itself. The secrets of the law are revealed unto the student and make him as an overflowing fountain, a never-failing river. They make him modest, slow to anger, and ready to forgive. They exalt and magnify him above all beings." [40]

CHAPTER IX

RABBI SIMON BEN YOHAI

THROUGH the rebellion of Bar Kochba and the calamities which followed it for the Jewish people in Palestine, the House of Hillel seems to have passed unscathed. The presidency of the Sanhedrin had practically become hereditary in the family of the great Babylonian Rabbi. He had won the office by his abilities, the wealth he amassed and transmitted to his descendants; and his admitted descent from David secured it afterwards for many generations to members of his family. Though no political power was attached to it, the veneration of the people made the patriarchate a shadow of royalty in Palestine. Its possessors were careful not to risk it by joining in the revolution attempted by Akibah, and when that was crushed by the Romans, the wealth of Hillel's descendants escaped confiscation. It was the Rabbis of the school opposed to the Hillelites, the House of Shammai, who had been chiefly prominent in the rebellion, and the House of Hillel, though it still enjoyed the respect of the masses as its spiritual leaders, was not an object of suspicion to Rome.

Among the devoted adherents of Akibah who survived him the most noted were Mair and Simon ben Yohai. Both had visited Akibah during his imprisonment, and both after his death received the degree of Rabbi from Rabbi Juda ben Babba.[1] The latter was an enthusiastic partisan of Akibah in the national revolution, and after its failure he continued to teach in defiance of the edicts of Hadrian against Jewish instruction.[2] His rigid observance of the ceremonies of the law was such that when the hours prescribed for prayer came he would omit every other employment to give himself to them. The Talmud tells that once, while travelling on the road, he thus stopped to pray there. A chieftain came by on horseback and courteously saluted him, but the Rabbi, absorbed in his devotions, made no answer till he had finished his prayers. The angry chief said then:

"Your law bids you be careful of life, yet you have been careless of your own, for there was none to hinder had I cut off your head when you answered not my greeting."

"I ask thy pardon for that; but answer me,—if thou wert speaking to the king, and a friend addressed thee, wouldst thou turn from the king's face to answer it?"

"It would be as much as my head were worth," answered the chief.

"Then if such be the risk for showing disrespect to a mortal king, what would I have deserved had I shown irreverence to the King of kings, who is from eternity to eternity? I stood in supplication before Him when thou deignedst to salute me."

The chief accepted the admonition in good faith and the two parted.[3]

Ben Babba continued to instruct disciples in the law, despite the persecution, and one day his school was surprised by a party of Roman soldiers. He saw them coming and at once pronounced the form of words over Mair and Ben Yohai which made them legitimate Rabbis. He then gave them his blessing and bade them flee.

"But what will become of thee, Master?" they asked.

"I stay like a rock," he answered.

The disciples fled, but Ben Babba was pierced by the Roman lances and died there.[4]

Ben Yohai, though an ardent disciple of Akibah and a devoted patriot, was the son of a Jew who had entered the Roman service, and held high position as an official. He seems to have neglected even the religious rites of his people, for in after years, when Ben Yohai was a Rabbi and a religious master in Israel, he had to rebuke his widowed mother for idle speech on the Sabbath Day.[5] Whatever his father's wishes, Simon early devoted himself to the study of the Jewish law. He won a name as an expounder in the rabbinical schools which attracted the attention of Akibah during his career of revolutionary propaganda. The son of the Roman official became the friend and disciple of the revolutionist, and was thirteen years in his company and under his instructions.[6] Akibah said to him in admiration on one occasion:

"As I live, it is only thy Maker and I that can understand thy ability."[7]

Such testimony speaks much for the abilities of Ben Yohai. Akibah, on the other hand, was adored by his disciple with his whole soul. He lost not a word that fell from his lips. He copied even the manners and gestures of the master, and, in after years, he boasted that his own manners were modelled on Akibah's.[8] Still he was not a slavish adherent. He did not fear to reject a decision of the master's when he believed it incorrect, or to give his own explanation as sometimes better than Akibah's.[9]

Simon ben Yohai, like Akibah, was a married man when he took up a life of study. The latter had his abode and school in the town of Benai Berack, far from Simon's residence, and Simon left his wife and children to dwell apart during the years that he gave himself to study. His wife at last urged him to return, as their daughter was of an age to marry and needed her father's care. Ben Yohai did not heed the call. Akibah heard of it, and, when his disciples were gathered together, he ordered Simon to depart.

"Let him who hath a daughter of age to marry return to his home till she be married," was his command, which Ben Yohai had to obey.

He returned to his house unannounced, and the surprise made his wife swoon. The tardy husband thought her dead, and exclaimed:

"Lord, is this the reward she receives who hath awaited me thirteen years?"

His wife fortunately recovered, and, then Ben Yohai laid down the sage rule:

"Enter not suddenly thine own house, much less that of another."[10]

It was not in Akibah's school alone that he grounded himself in knowledge. A curious anecdote of him in the Talmud illustrates this fact, and also gives an idea of the subjects of study and the methods of studying, of Hebrew scholars in the olden time. Rabbi Simon was explaining to his disciples the manner of observing the Feast of Tabernacles. The Law of Moses required all free men of Jewish race to reside in booths of branches during the days of that festival. The Rabbi laid down the law on the subject as he had heard it from Gamaliel II., the descendant of Hillel. He told how he had, when young, called on the president at Yamnai, and been asked to eat with him in his booth. Ben Yohai, with other guests, came with Gamaliel, and, when they entered the booth, they saw a slave, Tobi, asleep under the table.

"See," said Gamaliel, "what a scholar this slave is; he knows that he is not liable to the obligation of the festival."

From this Simon learned that only freemen, not slaves, were required to observe the precept of dwelling in booths for eight days, and also that to fulfil it it was necessary there should be no ceiling of boards like the table under which Tobi was sleeping in peace." The technicalities of the law, as elaborated by generations of Rabbis, must have rivalled the intricacies of an English Chancery suit. Another characteristic anecdote of the spirit of the students in the schools tells how Rabbi Juda bar Illai said contemptuously of Ben Yohai:

"He is like a grinder who throws out only a little

bran," meaning that his original remarks were of little value."[12]

Simon hotly asked his meaning, and was parried with the adroit explanation:

"I but meant that thou grindest much learning, and forgettest but little, and that of no worth, like bran." [13]

Ben Yohai was appeased, but the feud between the masters broke out later in another place.

After his ordination as Rabbi, Ben Yohai, despite the Roman persecution, established a school in Thekoa, a town in Galilee; either through his father's protection or the remoteness of the place, he was not molested.

The ardor of the Jewish students for the prescribed studies and the still glowing national spirit brought disciples around the favorite of Akibah. Ben Yohai gloried in preserving all that Rabbi's teachings, and he looked with contempt both on the scholarship and the political course of the Rabbis who adhered to the House of Hillel. When the decrees against Jewish schools were relaxed by the Emperor Antoninus in 138, Ben Yohai came among the teachers who gathered around the president in Yamnai. He was received with honor, his legal lore was admired, and in private his adhesion to Akibah won him many partisans among the stricter nationalists. With all his admiration for the revolutionary Rabbi, Ben Yohai had not committed himself to any act of open rebellion. His father was high in favor with the Roman authorities, and Ben Yohai conceived the audacious project of securing for himself the presidency of the Sanhedrin. Gamaliel, the holder of that office, died in 140, and an election was held to give him a successor. The patriarchate by common consent had been hereditary in the House of Hillel for a hundred and thirty years. Hillel was a descendant of David, and while a son of David held the highest office in the nation, though with no political power, the Jewish populace recognized a kind of continuation of his kingdom and felt that the sceptre had not altogether passed from Juda.

Ben Yohai scoffed at this sentiment. He derided the little learning and yielding character of Gamaliel the Patriarch, and when his son Simon claimed the vacant seat, Ben Yohai demanded it for himself, as being the most learned Rabbi in Israel. The members of the council were not ready to accept his claims; indeed, it could hardly be expected that the Roman authorities would tolerate a friend of Akibah in the chair of the Sanhedrin. Simon was elected president,[14] and Ben Yohai left Yamnai in anger and disappointment and went back to Thekoa.

He was called some time later to another meeting of the Sanhedrin in Yamnai to settle some important questions which had arisen.[15] Ben Yohai came, but anger over his defeat still burned in him. He bitterly criticised the learning and what he considered the political cowardice of his fellow-Rabbis, and he forgot, in his heat, that the Jewish religion only was permitted by the favor of the all-powerful Roman Empire. During the synod one of the Rabbis, Juda Ben Illai, spoke in terms of praise of the material civilization of Rome and Greece. The bitter feelings of Ben Yohai were not to be suppressed by considerations of danger. He denounced the works of the masters of Palestine with harsh contempt.

"The Romans," he said, "have done all their works for self, and self-indulgence alone. They have laid out streets and built fair buildings and baths and bridges, but their buildings are brothels, their baths abodes of sin, their bridges only tax offices to wring tribute from the poor. They have done nothing for either the glory of God or the help of man."

There were friends of Rome and enemies of Ben Yohai even among the Rabbis in their religious gathering. Juda ben Gorion bore to the prætorium the seditious discourse of the angry Ben Yohai, as well as the speeches of the other Rabbis. An edict went forth from the Roman governor:

"Let Juda, who spoke well of Rome, be promoted; let Josai, who was silent, be exiled; let Simon ben Yohai, who slandered Rome, be executed." [16]

He did not await martyrdom, however. With his son Eleazar, also a famous scholar, he fled to the mountains. There they remained hidden for many years. As he went he vented the bitterness which filled his heart at the forgetfulness of religion among the teachers of Israel and their readiness to worship the ways of the heathen. Ben Illai, the panegyrist of the Roman tyranny, and Ben Gorion, the treacherous spy, were equally hateful to him.

"Once I used to think," he said, "that had I been

with Moses at Sinai, I would have asked the Lord to give man two mouths: one to speak his own praises alone, the other to speak the affairs of men. Now I see my folly. For if man with only one mouth can nearly destroy the world by his false speaking, what further evil might not come had he two tongues!" [17]

Legend has woven a story of marvels around Ben Yohai in his cave. It is not easy to distinguish always the facts, be they real or supposed, which the Talmud tells of, from the figurative imagery with which it clothes their narration. It seems best to give them as told, for thus they throw light on the frame of mind prevalent among the Jewish people during the last days of their sojourn in the Promised Land as vassals to Rome. We are told that Simon and his son passed thirteen years in their cave, living on the fruit of a locust and the water of a spring within their resting-place. They sat and slept in the sand which covered its floor, and Simon's body became covered with sores [18]; but he heeded them not. He was absorbed in reflection on the law of Israel, and he discussed it daily with his son; gradually his mind was drawn away from the passing things of human life to the invisible things of eternity and the inner nature of man. He looked on his former existence, with the strifes, fears, sorrows, and deaths which had filled it, as only a dream of the night. The objects pursued by the majority of men, their loves and their hatreds, the greed of wealth and honors, even ordinary occupations of life, became sinful in his eyes. The one thing worthy of man's care was the study of the law. To that he gave himself up wholly. He went over in mind the lore he had gathered from his former teachers, he pondered and digested all in his cave, even while the Rabbis of Yamnai were bewailing that study had died out, and that the law of Israel seemed in danger of perishing for want of knowledge.[19]

Thirteen years had thus passed when word was brought to Rabbi Simon that his life was no longer threatened and that he was free to return to the abodes of men.[20] He and Eleazar came forth, but everything that met them was in such contrast to the bareness of their mountain abode that it pained, rather than gladdened, their hearts. The very birds and plants displeased their saddened souls. Ben Yohai recalled the ruin of the Holy City, the tortures and deaths that had fallen on its greatest sons, the misery that hung like a cloud over the people of Israel, the treachery of his own colleagues, and he found no cause for joy in life. He rebuked the joy his son showed at revisiting the society of man. Man has no right to rejoice in such a world as this, was his dreary verdict.[21]

He doubted, after all, whether it were good to exchange the calm of his hermitage for the affliction of seeing the law disregarded among men, and fear of Rome more powerful than Jewish national feeling. As he revolved these things in his mind he caught sight of an archer who aimed at a bird. The arrow missed its mark, and the bird flew away unharmed. Ben Yohai felt his fatalistic faith revived by the sight.

"If even a little bird cannot be slain without the

consent of God," he said, "much less need man fear danger from the malevolence of men." And so he went on his way."

Mystic power had come on him during the days of his solitary sufferings and study. Nature seemed to bend to his wishes, even passing ones. As he walked through the cultivated fields he saw men and women at work. His reflections on the vanity of passing things revived, and he said bitterly to his son:

"See these men barter eternal life for the idle things of a day. They plough and reap instead of studying the law, but their end will be death."

Hardly were the words uttered when the husbandmen fell down and died. The voice of an angel rebuked the intemperate zeal of the Rabbi.

"Return to your cave," it ordered. "Did you only leave it to destroy men?"

The wayfarers obeyed; they went back and dwelt in their wild cave a year more. Then they came forth and returned to it no more."

Though rebuked by the angel, Simon had not wholly removed from his heart the bitter zeal he cherished for the law. As he travelled, he came to a field where men were culling the after-crop. Now it was the Year of Release, when it is not lawful for an Israelite to cut the after-growth of his field, which is the inheritance of the poor and needy. Simon, however, when a Rabbi of renown, had pronounced that this precept was not binding. His decision had been overruled by the majority in the Sanhedrin, and therefore was valueless in religious law, but it was still quoted with approval by greedy agriculturists. Simon rebuked them.

"How dare you act thus?" he asked.

"Art thou not then he who taught us?" was their rejoinder.

"Even so," he answered, "others and the greater number rejected my teaching, and in Israel it is the ruling of the majority that makes the law. Know, then, that it is written of those who break the law that serpents shall sting them."

Then a multitude of serpents came and bit the law-breakers.[24] He went on and, as he approached Tiberias, he met Juda ben Gorion, the same who had denounced him to the Roman governor. Rabbi Simon looked on his enemy and said:

"Doth this man yet live?" and the traitor was suddenly turned to stone.[25]

A milder instance of this power was given in the case of some of his old pupils near the same town. They greeted him and told of the wealth they had acquired, and Simon said:

"Be such things worth prizing? Lo! I need but call and all this valley shall be covered with gold." So it was on the moment. Then Simon said:

"Take all you please, but I say to you that whoever takes even one shall forfeit his place in Paradise.[26]

Somewhat similar in its contempt of earthly things was his answer to the greetings of his son-in-law, Phineas, himself also a mystic and wonder-worker of fame. When Simon met him, Phineas was struck by the wretched appearance of the once famous master, covered with rags and afflicted with grievous ulcers.

"Woe is me to see my master thus!" he exclaimed.

"Nay, my son," said Simon, mildly; "rather say, 'Joy that I see thee thus'; for of a truth, were I otherwise you would find nothing worthy of honor in me." [27]

Phineas dwelt in Tiberias, and Simon remained there instead of going to Yamnai, the seat of the Sanhedrin. The air of Tiberias was mild; the town abounded in hot springs, and its surroundings were beautiful, but it was under a ban of superstition as a residence with the stricter Jews. It had been rebuilt in Roman style by Herod, on the ruins of an ancient city, and the Jewish Quarter was located on the site of a cemetery. For this reason the law made it unclean as a residence for priests, and the students likewise shunned it. Simon ben Yohai declared that tradition promised it would yet be made clean,[28] and he realized the prediction by having the old graves sought out and the bones removed to another place. Then he formally pronounced the city "clean," and opened his school there. His fame was widespread already, and crowds came to study at his feet. Tiberias became a centre of Jewish learning, which later overshadowed Yamnai and every other seat of instruction in Palestine.

The fame of Ben Yohai as a worker of wonders grew rapidly with the renewal of his active teaching. The Talmud, by a bold flight, represents him as even making the will of the Roman emperor bend to his mystic powers. It tells how Marcus Aurelius designed to renew the edicts of Hadrian against the Jewish rites, and that, in their despair, the people besought Rabbi Simon to go in person to Rome and plead for mercy. Simon consented on condition that the son of his old colleague, Ben Josai, the same who had held his peace when Ben Yohai denounced Roman ways in the Sanhedrin, should go with him. Josai feared some evil, but yielded at the prayers of the people. Simon and the son of Josai set out on their embassy.

He did not count on entreaties for the success of his mission. The Talmud tells how on his way he met a demon, Tamalion, and him he commanded to take possession of the daughter of the emperor. When the envoys reached the capital they found all its people in sorrow for the fate that had fallen on the imperial House. The daughter of Aurelius had suddenly become a maniac. Physicians were unable to alleviate the mysterious malady. The emperor was inconsolable at the affliction in his family. Simon applied for an audience with the emperor in the name of his people. It was near being haughtily refused, but Aurelius suddenly remembered the reputation for strange powers enjoyed by his Eastern subjects.

"The Hebrews have skill in medicine and in magic," he said, "perhaps this man may cure my daughter. Let him be admitted."

"Peace to thee, O lord," said Simon when he entered the council-chamber.

"There is no peace where sorrow dwells," was the cæsar's answer.

"What can thy heart desire in vain, mighty Emperor?" asked Ben Yohai.

"My daughter's restoration to health," was the reply.

"If thy daughter's illness be the only cloud on the august face of cæsar, let him be cheerful now," said the Rabbi, "for, by the living God of Israel, I will restore her to health."

"If thou canst," exclaimed the emperor, "thou mayest name what price thou willest and it shall be thine, though it be all the treasure of Rome. But beware of mocking my grief! If thou failest, not only thy life, but the lives of a thousand of thy Hebrew countrymen, shall pay the forfeit."

"Show me the maiden and thou shalt see the power of the Lord God of Israel," was Ben Yohai's answer.

The emperor brought him to his daughter's room. She was a raving maniac, and spurned her father's caresses and entreaties with insane fury. Simon approached and fixed his eyes on hers. Gradually the fury died out of her face, her eyes grew calm, and were fixed with an entreating look on Simon's face. He then commanded the evil spirit to leave her, and Tamalion obeyed. The princess threw herself into her father's arms, cured completely. Aurelius kept his word. The Jewish envoys were sent to the imperial treasury and bidden to take whatever they desired. They passed through and saw with sadness the plundered treasures of Jerusalem, carried away years before by Pompey and Titus. They shed tears over the sacred vessels, but they touched them not. Simon asked to see the record of edicts. He took therefrom the decree of persecution already prepared against the Jewish people. This he laid before the emperor as his reward. Aurelius cheerfully granted his desire and withdrew the edict.[29]

After Ben Yohai's settlement in Tiberias a gradual change came over his mind. The bitterness of his zeal gave way to mildness. His sayings are thoroughly racy of the soil of Palestine, but they are stamped with a liberality very unlike the spirit which doomed to death the offenders against the usage of the Year of Release. A few examples will illustrate this:

"He does not sin who bows before an idol through force."[30]

"Religion can never be a cloak for evil deeds. Unjustly gotten goods are not sanctified if offered for sacred uses."[31]

"The glory of the Lord accompanies the righteous to every land" is significant of the change which had come over Ben Yohai from the time he identified Palestine with the full observance of religion.[32]

Simon's attachment to the Jewish law was deep and lasting. In the troubled times in which his life was cast, many of the Rabbis feared to maintain the traditions of constant study and discussion of its precepts which had been so large a part of national life at an earlier period. They feared to draw down fresh persecutions from the jealousy of the Roman rulers if they drew crowds of disciples around their schools. They admitted the need of educating the youth of the nation in the law, but they feared the risk. They excused their timidity by the plea that God would Himself provide for the preservation of His law, and that efforts were not needed on their part for such a result. They sought, by casuistry, to minimize the duties prescribed for faithful Hebrews by their own law, and they held that the laws of the dominant heathen power had no moral force over Jewish conscience. They looked with indulgence on crimes of violence or fraud against the heathen, and bred hypocrisy among the people by teaching that outward obedience was all that was desirable from Jews to the foreign rulers. Simon held a braver course.

"Respect authority and be quick to obey," he said, which is almost the same as the precept, "Fear God and honor the king."

"Be gentle with the young and friendly to all men," was the complement of his precept.[33]

Yet he urged the strict observance of those regulations which rested on the Jewish law itself as ardently.

"One should not speak of worldly affairs on the Sabbath,"[34] and, "If all the people would but keep two Sabbaths properly their salvation would be at hand,"[35] are maxims in the thorough spirit of Judaism. He illustrated his meaning by a curious parable:

"The Fifth Book of Moses (*i. e.*, the written law)," he said, "appeared before the throne of mercy. It pleaded its cause: 'King Solomon hath destroyed my power over the people by his contempt of me. The law forbids many wives to a man, yet King Solomon hath taken exceeding many. It says the King shall not keep many horses, yet he keeps horses in exceeding number. It forbids to lay up much store of silver or of gold, yet Solomon is insatiable for gold and silver. Even as a man's testament loses force when part of it is made void, so am I made void among the people since the King has broken part of my precepts.'"

But the Lord comforted the Book and said:

"Solomon and hundreds like Solomon shall pass away, but not a jot of thee shall pass or be forgotten." [36]

Simon urged from this the constant study of the imperishable law of God as the highest duty.

"He who, as he walks, stops his contemplation of the law to speak of the beauty of flower or field, sins," [37] is his maxim on this head.

Human diligence must co-operate with God's will.

"To live up to the law," he adds, "is better than to know the law." [38]

On another point his dislike of usury, which was forbidden to Jews among themselves, was expressed in the command:

"A borrower shall not be the first to salute when he meets him who hath lent to him, nor shall he so salute through other men's agency." [39]

The precepts of general morality laid down in his sayings are marked with a stamp of mildness very unlike the character of his early bitter zeal. Experience had evidently softened the harshness of his temper, and the Christ-like tone of his later utterances is remarkable.

"Life is earnest, and it is sin to be frivolous in a world of sorrow." [40]

"Love is a jewel in Heaven's treasury which every man can win if he seek it truthfully." [41]

"It is a higher duty to honor parents than to make offerings to the Lord. If a man be poor he sins not when he offers nothing, but, rich or poor, he must pay the debt of honor to his parents." [42]

"Speak ill of no man, however evil be the times; even though children do not honor father or mother," [43] shows how strongly Simon regarded the obligations of children to parents. He classes its neglect as the worst form of social demoralization.

"It is worse to rob a man of his good name than of his money," is another injunction against slander. [44]

"Rather throw thyself into a furnace than bring thy fellow-man to shame." [45]

"If thou hast wronged another, confess thy wrong aloud, but if thou hast helped him, let thy kindness be hidden" is very like the precept, "Let not thy right hand know what thy left hand doeth." [46]

"Confession of sin should be whispered, lest others hear and afterward bring the penitent to shame." [47]

"It is unworthy of man to make earthly things his aim, even though they be the necessaries of life." [48]

"The proud man is an idolater. He worships what is of no worth [himself]." [49]

"A sinful soul lives in fear; for conscience is its constant accuser. A pure soul needs not fear, for piety is its guardian." [50]

"A stainless name is better than a priestly crown," [61] and,

"Great is work, it honoreth a man," [62] are two more of his precepts. The latter he carried out in his own practice by daily carrying his own satchel to his school, notwithstanding his dignified position. It was given in answer to the criticism of this habit by some of his pupils.

"It is the punishment of liars to be disbelieved even when they speak truth," [63] is a pithy adage which may refer to the men who had offered Bar Kochba to Israel as the Messiah. In the movement for independence lying promises had beguiled the people, and the just causes of complaint had been forgotten in the falsehoods which were coined to accompany them. Akibah and his fellows had seen visions and dreamed dreams, and they had given them to the people as revelations.

"Dreams are but echoes of idle words,—grains of fact on the straw of fancy," was Ben Yohai's pithy remark. [64]

An example of a moral precept as illustrated by a tale is interesting as a specimen of the literary forms of Eastern people:

"A ship was crowded with passengers, each in his place. One sat apart and was sullen and silent. Suddenly he took an auger and began to bore through the vessel's side. The other passengers saw his work and asked what he meant.

"'It is not your business,' said the man; 'you have your places and I have mine. I have paid for it. Can I not do as I like with my own?'

" 'Not so,' the passengers cried, 'for thy deed will destroy us all with thee. The waters will come on us as well as on thee.'

"Thus," said Rabbi Simon, "if one man in a city sins and is not restrained, the other people of that city must share in the punishment of his sin." [55]

These quotations give an idea of the form taken by the mental activity of the Jewish race. Widely as it differs from Western forms of expression, Oriental wisdom is not the less genuine. Among the Hebrews the proverbs which are the delight of all Eastern people take on a certain authoritative tone from the intimate connection between the scholars, or wise men, and the expounders of the divine law. It is this rather than any other cause which has made literature so great a power among the Jewish race in all ages, as it continues to be to-day.

An anecdote of Simon's career as a judge shows that his practice was in keeping with his preaching.

When holding court in Sidon, a man applied to him for a divorce. The wife had reluctantly consented to the proceeding. She loved her husband, but as they had lived together for ten years without children born the law granted him a right of divorce. The facts in the case were easily proven. The man had other wives, and children by them. Simon disliked to separate them, and talked earnestly with the man to change his mind, but to no purpose.

"As you will," said the Rabbi, "but since you have lived together for ten years I advise you to let a feast precede your divorce; be joyful once more as on your wedding day, and then, if you will, part in peace."

The Rabbi's suggestion found favor with the man. He invited his friends and gave them a feast. Old wine was freely drunk by host and guests. They drank the health of the woman who was about to go from the house, never to return, and as the husband lifted his cup, while bending his face to his wife's, a sudden feeling of regret filled his heart. They had been happy together, and but for his desire to have children, he had no cause to send her away. But as divorce her he must, she should at least not leave his house like a beggar; she should have anything her heart desired, though it were half his fortune.

"Choose the dearest object in my house and it shall be thine," he cried.

She bade him drink more wine.

Soon the strong wine had its effect and he became unconscious. Thereupon the woman took him on her back and carried him to her father's house.

After drunkenness had left him and the husband realized where he was, his wife said to him:

"Behold, I did as thou didst command. I took from thy house the one object I hold dearest on earth,—thee, my husband."

Obviously the Rabbi's ingenuity had been at work to the happiness of both husband and wife.[55]

The change which had come over Ben Yohai's mind since the days when he left his cave to smite transgressors of the smallest points of the law with death is very striking. By a strange contrast Eleazar, his son, whose joy at leaving their mountain retreat had earned the stern rebuke of Ben Yohai, seemed to grow more bitter in his zeal as the years passed over him. He scorned the Sanhedrin which had refused to choose his father to preside over it. He especially despised Simon, the actual president, and Juda, his son. In youth Juda and Eleazar had been fellow-students, and the superior abilities of the latter had been acknowledged. He had humbled the son of the House of Hillel before his fellows, and in after years he scorned to do him honor even though head of the Sanhedrin. While Ben Yohai lived, he restrained the harshness of his son's character, but when he was gathered to his fathers Eleazar gave full sway to his antipathy to the men in authority among the Jews. He professed a fanatical zeal for the law, but he coupled it with a hatred for his people which he veiled under the name of hatred of sin.

The public law of Palestine was the Roman, and Roman officials chastised law-breakers without mercy. The majority of the Jewish Rabbis, while insisting on the observance of the law of Moses under penalty of grievous sin, made light of offences against the laws of the heathen. The Sabbath-breaker was accursed, but the robber or assassin, if his victims were not of the House of Israel, found indulgence from the Rabbis.

"A Jew is a Jew, they said, and before the Lord, who is the Father of Israel, the wrongs he may do in his dealing with the heathen will not be laid up against him." Eleazar, whose family had been long associated with the Roman officials, sternly rejected this laxity of moral teaching. Israel to him was as a chosen vineyard from which it was a sacred duty to root out sinners as the husbandman roots out weeds. Sinners to him were sinners, whether it was the law of Moses or that of Rome which they offended.[57]

He did not confine his zeal on this point to theory. Following the example of his grandfather, he joined himself to the Roman rulers of the land, and was made a captain of their soldiers. His size and strength were enormous, and his earnestness in carrying out the Roman laws in the fullest vigor was unbounded. Since the rebellion of Bar Kochba the land was full of Jewish outlaws, who supported themselves by plundering travellers, and regarded themselves in a sense as patriots in their resistance to the hated foreign law. Eleazar hunted down this band without mercy. His knowledge of the country and the ways of the Jewish people made him a singularly efficient agent for the Roman government. No man could deceive his vigilance by smooth speech, such as satisfied the Roman officials. His instructions to his men were emphatic:

"Visit the houses before noon. If you find men sleeping, then ask if they be scholars or laborers. If they be, let them alone, for work brings sleep. If they cannot show they are such, arrest them at once, for surely they are robbers."[58]

The vigilance of Eleazar cleared the country of malefactors, but it excited keen resentment in the minds of the more patriotic Jews. The son of Akibah, Josua, sent a message to Eleazar in stinging language.

"Vinegar, son of wine, how long wilt thou continue to deliver God's people to death?"[59]

"I only destroy the weeds in the vineyard," was the short reply, to which Rabbi Josua rejoined:

"Leave the owner of the vineyard [God] to destroy the weeds." [60]

The nickname given by Josua soon became common among the people. One day a countryman applied it to him in public. Eleazar was angry and bade his men seize the insulter.

"His impudence shows him a robber," he said, and the man was taken to prison.

After a while his anger cooled, and he went to the prison to release the offender. He learned he had been just executed as a robber. Remorse seized him and he wept. The jailer, who was a Hebrew, to console him, told him that the man executed had been guilty of an atrocious crime against a Jewish maiden, which merited death by the law of Moses, so that his punishment on another charge was substantial justice.

"Rejoice, my soul," said Eleazar, "for, after all, I was in the right." [61]

The occurrence, however, made a deep impression on his mind. He resigned his position among the Roman soldiers, and sought reconciliation with his countrymen. A curious statement in the Talmud may either symbolize his change of heart or tell of an actual surgical operation. It says that he was so fat that he had his stomach opened by surgeons and many layers of tissue removed.[62] He gave himself up afterwards to prayer and penances. Gradually the people recognized him again as a Rabbi and teacher, and his fame grew in the land. He continued his hostility, however, to the president of the Sanhedrin.

"The Messiah will not come," he said, "till all judges and officials have disappeared from the congregation of Israel." [63]

This was in accord with the utterances of Ben Yohai against Simon, the president of his day.

"The man who lacks knowledge of the law had better not discuss the law," [64] and,

"It is as much a duty not to discuss what one does not understand as to discuss what one understands." [65]

Rabbi Juda, the son of Simon and his successor as president, could not pardon the attacks of Eleazar. He branded him as "The evil-doer who destroyed many of the seed of Israel." [66] Phineas ben Yares, the son-in-law of Ben Yohai, also refused to have anything to do with Eleazar, and his life was embittered by frequent criticisms.

A tale in the Talmud may illustrate his position and the feelings of the people towards him.

Once, it runs, Rabbi Eleazar was riding from Migdol Goser, and, as he came to a river, he dropped the rein to let his mule eat grass. Pride and gladness filled his heart as he thought of how much learning was his. As he pondered on the decision of his masters, a misshapen man passed that way and saluted him, but Eleazar paid no heed to the salute. The man made a sharp comment on his rudeness, and Eleazar was angry.

"Are all the people in thy town as ugly as thou?" he asked.

"I know not," the man replied, "but if my body does not please thee, thou art at liberty to ask my Maker why He hath made me an ugly vessel."

The answer made Eleazar conscious of the ill grace of his words. He sprang from the mule and humbly begged the man's pardon.

"I will not pardon thee," said the man, "until thou hast made complaint to my Maker of the ugliness of His handiwork."

He walked on, followed by Eleazar, who again begged to be forgiven; for, according to the law, he had to receive the man's forgiveness ere he could hope to be forgiven by God.[67] But the man was obdurate, and there was nothing left for Eleazar but to keep up his plea until they reached the city, and there ask the man's pardon publicly: should the latter persist in his refusal, the conscience of the Rabbi would be clear, as the humility would offset the offence. The town was Eleazar's rabbinical seat, and the people, having expected him, had gathered in numbers to salute him

"Hail, our Rabbi and our Master!" they cried.

"Whom call ye Rabbi and Master?" the ugly man asked.

"He who follows thee," the people replied.

"If he is a Rabbi," said the man, "then may there be none like him in Israel!"

They asked him why, and he told what had taken place on the road.

"Yet we beg of thee to forgive him," the elders pleaded, "for he is a great man and learned in the law."

"For your sake, then, will I forgive him, but on condition that he never do such a thing again," said the man.

When Rabbi Eleazar heard these words a great joy filled his heart, and forthwith he preached a sermon in the public square, the burden of which was mercy and forgiveness. "Let man ever be yielding as a reed and not hard and unbending as the cedar," he cried.[68]

This anecdote illustrates the mingled respect and dislike with which the son of Ben Yohai was regarded. His father had died in 165, and the people bore his body to the cave where he and Eleazar had dwelt so long. It became a pilgrimage for the religious among the people, for Ben Yohai's fame was great as a worker of miracles. It has lasted. A correspondent of the *Alliance Israélite Universelle* in 1888 says:

"During the month of April, Jewish pilgrims leave this city [Damascus] for the purpose of celebrating the thirty-third day of Omer at Mitan, where they visit the tomb of Rabbi Simon ben Yohai. It is a touching sight to behold invalids of every description undertaking the long journey, full of hope and firm in the faith that the proximity of the sacred tomb will cure them of all their infirmities."

Eleazar felt keenly his position, and his health declined through grief. He found his end approaching and he knew that his body would not be allowed to rest with his father's. He called his faithful wife and told her his wishes.

"I have been a proud man all my days and have

done what was right in my eyes without fear. I have never failed to correct my course when I thought I had erred, but the men around me will not forgive me. Meanly they have acted during my life, and meanly they will do when I am no more. I know they will not accord my body the respect due to my learning and the honor due to the son of Ben Yohai. I charge thee, dear and faithful wife, to make no announcement of my death, nor to bury my body, but, wrapping it in the shroud, thou shalt put it on the floor of the attic. Fear neither decomposition nor other ill; for neither will come so long as the secret is kept and my body remains undisturbed."

Tearfully the Rabbi's wife promised to fulfil his request, and while the ashes of Ben Yohai were resting in the cave of Meran that had sheltered him and his son for so many years, the body of Eleazar lay in the garret, unknown and unmourned by any but his faithful wife, whose love had outlasted death.

After many years,[69] however, the secret became known to the Rabbis. It is said that Ben Yohai appeared in a dream to the Rabbis and said to them:

"I have a little dove in your midst and you refuse to bring it to me."

The Rabbis investigated: they found the body and carried it with ceremony to the cave of Meran, "to let a worthy son rest by the side of a worthy father," as the Talmud has it.[70]

After Rabbi Eleazar's burial, Rabbi Juda the Prince sent a messenger to the widow asking her hand in marriage. She answered that she would count such an alliance a personal degradation."[71]

The prince persevered; he sent another message: "Thy husband may have been more learned than I, but he was not more charitable; he did not excel me in works of practical righteousness," was his plea.

"Whether he was more learned than thou," she replied, "I know not; I am a woman and unable to judge; but for practical righteousness thou couldst never hope to be counted his equal; for he underwent bodily pain to serve humanity, while thou but givest of thine abundance."⁷²

Thus the enmity between the son of Ben Yohai and the son of the House of Hillel continued even after the former's death. The rivalry between Juda and Eleazar dated from boyhood.

Once, when both were students, Eleazar had publicly affronted the son of the president of the Sanhedrin. He told him contemptuously that he did not comprehend the subject which he was discussing before the school.⁷³ Juda on his return home complained to his father, the president. The latter answered:

"Take not this to heart, my son; Eleazar is very learned, but remember he is a lion and the son of a lion, while thou art a lion, but the son of a fox."⁷⁴

This remark expresses the policy of the House of Hillel. It was not force, but diplomacy, that had maintained it in power and wealth so long. It was diplomatic skill, the cunning of the fox, that had carried its fortunes through the storms of Roman conquest and of Shammaitic intrigue in the Sanhedrin itself. That skill had made the Davidic descent, which could not be taken away, to be regarded as the first qualification for the presidency. Ben Yohai might be more learned than Simon, but he could not claim descent from David. Simon may well have felt that in the condition of Israel the skill of the fox was more desirable than the roar of the lion, and he impressed the lesson on his son.

Did the prince follow his father's advice? Did he employ the cunning of the fox in his dealings with Jew and heathen? Did he hold tenaciously the dignity bequeathed to him by his father? Did he make the House of Hillel great? The life of the prince shall answer these questions. The work he executed stands to-day as a marvel, and will last as long as the Jewish race.

CHAPTER X

RABBI JUDA THE PRINCE

THE title of Prince, associated with the name of Rabbi Juda alone, in Jewish history, is not an empty form. It is true that it was officially borne by every president of the Sanhedrin, but in Juda alone it carried a certain half-royal character that belonged neither to his predecessors nor his successors. His succession to the office at the age of twenty-five was due not to his talent as a teacher or judge, but mainly to the hereditary principle which had been gradually introduced among the people by Hillel and his family. Among the learned doctors who constituted the national assembly, the young president was accepted as chief, as a prince is allowed to occupy his father's throne. His bearing, his character, and his weaknesses were those of a prince rather than of a scholar or judge, such as other masters in Israel. His life-work, too, was in keeping with his character. It has been felt in the life of the Jewish race through centuries and its result made the title a part of his name. As the great Frankish emperor remains the great Charles (Charlemagne) through history, so is Rabbi Juda "the prince" in Hebrew annals.

A few words of explanation are needed to make clear the actual office of Juda. Under the last Jewish kings of Palestine, the Sanhedrin, an assembly of learned doctors of the law, selected for their learning by choice of its own members, was practically both the Supreme Court and the Legislature of the Jewish nation. The Law of Moses was supreme for all Jews, king and peasant alike. It might not be added to or diminished by human authority. It had, however, to be interpreted and applied in the changing circumstances of ages, and the right of such interpretations and special application was vested in the Sanhedrin alone. The majority of that body pronounced what the law was, and from that law there was no appeal. A king might obey the law or defy it, but the Jewish people could not conceive him as making it. The priests and Levites, even the High Priest, were equally destitute of such power. The ceremonial prescribed by the law was their care,—not its teaching. The learned men from whom the members of the Sanhedrin were chosen were Rabbis, or teachers. Jews of any class might enter their ranks by study and attending the lectures of the Rabbis in which the decisions of the past on everything connected with the law were taught orally. Writing was reserved mainly for the Scriptures themselves; the comments on them were preserved by constant memorizing and repetition, as the Celtic Druids transmitted their lore in other lands.[1]

When Palestine fell under the Roman sway, the new masters left the Sanhedrin intact. The law of

Rome was supreme, as in other parts of the empire, and Roman citizens obeyed no other, but in the internal affairs of the Jewish people, the Sanhedrin was left to direct as under the Hebrew kings. Its external powers were not enforced by Rome, but the Roman authorities were willing to leave their Jewish subjects to their own customs and rites. Hillel had become president of the Sanhedrin in the days of Herod. He was of the stock of David, and when the sceptre of political power was taken from Judah, the presidency became all the more important in the minds of patriotic Hebrews. Hillel had won it by his intellectual abilities and learning. He transmitted it to his family, who retained it rather by diplomatic skill than legal learning. Their Davidic descent was magnified as a qualification for the leadership in Israel apart from personal talents, and the wealth which Hillel had transmitted to his family aided materially in the election of successive presidents. Gamaliel II. decreed that adherence to the House of Hillel should be a necessary qualification for admission to the Sanhedrin.[1] His son Simon surrounded his office with new forms and ceremonies well calculated to impress the popular mind. When, on the death of Gamaliel, Ben Yohai, the most famous Rabbi of his day, attempted to dispute the election of Gamaliel's son, he was defeated by the votes of his colleagues. When Simon ben Gamaliel came to die, his son, the youthful Juda, was put in his seat without opposition as the natural head of the congregation of Israel.

Juda was born in a time of calamity for his people.

Tradition tells that it was on the day of the execution of Akibah, the last champion of Jewish independence.[3] His father, Simon, and the chief Rabbis of his party had not joined in the revolutionary movement and were not molested by the victorious Romans. Hadrian, however, vigorously proscribed the exercise of the Jewish religion or rites in Palestine after the defeat of Bar Kochba. Toleration of the religion of conquered peoples was the usual policy of Rome, but Hadrian departed from it in this case. In the stubborn resistance of the Jews to Roman rule, he recognized the workings of their religious faith. Though he could not comprehend its workings, he saw its results, and he strove to root out the practices of the Jewish law, that he might make the Jews as other races. Circumcision was strictly forbidden, among other rites, but Simon ben Gamaliel, however yielding in political affairs, was a strict adherent of the Law of Moses, and his infant son was duly circumcised. It came to the knowledge of the authorities, and punishment was threatened. Simon's wife went to Rome and appealed for mercy to the wife of the emperor Antoninus. She obtained pardon for her family, and Antoninus even revoked the edicts against the Jewish religion.[4] This circumstance contributed not a little to the popularity of the child among the people, who saw in him a sun rise again in Palestine.

Simon, his father, spared no pains in preparing his son for the office which awaited him. He educated him carefully in all the lore of his time, both Jewish and Roman. He learned many languages and sciences.⁵ Greek was his favorite of foreign tongues, but Hebrew was the special object of his admiration. He hated the Aramaic jargon which prevailed in Palestine, and when he grew to man's estate nothing but the pure Hebrew tongue was spoken in his house. The very servants spoke it with elegance.⁶ When scholars used Aramaic in his presence he was outspoken in his displeasure.

"Why speak that jargon," he said, "when one has Hebrew or Greek at his command?"⁷

He also studied the physical sciences of Greece, and, with all his patriotic feelings for his native tongue, he did not hesitate to give preference to the astronomers of Greece over those of Palestine.⁸

The Hebrew law was naturally the largest part of the education of one who was to be a prince among his people. His father sent him to the various schools in succession. The first Rabbi whose lectures he attended was the famous Ben Yohai, who had been the rival of his father. In his school he had to face cutting sarcasm from his schoolfellow, Eleazar, the son of Ben Yohai, who took delight in humbling the pride of the House of Hillel in his person. When the haughty Juda complained of this treatment to his diplomatic father, the latter bade him remember that though a lion he was the son of a fox. Other distinguished masters helped to store his mind with Jewish lore. Among them were Mair, Juda and Jacob ben Corshe.⁹ It was with a mind well stored that he assumed the office of president at the death of his father in 165, though a Patriarch of twenty-five was indeed an innovation in the Council of Israel.

The prince accepted his election as a matter of right divine. One rival, he admitted, might have a better claim, but only one, and that was one who made no pretence to seek the office. The Jewish colony in Babylonia, which had been settled there since the captivity, was regarded as the legitimate aristocracy of the Hebrew race. They enjoyed a far greater degree of liberty under the Parthian kings than was the lot of their co-religionists in Palestine. A prince descended from David ruled the Babylonian Jews with kingly power under Parthian suzerainty. His descent from the Prophet King was more direct than Juda's, as it came through the male line.[10] Juda declared that he would recognize his right to the presidency of the Sanhedrin if he should come to claim it.

"For no man would I do," he said, "what the Sons of Bethyra did for my ancestor Hillel, when they yielded the presidency to him. Were I in their place, I would not have given it up. To no man would I resign it except Huna the prince of the captivity came here to demand it. To him I would give place."[11]

There was a good deal of diplomacy as well as pride in this assertion. The recognition of descent from the royal prophet as the necessary qualification for the presidency of the Sanhedrin was a principle which could only confirm the authority of the House of Hillel. There was no likelihood that the aged prince of the captivity would ever come to ask the votes of the Jewish doctors in the Sanhedrin. However, the prince's proclamation was made the occasion of a mortification to him at a later date. The old Huna died, and his body was carried for burial to the land of his fathers. One of the Rabbis, Hiyah the Babylonian, learned of the arrival of Huna's body in Palestine. He went at once to the Sanhedrin when the prince was addressing its members, and informed him that Huna was here. The prince staggered and nearly swooned. Hiyah relieved his fears by explaining, "Huna is here in his coffin." [12] The prince, however, would not forgive the insult. He forbade Hiyah his house, and it was years before he allowed him to return to it. The sons of Hiyah repaid the prince's severity with interest. At a feast one of them was asked to speak, and he told the company:

"The Messiah will not come till there is neither a prince in Babylon nor one in Palestine." [13]

The feeling which made Juda refer repeatedly to his descent was not mere conceit. When he scoffed at the insolence shown to his grandfather by the famous Rabbi Josua on the ground that it was not for a smith to argue with a prince, it was not a mere expression of personal pride. He looked on himself as the natural ruler of his people, and he felt that loyalty to his house was a moral duty for every conscientious Jew. The continuance of the rule of the House of David was, he believed, a necessity for the ultimate well-being of Israel. It was to support its dignity that he was ready to admit his inferiority to a foreigner in Babylon, provided he possessed Davidic descent. To no other would he condescend to bend or apologize. With all his pride of birth Juda was affable to the multitude. He gave freely of his vast wealth, and the people adored him, whatever opposition he might have to meet from rival Rabbis or offended dignitaries. He was skilled in the art of diplomacy, too, and if his learning did not dazzle the Sanhedrin, he knew how to make it endorse the policy which he deemed suitable to the needs of the people. He was emphatically a prince in his ways.

His policy in the limited sphere which Roman power left to him was that of his great ancestor Hillel. He had no thought of building up a kingdom in Palestine or emulating the patriotic fervor of Akibah. His object was to secure the perpetuity of the religion and language of his race, not the independence of Palestine. A cosmopolitan Jewish people, he hoped, might continue to exist though a Jewish nation could not be maintained. He sought to mould the law, of which he was the guardian, to the changed conditions that must come when that people should be spread over the world instead of being dwellers in the narrow limits of Palestine.

Though zealous for the Jewish law, he cared little for the ceremonial of the Temple worship, which to the national party in Palestine was the centre of religion itself. He practically annulled as obsolete the laws referring to priestly service in the Temple.[14] He placed the education of children in the right path, —above mere ceremonies.

"Interrupt not the teaching of the children, even

were it for rebuilding the Temple," was a maxim of his,[15] and,

"The world depends on the breath of the school-children." [16]

What teaching meant was summed up in the law:

"Every one is bound to instruct his children in the ways of the land wherein he dwells." [17]

This was a bold regulation for the times when the narrow thought of many Rabbis identified the land of Palestine with the observance of the law in its fulness. Equally so was his precept for moral conduct.

"Observe three things in thy conduct and thou shalt never sin: Know there is an Eye everywhere that seeth thee, an Ear that heareth thee, and a Hand that registers every wrong of thine." [18]

Whatever opposition Juda experienced in his own time, later generations recognized the wisdom of the Prince's laws. His decisions were given precedence over those of all other masters except his father, Simon. Even the famous Rabbi Mair's authority had to yield to that of his pupil, Juda the Prince, in the schools of the Rabbis who interpreted the law for the scattered people of Israel.[19]

The whole policy of the prince in his legislation, as it may be seen from the foregoing, was to make the law of Israel more flexible in its application. Originally given to a pastoral people dwelling in one small land, many of its regulations could not be carried out in other circumstances. The ingenuity of many generations of disputing doctors had elaborated these local and temporary laws almost to the dignity of divine commands. Man was made for the Sabbath, not the Sabbath for man, in their eyes. Juda, like Hillel, strove to give the questions of local ceremonial and pedantic deduction their fitting place as accessory, not essential, to the due observance of the law. He looked to the people scattered over the earth rather than to the land of Palestine. For this reason, though religious in practice, he was rather unfriendly to the sacerdotal class. The Rabbi class to which he belonged had nothing in common with the priesthood of Aaron. The public worship which centred in the Temple was the province of the priests in Israel and that alone. The learned men, the Rabbis, or teachers, were the judges, the legislators, and even the preachers of the law. The Temple had perished, the priests had little practical importance, and Juda cared little for their favor. He showed no special zeal for the restoration of the Temple, the dearest wish of the priests and the nationalists. He even urged the abolition of the Fast day instituted to recall its destruction on the ninth day of the month of Abh. Though the opposition in the Sanhedrin prevented this bold measure,[20] it shows the policy of the prince clearly that he proposed it. He would not even admit priests, however learned in the law, to the dignity of Rabbi. He refused it to the learned astronomer and doctor, Mar Samuel, apparently on no other grounds.[21] He restricted the power of giving the degree of master to himself instead of leaving it to the discretion of other Rabbis.[22]

The tendency of Juda's legislation was shown

further by the modifications he introduced in the Sabbath observance. It had been developed to fantastic proportions by the casuistry of earlier doctors. Faithful Jews might have no fire kindled on that day or touch objects used on other days. These prohibitions were abolished by the Sanhedrin under Juda's rule. The regulation which obliged travellers to halt and prostrate themselves at the hours of prayer was in force among the Jews of his day, as among the Mohammedans of ours. The prince pronounced it needless. A traveller should pray, but might pray as he travelled.[23] Travel on the Sabbath was permitted and the heating of food.[24] In fasting, he also lessened the minute details of the national Rabbis.

"Burden not the congregation with over many fasts," was his dictum.[25]

Another important ruling was that circumcision, which had been absolutely required of every Jewish family, might be omitted in case of danger to life.[26] The older Rabbis admitted that this and similar ceremonial laws might be omitted to save life, but on no other grounds. Juda enlarged the exemption by decreeing that danger to life warranted its use.[27]

It need not be thought that with all his wealth and official dignity Juda carried out these measures without opposition. The graybeards of the Sanhedrin felt their professional pride offended by the legislative activity of one whom they regarded as but a boy. His Davidic descent, though honorable, they did not count as filling Juda with wisdom like theirs. By old practice, election to the council depended solely on personal merit, as in the Catholic Church to-day any priest, or even a layman, may be raised to the Papal office. They favored not the claim of the prince to give the rabbinical dignity at his personal will alone. They recalled how his grandfather had been deposed from office by a vote of the Assembly, and they did not fail to remind him of the fact when his autocratic manners were too freely exercised. Criticism of his pride and his inferiority in learning to the famous masters was common in the schools. A certain Bar 'Haninah criticised his pronunciation of Hebrew as not according to the correct Babylonian standard. Juda told him he would never make him a Rabbi till he returned to his masters in Babylon.[28] He had to call in the medical service of Mar Samuel to whom he had refused the same honor, and he tried to excuse his action to the physician. The latter sarcastically told him:

"It is written in the Book of Adam that 'Samuel shall be not a Rabbi, but a sage through whom the prince shall be healed.'"

It was the gibe of a scholar, and Juda bore it patiently.[29]

It was different with Bar Kappara, a celebrated wit, who took occasion at a feast to insult him in his own house. The son-in-law of the prince asked Bar Kappara to frame a riddle for him to repeat before the guests. The malicious wit made one, the solution of which was insulting to his host. Juda never forgave the affront, and in after years when Bar Kappara sought the rabbinical office he was curtly refused.[30]

The opposition he had to encounter in the Sanhedrin to his legislative reforms was strong. When he sought to lessen the rigors of the Sabbath observance, the nationalists told him:

"Thou permitted what thy ancestors prohibited."[31]

The prince met the objection boldly:

"Hezekiah destroyed the brazen serpent that Moses made in the desert because the people of his day adored it as a god. There were other worthy kings and destroyers of idols who feared to destroy that serpent. Hezekiah's merit, then, is special to him alone. So is my work peculiar to me, and I fulfil what my ancestors began."[32]

The nationalists took another course. They proposed changes more radical than those of the prince. They suggested the emancipation and admission to Jewish citizenship of the serfs, the Nethinim, who had been a subordinate body for centuries.[33] The prince opposed it on the ground of expediency. Another proposition submitted was to declare that the Davidic descent of those who had remained in Palestine was purer than that of the children of the captivity in Babylon. This was in keeping with the narrow tribal sentiment which would identify Jewish faith with Palestine. It also aimed at the title of Juda; for his ancestor, Hillel, was one of the captivity. The prince opposed it with all his power.

"You would put thorns in my eyes," he told the Rabbis, and they yielded to his will.[34]

In a more friendly fashion a famous Rabbi, Jonathan ben Amran, conveyed a rebuke to the princely president. During a year of famine, the latter opened his grain stores to all students of the law. He forbade the Men of Earth, the ignorant rabble, to enter with them. Jonathan made his way in disguise and said:

"Master, give me to eat, for I hunger."

And the prince asked, "Hast thou read the law?"

And Jonathan said, "I have not."

"Hast thou read the Mishnah?"

"No."

"Then how can I feed thee who hast not fed thine own people?"

"Master," said Jonathan, "thou wouldst feed a dog or a raven. Feed me likewise, for I, too, am a creature of God."

And the prince gave him alms. But when Jonathan had gone the prince repented and said:

"Woe is me! I have fed a Man of Earth."

But one of his disciples told him it was Jonathan, his disciple, who would fain conceal his learning. The prince changed his mind when he heard this and he said:

"Now let all men enter my stores and be fed, for it is not for man to discriminate between God's creatures for his own caprice." [35]

In other ways he showed a kindly temper, unlike the character which the hostile critics of his power gave him.

He was willing to learn from his own pupils and acknowledged it freely.

"I have learned much," he said, "from my teachers, more from my equals, but most of all from my pupils." [36]

When the king, Artaban,[37] sent him a jewel as a gift, the prince returned a scroll of Scripture. The king was surprised and sent him a message:

"I have given thee a jewel of price, and thou sendest me a thing of less value than the case that holds it."[38]

"Nay," the prince replied, "thou hast sent me a gift which I must guard, but I have sent thee one which will guard thee, as it is written, 'It will guide thee wherever thou goest.'"[39]

With the members of his race who professed their belief in Christ as the Messiah, Juda maintained friendly relations. He evidently regarded them as countrymen and brothers in the Law of Moses. It is recorded that at his table he asked once a Christian friend to say the blessing over the wine, which, among the Jews, was regarded as a high honor to a guest. So high was it that by custom a fine of forty pieces had to be paid as an offering by any guest who declined the duty offered. The blessing included an acknowledgment of the rite of circumcision which had ceased, at least as an obligation, among the Christian Jews. The prince then coupled his invitation with the assurance that he would pay the fine himself if his guest had any scruples about repeating the form of prayer. The Christian assured him that he had none.[40]

The relations between Juda and the Roman rulers of Palestine must not be passed over. The Talmud represents him as holding long conferences with the emperor Antoninus. It is impossible to say if he really met the emperor, and the hyperbole of the story cannot be reduced to historic accuracy,[41] but it is so interesting as a specimen of Jewish philosophy at the time that we give the dialogue.

Antoninus said to the master:[42]

"It is easy for man to evade judgment for sin after death. The body can plead, 'It is the soul that hath sinned, for since it left me I have no more desire than a stone.' The soul can say, 'Since it left the body it is stainless, sinless, and free.'"

The master replied:

" I will answer thee by a parable. A king placed two guards in his garden, one blind and one lame. The lame man said to the blind, 'I see much fair fruit; carry me to it and we will eat.' So the blind bore the lame man to the tree and they stole the fruit and ate it. And later the king came and saw that the fruit was gone, and he asked the guards where the fruit was he had put under their care. And the lame man asked, 'Could I walk to steal it?' and the blind man said, 'Have I eyes to see it?' Then the king put the lame man on the shoulders of the blind man and he punished them as one man. Even so will the Lord, blessed be His name, put again the soul within the body and judge them together as they have deserved when together."[43]

Again Antoninus asked the Master:

"Why does the sun rise in the east?" and the master told him that if it rose in the west he might ask the same question.[44]

The emperor then asked advice on a personal matter. He told him he desired two things from the senate, but that they would only grant one

request. He desired the succession of his son secured, and also that the province of Tiberias should be made a Roman community. The master called two men. He made one mount the shoulders of the other, and then gave him a dove. He next bade the lower man tell the other to release the bird. Antoninus comprehended the hint and said:
"I will ask the senate to recognize my son, and then bid my son to enroll Tiberias as a province." [45]

Another anecdote tells how the emperor sent the master a sack of gold covered with wheat each day, and the Master said to him:
"I need it not; I have grain and gold enough."

And Antoninus bade him take it for his children, that they might give it in tribute to his own children.[46] The suggestion in this tale is manifest.

It has been seen that the policy of Juda in the Sanhedrin was mainly directed to making the yoke of the law lighter on the people and loosening the bonds which held them in Palestine. It was not in his power, had he willed it, to stem the tide of emigration which was carrying the Jewish race away from its ancestral home. The superior profits of foreign trade, made easy by the extension of the Roman dominion from the Euphrates to the Atlantic, drew keen Hebrew emigrants away. The oppression at home which followed the campaigns of Hadrian stimulated the movement. The Jews streamed from their native land in the days of Juda, as the dense population of Europe has poured across the Atlantic in our own day. The patriotic sentiments of the prince, his faith in the future of his people, made him seek every means to prevent the scattered children of Israel from losing their nationality and being lost among other races as the kingdom of Israel had melted away in the old days.

To this end it seemed to him the most effective means would be to make a literature for the Jewish people. Down to his time, though study and mental activity were pre-eminent in Juda, little attention had been paid to literature or written thought. Writing was reserved for the sacred Scriptures. The interpretations of the law, the sayings of the wise, the story of the people since the captivity, were handed down by word of mouth from generation to generation. The schools of the Rabbis in Palestine had preserved the wisdom and history of the past by careful repetition. The Jews of other lands near could come there to share in them as Hillel had come from Babylon, but with the exodus that was going on there was small likelihood that the schools themselves could continue long. It was harder, too, to come from Rome and Cadiz and India and the other lands to which the Jews were now moving than from Egypt or Babylon.

The prince determined to collect the whole body of oral Hebrew lore while there was yet time and secure its perpetuity by committing it to writing. To that task his life was devoted, and by it he deserves to be regarded as a foremost agent in the marvellous preservation of nationality without a country which has marked the Hebrew race from all others.

The work which he thus compiled, with the help of the numerous scribes whom his wealth enabled him to employ, is known as the Mishnah." Its main object is the interpretation of the Law of Moses, but its character as the record of the sayings and doings of so many generations gives it the nature of a rude encyclopedia. It deals with the whole system of human moral action; it touches on the sciences, and the events of successive generations. When Rabbi Juda began his task there was no Hebrew literature. The Bible was not within the reach of the mass of the people. The ceremonial practices of the law were the greater part of their worship. They had to learn practically that the God of the world is not confined to temples made by hands, nor His favor bounded by the narrow limits of Palestine. That the knowledge of the law could be spread among them, it needed more than the gatherings of a few learned men in Jerusalem or Yamnai: it needed literature, and as the founder of that literature Rabbi Juda the Prince deserves a place among the greatest of his people.

It was a colossal task for a man to gather up from a hundred sources the traditions of centuries, to compare and systematize the thousands of often contradictory decisions that had been handed down from famous doctors, to form them into a consistent whole. Juda had no native model in his task. A few, like Akibah, had written some decisions, but there was no model to guide him. That his work is not like the literary monuments of Greece or Rome is not to be wondered at. Yet it has a style and merits of its own of unmistakable worth. Its language is the purest Hebrew, and in spite of the mass of subjects treated, its style is uniform and terse. Like other Semitic races, the Jews liked to express their thoughts in short, half-enigmatic phrases. Parable and simile and proverb were the common form of Jewish speech. That it left room for study to the listener, and called his mental activity to work before its meaning could be clear, was regarded as a gain rather than a loss. The Talmud was composed according to this idea. It was to furnish food for thought to others, to be elucidated and commented on by successive generations, and so it is no cause for surprise that to the modern student, be he Jew or Gentile, its meaning is often hard to determine. Still no one can fail to admire its wide scope, its classic language, its poetic form, and its grasp of the varied forms of human thought.

A commentary to the Mishnah known as the Gemara[18] was begun by the Rabbis in Babylon within the lifetime of the prince, and the two combined are since known as the Talmud, or Babylonian Talmud. A somewhat similar work was later undertaken in the Aramaic dialect of Palestine, and is known as the Talmud of Jerusalem, but neither in style nor matter can it rank with the Babylonian Talmud.

Though the Mishnah purports to be a summary of Hebrew law, it has no resemblance to a legal treatise in modern ideas. The Jewish conception of law was indeed wholly different from that of the nations of the West. It was no mere collection of edicts or decrees of kings or senates. It was the rule of human life in all its manifold activities; for every human act has a moral character in the divine system, of which a part was directly revealed to the Hebrew law giver. The constitutional provisions which made the interpretations of the majority of the doctors of Israel a part of that law broadened out its fabric to almost boundless proportions in the course of ages. The cultivation of the fields, the care of domestic animals, the preparation of food and clothing, the dwellings of men and beasts, the care of health, of personal cleanliness, of social intercourse, and myriad similar points foreign to our notions of legislation were discussed and regulated by solemn law among the people of Israel. To cast this law into a literary form was the colossal work of Rabbi Juda.

It is cast in systematic form, but the system is widely different from the divisions and subdivisions of modern science. The Rabbis had found the need of system in their teaching, even when the body of the law was preserved by oral tradition, but their system was formed on the association of kindred ideas around a particular easily remembered subject. The cultivation of memory was of the highest importance when decisions had to be handed down by repetition alone. The highest praise for a teacher was that his mind was a cistern which lost no drop of the words poured into it. Thus the classification followed in the Talmud is largely based on a mnemonic system. The subjects associated in a section seem often as incongruous as the union of "Papal Country Seats and the Bite of the *Tarantula*" by a modern Italian writer. To the Jews of the day, however, these associations seemed perfectly natural as aids to memory, and their perpetuation in the Talmud was in keeping with old habits of thought.

There are six divisions of the whole Mishnah, each bearing a name indicative of its subject-matter.[19] These are subdivided into a varying number of Books similarly named by keywords. The Books are divided into sections by numbers only. The general names of the six divisions are Seeds (*Zeraim*), Feasts (*Moed*), Women (*Nashim*), Wrongs (*Nezikin*), Consecrations (*Kodashim*), and Purifications (*Taharoth*).

The subject of the first division is the common life of the mass of the people who in Palestine were mostly dependent on the cultivation of the soil. To the cultivator, seed-time and harvest are the chief epochs of the year and "Seed" the first requisite of his work. The eleven books which make up the division bear the names, Blessings, Cultivation, Uncertain Things, Blending, Sabbath Year, Ablutions, Tithes, Second offerings, Dough, Birds, and First Fruits, respectively.

The first prescribes the numerous forms of prayer to be used in ordinary life, and is subdivided into nine sections. The book "Cultivation" describes the times and places for sowing and reaping and the provision for the needy which the agriculturist was bound to leave at harvest-time. "Uncertainty" deals with the subject of when the fruits of the earth are fit for human use by the Mosaic law. "Blending" prescribes the manner of crossing plants and animals, and of woolen and linen in dress. The ten sections of the "Sabbath Year" deal with the regulations of periodic fallowing prescribed in Deuteronomy. "Ablutions" in eleven sections describes the offerings due to the Aaronic priesthood from cultivated fields. "Tithes," in five sections, prescribes the amount and conditions of the "tenths" of the fields and flocks which had to be paid for the sustenance of the tribe of Levi. "Second Offerings," in five sections, deals with the portion of the harvest which had to be eaten in Jerusalem, and "Dough," in three sections, speaks of the offerings to the priests on account of bread-making. "Buds" gives the rules for determining at what age fruit of trees should be held fit for human food, and "First Fruits" tells the methods of harvesting and using the first products.

The second division, "Feasts," deals with the festival and fast days prescribed in the law, their mode of observance, and other particulars. "Sabbath," its first book, describes the law of observance of the seventh day of rest, in twenty-four sections, and "Erubin," the second book, continues it in ten sections as to the distance of travelling on that day. The third book, "Passover," prescribes the observances required for the passover. The fourth, "Shekels," the tax to be paid by the people. The three following books give the rules for observing the other great festivals, namely, Atonement, the Tabernacles, and New Year. "Festivals," the seventh book, gives general laws for all feasts, as the ninth, "Fasts," does for all days of penance. The tenth regulates the observance of Purim, the eleventh that of half-holidays, and the twelfth that of the pilgrimage to Jerusalem.

The third division of the Mishnah deals with the relations between the sexes: Marriage, divorce, dowries, engagements, rights of married people, and their duties. Its books are:

1. "Sisters-in-law," referring to the rule requiring brothers to marry such in case of widowhood. 2. Marriage contracts. 3. Vows. 4. Abstainer, the continence required of married persons. 5. Adultery. 6. Divorce. 7. Sanctifications.

The fourth division, "Wrongs," has ten books. The "First Gate" deals with damages for offences, the "Second Gate," with borrowing, renting, giving in trust, and articles found by the way. The "Last Gate" gives the laws of deeds, gifts, and inheritance. The fourth book, "Council," the administration of the law, the duties of Judges, and the constitution of legal courts. The fifth describes the various legal penalties for crimes. The sixth treats of oaths, their nature, and form. The seventh, "Common Law," of the weight to be attached to precedence and usage in the courts. The eighth, "Idolatry" and its punishment. The "Books of the Fathers" is made up of moral precepts and maxims of the sages of Israel. "Decisions" is the tenth book, and is a record of such by various distinguished judges. "Consecrations," the fifth division, contains eleven books: namely, offerings of animals, offerings of fruits and liquids, diet and food. The "First-Born," prescribing the action to be followed in the matter of first births, both in human beings and animals. "Values," that is, the money price to be paid for redemptions of the former under the

Levitical law. "Exchanges," how to act in the matter of substitution of profane for consecrated animals under the same law. "Destruction," how the penalty of death may be incurred and in what cases it may be commuted. "Malfeasance," prescribing penalties for the theft of sacred things. "Sacrifice," describing the rites of worship in the Temple. "Measures," a minute description of the Temple, its site, buildings, treasures, guards, and pilgrim services therein. The last book, "Nests," relates to the doves and other birds prescribed as offerings for the poor among the people.

The sixth Mishnah division, "Purifications," [50] embraces twelve books named, respectively, "Vessels," "Tents," "Skin Diseases," "the Red Cow" (*i. e.*, the sacrifice of that animal prescribed in Numbers), Purifications, of impurities in detail, "Wells," waters used in purification of men and things. "Separation," of married people at certain periods. "Capacities," objects which make other things unclean by contact. "Fluxes," "the Bath," "Hands" and "Stalks" or "Shells." All of these deal with the impurities mentioned in the Mosaic law. They describe their nature, how they may be incurred by men or inanimate objects, how the uncleanness may be removed by purification, and the various forms of the purifications themselves.

Wide is the usage of subjects embraced by these heads. They are far from giving the full contents of the Mishnah. It is the record of the thoughts of the Jewish race, not only on these points of law and doctrine, but on all subjects in any way connected with them. The Rabbis wove their judgments and thoughts into fables and similes, like all Easterners. They found hidden meanings in the words and actions appearing indifferent in themselves, and they delighted in exercising their minds in such researches. The whole life of the people finds illustrations in the anecdotes or parables in which learned Rabbis decided how many yards it was lawful to walk on the Sabbath or at what age the fruit of the olive might be pressed for oil. If Akibah could draw countless precepts from every letter of the Hebrew alphabet, as his colleagues said, it passes calculation to guess what subjects might fall within the scope of the whole body of the Law.

The colossal proportions of the task impress us very strongly even at present, but its difficulty was enormously greater than we can at first sight comprehend in an age when literary composition was in its infancy. The task of the Athenian prince who collected and edited the scattered ballads that under the names of Iliad and Odysey have been the foundation of all our Western literature seems small, indeed, beside that of Rabbi Juda in Palestine. He had a far wider range of subjects, which called for close investigation in every part, not the ballad history of a famous campaign, as his task. He put a system all his own into the mass to which he thus gave literary form. He dwelt not much upon precise dogmas and took little heed of the hair-splitting casuistry of the meaning of words and laws which other Rabbis delighted in. He did not enter much into metaphysical speculations on abstract points.

His object is apparent: it is to record all that he could gather of the experience of the past of his race, which might bear on the conduct of his own and future generations of his people. The text of Scripture itself is the framework of his compilation. The Word of God to him was the unchangeable Law. The comments of men, even the wisest, were but partial elucidations of its full meaning. Those he collected were to guide man in his path through life practically from the cradle to the grave, to direct his aspirations and the work of his mind and hands, his spiritual and intellectual as well as his material life. His planting and reaping, his eating and sleeping, his joys and his sorrows, all are regulated by definite laws, and in all faith recognizes protection from on high and the rewards and chastisements that fall from the Father's hand for human action. For this reason, the Talmud goes into minute details of daily life. It recalls the ways and the men of former days and shows how some lived after the heart of God Himself, and how far others failed to do so. It tells of hopes that were realized and hopes that failed among the people, of its errors and its true judgments. It discusses the meaning of the text of Scripture itself, and points out what remained for further analysis and comment. Its matter is no less than the material, intellectual, and moral life of a people.

That in his work the Prince had thoroughly entered into the spirit of the Hebrew race has been proved by the reception accorded to it. In his own lifetime the Gemara was commenced as a commentary on it in Babylon, and the two have since been combined into the Talmud as the literary and moral guide of the Jewish race. The comments on the Talmud since are beyond reckoning. Indeed, the intellect of the race in literary work mainly centred around the work of Rabbi Juda. In widely separated lands the scattered children of Israel pondered over its pages, as, in earlier days, they had crowded the schools of the Rabbis. Its spirit kept their faith living, and strengthened them to endure persecution. Neither Jewish history nor Jewish religion can be understood without a knowledge of the Talmud. At times the reverence which surrounded it, made the reading of it of even greater merit than the reading of the Scriptures. Through centuries the race survived as a dweller in lands not its own, as the subjects of alien masters. It was not bodily strength or endurance that carried them through, but the intellectual force which they drew from their literature. In study the Jew forgot his slavery; he recognized a higher power than that of the temporary oppressor, and he lightened his load by the hope of a brighter future. When all around threatened destruction, he asked the advice of the men of old from the pages of the Talmud. Their answer was, "Learn, endure, and pray." These counsels have been the staff which supported the Jewish race from Hadrian's to our own time. The remarkable national existence which has been preserved for eighteen centuries without a country may fairly be said to be due in great part to the Talmud.

Were it not for the Talmud, the spirit of which

permeated the Jewish heart, the Jew could never have manifested his unshaken fidelity to the Word of God. Without the Talmud, the power of which fortified his soul, the Jew could not have endured his ages of martyrdom. Without the Talmud, the knowledge of which gave him ever-increasing faith, the Jew could hardly have withstood the temptations to the renunciation of his religion. Without the Talmud, the light of which illumined the darkness of nigh two thousand years' wanderings, the Jew could not to-day show a history which is the grandest expression of tragedy the world has seen.

Where else shall we find a tragedy the scenes of which are so varied; the time of which has lasted so long; the actors of which included so many heroes, kings, sages, men and women, old and young, who rose again, day after day, night after night, only to face the same hisses, the same jeers, the same curses, and to meet the same hand that struck them to the ground?

If the Jews have survived the atrocious treatment of their fellow-men, have borne the moments of sorrow and despair in the dark ages, it is because they had faith; because they read the written word and believed its promises. And the book that contained the elucidation and reassertion of these promises was the Talmud, the foundation of which was laid by Rabbi Juda, whose memory will last as long as the Hebrew language.[51]

The prince did not neglect the interests of his own house in the ardor of literary work. He steadily increased the powers of the patriarchate among his

countrymen. Down to Hillel, the president and
Judge in the Sanhedrin had been nearly equal in
power, and both depended for office on the will of
the majority in that body. The superior authority
of the patriarch had been established by Hillel.
Rabbi Juda made himself practically the master of
the national council. He claimed the sole right of
selecting its members. He decreed its decisions,
and when near his end he named not only his own
successor, but also the Judge and Lector. He forbade, in the name of the law itself, any one to set
up as a Messiah henceforth.

"Read his name Liar, not Star of Jacob," was his
sentence on the memory of Bar Kochba.[52]

The power which the Sanhedrin had long exercised over the Jewish people thus became centred
in the person of Juda the Prince. The patriarchs
who succeeded him were recognized by the Roman
authorities as pontiffs and heads of the Jewish people throughout the empire. Taxes were laid on the
various Jewish congregations for the maintenance of
the patriarchate and enforced by the Roman officials.
Juda himself was a great man in Syria. Foreign
kings sent him messages and gifts, and he often declined the latter in regal fashion. The intercourse
between the Jewish Rabbi and the Roman emperor
has been already noted. The dignity thus attached
to the office of patriarch was continued for two
hundred years after the death of Juda. The Emperor Julian even addressed the Jewish patriarch
Hillel II. as "brother" when he was planning the rebuilding of the Temple at Jerusalem. The office

was finally abolished by Theodosius the Great in 425. Before it ended the House of Hillel had enjoyed a life greater than falls to most kingly dynasties.[63]

The family of Rabbi Juda consisted of only two sons, Gamaliel and Simon, and a daughter, the wife of Bar Elasa. When advanced in life and a widower he sought in marriage the widow of his old opponent, Eleazar ben Yohai, and, with all his wealth and honor, had to undergo the humiliation of a refusal. The widow declared she would regard herself as degraded by an alliance with the patriarch. He found another wife, however, whom he recommended to the care of his children in his last instructions. His life was prolonged to an advanced age though for many years he suffered from continuous ill-health. The Talmud says he could only sleep the time of sixty respirations in his later days,[64] and it records how Mar Samuel, whom he had long excluded from the council, was called to relieve him from an affection of the eyes. He had to change his abode to the mountain town of Sephoris, where the last seventeen years of his life were spent. Constant pain increased his natural irritability to a marked degree, and the shadow of opposition to his will drove him to fury. Yet withal he was placable when his passion abated and the love of the people surrounded him. The people of Sephoris were said to have vowed to kill whoever should bring the tidings of the death of their adored prince.

When his end approached he named his successor in autocratic style.

"Gamaliel, my son, shall be prince when I am

dead. Simon, my son, reader, and my disciple, Hama bar 'Haninah, judge in the Sanhedrin.[55] Let this be opened thirty days after my death and let there be no mourning in the towns."

He gave instructions in the duties and rights of his position to Gamaliel and especially advised him to rule the Rabbis with a strong hand.

"Be strict with the disciples," was his warning to his successor, which the latter faithfully carried out.[56] His other instructions were brief to his sons.

"Honor your mother. Make her happy, make no change in your household. Joseph of Kaipha and Simon of Efrath, who served me in life will arrange my body for burial."

It was in the year 220 that the prince was gathered to his fathers.

His death was widely regretted by the Jewish people, who recognized in him a representative of the royal house, and admired his liberality and industry. With all his ambition of power, Rabbi Juda showed no desire to amass wealth. He regarded himself as beyond the need of treasures and he distributed freely.

"Lord of the world," was his exclamation on his death-bed, "Thou knowest I have worked both my hands for the law but have not used even a finger to gain temporal wealth."[57] It was no unfitting boast. When the rivalries of the moment had passed, the Jewish race recognized the merits of the prince ungrudgingly.

"He it was who brought forth the Law for Israel," was the common sentence. The famous

Maimonides, who codified the Talmudic laws a thousand years later, did not hesitate to say of him: "He was alone in his time and generation. In him dwelt all the highest qualities, and those of his time styled him Our Master, the Holy One." [58]

NOTES

CHAPTER I

1. See Talmud Babli, Synhedrin 5; Talmud Jerusalemi, Khilaim 9; the same, Talmud Kethuboth, div. 12, and Midrash Rabba, Genesis, div. 33.
2. See Sotah 21.
3. It is a little perplexing to accept the general rendition of the text, שככל יום ויום היה עושה ומשתכר בטרפעיק (Yoma 35), "And it was said of Hillel that he worked and earned daily a tropaicon." A tropaicon, says Rab Shesheth (Kethuboth 64), is an Astira ($\Sigma\tau\alpha\tau\acute{\eta}\rho$), and what is an Astira? Half a Sus. But this was exactly what it cost to hear the daily lecture. If Hillel earned but a tropaicon, which he was forced to pay the doorkeeper of the academy, what did he have to live on? And from the text it is evident that he had as much more for himself and family. It seems to us that this bad sense in the text is merely due to a mistake of the copyists and later of the printer. It should read: "And he earned two tropaica (טרפעיק ב״)." The printer failed to put the divisional marks on top of the ־ ־, as may be seen in Yoma 35, where the phrase ר׳ יהודה אומר ג׳ טרפעיקין is found, and really gives an indication of the other reading.
4. See "Rabbi Josua ben 'Hananiah" in this volume.
5. See Yoma 35.
6. Ibidem.
7. See Sifra to Thasriang, div. 9; Talmud Jerusalemi, esachim, div. 6, 1; Tosephta Negaim; Pesikta to Thasriang.
8. See Jeruṣalemi, Pesachim, div. 6, 1.

9. Ibidem, and Talmud Babli, Pesachim 69. Later Rabbis praise the resignation of the Bethyrahs as an act of graceful condescension. There seems to have been no condescension whatever; rather was it a religious and political necessity to have a Davidic descendant in the presidential chair, considering also that Hillel stood much higher in the estimation of the people than the Bethyrahs, who had not attended the academy of the old masters, though they had had the fullest opportunity, being residents of Jerusalem and very wealthy, whereas the Babylonian, who had struggled and suffered, could boast of the advantage from the masters, Shemaiah and Abtalion.

10. See Talmud Babli, Sabbath 11 b.
11. See Patristic Chapters, 1.
12. See Talmud Babli, Sabbath 31; conf. Aboth de Rabbi Nathan, div. 1.
13. See Patristic Chapters, 1.
14. Numbers 18, 7.
15. Talmud Babli, Sabbath 31.
16. The Talmud (Yoma) expresses this in the maxim, וחי בהם ולא שימות בהם, "Ye shall live by them (the laws) but ye shall not die by them."
17. Talmud Babli, Sabbath 31; Aboth de Rabbi Nathan 1.
18. Talmud Babli, Gittin 36; Shebiith 10, 3.
19. Talmud Babli, Erachin 31.
20. Talmud Babli, Baba Metziah 75; Sabbath 148.
21. Sotah 48; Tosephta Sotah, div. 13.
22. Talmud Babli, Synhedrin 16.
23. Berachoth 60.
24. Derech Eretz Rabba, div. 6.
25. Talmud Babli, Sabbath 30 b, לעולם יהא אדם ענוותן כהלל ואל יהא קפדן כשמאי.
26. Sabbath 31 a.
27. Midrash Rabba, Leviticus, div. 24.
28. Ibidem.
29. Talmud Babli, Kethuboth 67; Talmud Jerus, Peah, div. 1.

30. Tosephta, Berachoth, div. 2; Derech Eretz Sutta, div. 8.

31. Talmud Babli, Sabbath 16, and Sifri at the end.

CHAPTER II

1. Talmud Babli Abodah Zara (ed. 1520); En Yacobh II, p. 348 (ed. 1519) Hagadoth ha-Talmud (ed. 1511) and Midrash Rabba Koheleth (ed. 1519). Compare also our note to Chapter V.

2. This Josua ben Perachiah can hardly be the same who was the colleague of Nita the Arbelite, who was the President of the Sanhedrin about one hundred years before Christ. The notice in Sanhedrin 107 b, referring to Josua's harsh treatment of Christ and the disapproval thereof by the Rabbis, gives room to one of two suppositions, either there was in the time of Christ a man of the same name, or the writer, regardless of chronology, set down the maxim not to deny salvation to any one, notably not to so learned a man as Jesus, though he was guilty of giving a decision without having been asked by his Master to do so, and for which the loss of Paradise was the penalty. But all this shows that the Rabbis frequently discussed the merits and demerits of Christ who, they held, was a secessionist and heretic, and could hardly be a sharer in the bliss vouchsafed only to the strictly orthodox. To Jesus they applied the saying of Rabbi Josua ben Perachiah, "Keep away from a bad neighbor, keep no company with the godless, and do not believe that they go unpunished" (Aboth I). They go even so far as to discuss the form of punishment to which Jesus is subjected in Hell (see Babli Rosh ha-Shanah 16; Jerusalemi Sanhedrin I). This harsh measure is condemned by other Rabbis, who hold that, "if thy right hand pushes away a person, let thy left be ready to receive him

back again" (Babli Sanhedrin 107). But the strict adherents to the letter of the law persisted that the action of Ben Perachiah was justifiable. Thereupon the gentler disposed Masters exclaimed, "Then let no man be like Josua ben Perachia who pushed away Jesus with both hands" (ibidem). This decision seems to settle the question of the fellowship of Jesus whom the Rabbis admittedly held worthy of consideration. And as Jesus was not a heretic (Min), he having lived in accordance with the laws of Moses, the rule laid down by the Rabbis as to those who are doomed to the fires of the Ge-Hinnon (Hell) does not apply to Jesus (see Babli Rosh ha-Shanah 16). Regarding the death penalty the Talmud is equally emphatic, showing unmistakably that the condemnation of Jesus did not find general approval by the later Rabbis, and such Masters as Rabbi Akibah and Rabbi Tarphon are reported as saying, "Had we been members of the Sanhedrin, there never would have been passed a death sentence" (Mishnah Makkoth 1, 10).

3. Talmud Babli Sanhedrin 43 and 67.
4. Josts Geschichte des Judenthums und seiner Secten, Vol. I, f, p. 405.
5. Midrash Rabba Koheleth.
6. Talmud Babli Abodah Zara 17.
7. Aboth de Rabbi Nathan 4.
8. Mishnah Rosh ha-Shanah IV, l.
9. Talmud Babli Sotah 47; comp. Josts Geschichte etc. Vol. I, p. 399.
10. Ibidem Pesachim 57; ibidem Jost.
11. Ibidem Sotah 22.
12. Megillath Taanith XII, 6.
13. Talmud Babli Nedarim 39; ibid, Pesachim 54; Targum Jonathan ben Uziel to Isaiah 42, 1, 2.
14. Talmud Babil Sanhedrin 97; Midrash Rabba Echah II, 2.
15. The eight hundred Pharisees crucified by Alexander Yannai were too fresh in their memory to let the Pharisees

sanction such an atrocious act even though they had differed as to his Messiahship.

It is evident from that alone that there were no Pharisees at the trial. Such a flimsy charge as the one by which was specified that Jesus called himself the "Son of God" would not have been sustained by the Pharisees. Every Jew was in the habit of calling God "Father." The words "Our Father" (Abinu Malekeynu) and "Our Father who art in Heaven" (Abinu sheba-Shamaüm) were words frequently spoken by the Hebrews in their prayers. Nor was it very extraordinary to call one "Son of God," since the Jews are often called "sons of God," בנים אתם ליהוה אלהיכם (Deut. 14 1), and also the "first born and beloved son," כי נער ישראל ואהבהו וממצרים קראתי לבני (Jer. 51, 20). The accusation of being a false prophet, נביא שקר, the Pharisees would not have sustained against Jesus; for he merely deplored the sad condition of the Hebrews spiritually, particularly those in power, and the Pharisees fully coincided with him in the matter. Any one could see whither the Jews were drifting by their negligence of the Law of God. But even had the Pharisees sided with the Sadducees in the charge that Jesus was a "perversionist," מסית ומדיח; that he led people from the true faith to a false hope; that he diverted the Messianic belief and incited the people to rebellion against the existing authorities; had the Pharisees been willing to forget so far their own interests in the interest of their enemies, they could not have convicted Jesus of that charge, at least without going against the plain law of Moses which provides the death penalty only in cases where a person had been guilty of leading the people from the faith in God to the worship of idols (Deut. 13, 2–12), and no one could have said such a monstrous thing of Jesus.

16. Neither the term σὺ εἶπας nor ὑμεῖς λέγετε are rabbinical affirmatives. This form of expression is seldom met with in talmudical writings. Nor is it an affirmation according to Matt. (26, 25) and John (18, 37). If the expression of Jesus, "thou hast said," meant affirmation, it would stand in glaring

contradiction to the thoughts expressed in John 18, 37. There is but one instance in rabbinical writings where the phrase "ye have said it" (אתון קאמריתון) appears, and there it is a distinct negative, as is evident from the addition, "I did not say so" (אנא לא קאמינא). This is the case of a certain scholar, Bar Kapara, by name, who takes it upon himself to announce to the people of Sephoris the death of Rabbi Juda the Prince. The Sephorites had vowed to kill the man who should bring them the sad news, so much did they love the Prince. It is therefore evident that, had Bar Kapara intended to affirm their question regarding the Prince's death, they would surely have killed him (vide Midrash Rabba Koheleth 7, 7; Talmud Babli Sabbath 134 *a*; Talmud Jerusalemi Kilayim 9, 4, fol. 32 *a*; Talmud Babli Kethuboth 104 *a*). It merely shows how quick-witted scholars made use of the phrase to get out of serious situations. In the case of Christ the reply also confirms the simple fact that he never spoke of his Messiahship in public, but that it was the High Priest who made the statement public for the first time. Jesus, therefore, says, "Thou hast said."

CHAPTER III

1. Talmud Babli Rosh ha-Shanah 21; ibidem Sanhedrin 41.
2. Ibidem Succah 28.
3. Ibidem Berachoth 17.
4. Ibidem Yoma 39.
4 a. Ibidem Sotah 47, משרבו המנאפים בטלו המים המרים.
5. Talmud Jerusalemi Succah IV, 6; Talm. Babli Pesachim 28.
6. Palmud Babli Gittin 56. The historian Jost (Geschichte des Judenthums und seiner Secten, Vol. I, p. 444) ascribes this

NOTES 281

act to Josephus. This is incorrect. Josephus neither asked for nor was he granted by Vespasian the favor of founding a school at Yamnai. He spent the latter part of his life in Rome, the pensioner of several Emperors, devoting his time to the writing of his histories. Comp. Graetz' History of the Jews, English translation, Vol. II. p. 288.
7. Midrash Rabba Koheleth.
8. Aboth de Rabbi Nathan 4.
9. Ibidem.
10. Talmud Jerusalemi Nedarim VIII, 7.
11. Aboth de Rabbi Nathan.
12. Talmud Babli Berachoth 28.
13. Ibidem Sotah 49.

CHAPTER IV

1. חסידות מביא לידי טהרות, "Piety leads to Purity" (Sotah 10).
2. The Hillelite school held with the ancient masters, Shemaiah and Abhtalion, that "man liveth by the laws—וחי בהם ואל ימות בהם—but he shall not die by (on account of) them." The Chassidaic races, on the other hand, held that one should die rather than break the law: as it is written (Deuteronomy 6, 4), "And thou shalt love the Lord thy God with thy whole heart and with thy whole life"; the words "thy whole life" signify that thou shalt not break the law of God though thy life be taken from thee, בכל נפשיך אפילו נוטל את נפשיך. Berachoth 61.
3. Ibidem. The Chassidaic maxim was, "Practical righteousness is preferable to study," ולא המדרש העיקר אלא המעשה (Patristic Chapters).
4. See Berachoth 34.
5. Ibidem, 3, 11, 12, 13.

6. Talmud Babli, Berachoth 24.
7. Ibidem 18.
8. Taanith 25.
9. Midrash Rabba, Koheleth 1.
10. Taanith 25.
11. Talmud Babli, Berachoth 33.
12. Taanith 24.
13. I believe there is a play on the name, and איבו really stands for איכא or אית־בא, "'tis here."
14. This story found many doubters. The Talmud is not quite ready to vouch for its truth, and thinking the unbelievers in this miracle entitled to some consideration, the Rabbis put in the guarded phrases— ויש אומרים: סניפין עשאום "And some (of the Rabbis) say, the beams were joined" (by the carpenter, of course). (See Taanith 24.) This certainty solves the problem in a rational and practical manner. But to throw cold water on a proposition which is intended to perpetuate the belief in the extraordinary powers of the Rabbis, particularly those of the Chassidaic-pharisaic sect, would not be in harmony with the spirit of the Talmud. Wherefore an addition is made to sustain the miracle, though it does not directly contradict what the "Some" say, as quoted above. The witness in the case is a certain holy man by the name of Plimo (Second Century A.C.), who unequivocally testifies as to the projection of the beams. "I have seen that house," says Plimo (Taanith 24), "and the beams projected to the measure of an ell on each side. And the people told me that this house was 'beamed' by the prayer of Rabbi 'Haninah ben Dosa"; בית זה שקירה רבי חנינא בן דוסא בתפלתו. By this it will be seen that the miracle is based upon "hearsay," while the main facts in the case, namely the projection of the beams, is supported by the "best evidence."
15. Here again some one evidently casts doubt upon the veracity of the report. "How came Rabbi 'Haninah by goats, since he was poor?" some doubting Rabbi asks. "And our sages have said," he continues, "that small cattle are not

raised in Palestine." (Taanith 24.) But here again a witness is found who gives a plausible explanation. Says Rabbi Pinehas: It happened that a man stopped at 'Haninah's house and left there some chickens, which 'Haninah's wife found, and of which she at once informed her husband.

"We can eat neither the chickens nor the eggs which the chickens have laid; they are not ours," he said.

And thus it came to pass that a great many eggs accumulated from which came many chickens, much to the annoyance of the saint and his wife; but they touched them not as food. However, to rid themselves of the chickens they sold them and with the proceeds bought goats. Some time after this the original owner of the chickens came back that way, and Rabbi 'Haninah heard him say to a fellow-traveller: "In this place have I lost my chickens."

"Couldst thou identify them?" asked the Rabbi.

"Aye, Rabbi, I can do that easily," the man replied, and forthwith described the chickens. Thereupon the Rabbi told the man of the disposition he had made of the chickens, and bade him take the goats instead, which the man gladly accepted. And these were the goats, the Talmud adds, which carried bears upon their horns. (Ibidem.)

16. משחרב בית המקדש נתבטלה נבואה, "Since the destruction of the Temple, prophecy has been abolished" (Baba Bathra fol. 9), is indicative of this policy. It was precisely this idea which the Rabbis advanced against Christianity. Granting that Jesus was a prophet, the Rabbis held that he had no authority to dissolve the old dispensation and to place in its stead a new form, אין נביא רשאי לחדש דבר מעתה (Megillah 2 *b*). But since, by the testimony of Jesus himself, he had not come to destroy but to fulfil, those claiming and advocating a new form in his name were deceivers.

17. Talmud Babli, Yebamoth 121.

CHAPTER V

1. Talmud Babli Hagigah 14.
2. Patristic Chapters II, 19.
3. Josephus Belli Jud. IV. 1, 3; Ant. XVII, 21, 3.
4. Talmud Babli Sabbath 114; ibidem 147: Aboth de Rabbi Nathan 14; Midrash Rabba Koheleth p. 101.
5. Talmud Jerusalemi Shebiith 1; ibidem Terumoth at the end.
6. Talmud Babli Baba Metziah 59.
7. Pirkey de Rabbi Eliezer I.
8. Talmud Babli Gittin 56; Midrash Rabba Koheleth, 7, 11.
9. Pirkey de Rabbi Eliezer II.
10. Ibidem.
11. See Chapter III this volume.
12. The historian Graetz errs in stating that Gamaliel II disciplined Eliezer ben Hyrkanos as one opposed to his authority in matters which had been decided by Ben Zakkai. Such could not have been the case, inasmuch as Gamaliel II was placed upon the presidential chair by Ben Zakkai himself, and Eliezer opposed nothing enacted by his Master. It was Josua ben 'Hananiah who forced the President to pronounce the ban over Eliezer, and as we believe, much against his inclination.
13. Talmud Babli Baba Metzia 59 a.
14. See Chapter I this volume. Hillel says, "So have I heard it from the mouth of Shemaiah and Abtalion."
15. The reference to the "bread-fruit tree," חרוב, is a very happy one and makes the meaning quite obvious, since it points to an historical fact. The time of Eliezer's trial took place shortly after the destruction of the second Temple, about seventy years after Christ, hence Eliezer's reference to the bread-fruit tree which requires seventy years for maturing and the bearing of fruit.
16. Patristic Chapters I, 1; Abodah Zara 36, the statement

NOTES   285

is found that Moses was shown every jot and tittle of the Law, and all that which the learned men in coming generations would add and explain ; מלמד שהראה הק״ב״ה למשה דקדוקי תורה ודקדוקי סופרים ומה שעתידים לחדש.

17. The notice, "Rabbi Eliezer, the Shammathite, for he was of the House (i. e., of the opinion) of Shammai," רבי אליעזר שמותי דהו מבית שמאי (see Talmud Jerusalemi Shebiith I, at the end ; ibidem Terumoth V, 4), indicates that the strict Shammaites suited Eliezer's ideas far better than those of the lenient Hillelites, and from what we know of his character, there is no doubt but that he was "a Shammaite in the House of Hillel."

18. Josua had a secret contempt for the wealthy Gamaliel, and once this became manifest in a very unpleasant form to Gamaliel, when he was forced to beg pardon of the learned blacksmith, who, though he forgave the public insult to which the President had subjected him, cried, אוי לדור שאתה מנהיגו, "Woe to the generation whose leader thou art" (Talmud Babli Berachoth 36).

19. Rabbi Eliezer had often reminded Akibah of his former occupation, which was that of a cattle herder, by saying, "Thou hast not demonstrated to me thy fitness of even herding cattle," ועדיין לא הגעת לרועי בקר. Akibah took the rebuke good-naturedly, and said, "No, I am not fit even to herd sheep" ואפילו לרועי צאן (Talmud Babli Yebamoth 16).

20. A later hand evidently added the words, ועדיין מטין ועומדין, "And they have remained in the same bent position." There is no doubt but that this is a mere figure of speech; for Roman legions soon after swept over the country and destroyed every school in the land and nearly every Jewish home as well. But the two divisions in Israel have remained unto this day. There are even now many who waver between the parties, and are loth to identify themselves with either the zealots or with those who have foresworn the ancient faith altogether. These remain religiously inert until awakened by a force with which they had thitherto not reckoned.

21. Exodus XIII, 2.

22. Talmud Babli Baba Metziah 59 *a*.
23. Talmud Jerusalemi Pesachim VI, 4.
24. Ibidem.
25. אדם שאינו הגון. "An improper person" might readily confound the decisions, and thus bring chaos where order was desired most. For it was necessary to report to Eliezer the whole proceedings, and as an ignorant person could not possibly give an accurate rendition, people might say, the Rabbis condemned Eliezer unjustly. Akibah particularly desired to lessen the shock to his Master and take the cruel sting from the awful message. It was no small matter, this anathemizing so great a man as Rabbi Eliezer, the most learned and the most pious man in Israel of that day. And though the ban was conditioned upon recantation, Akibah rightly feared that the shock might prove fatal to Eliezer's life, in which case a whole world of learning would be destroyed, ונמצא מחריב את כל העולם כלו. The Rabbis accorded as great a veneration to the person of the scholar as to his learning, and the later Rabbis, disregarding the causes of this unfortunate occurrence, give unstinted praise to Rabbi Eliezer, משמת רבי אליעזר נגנז ספר תורה. "With the death of Rabbi Eliezer the book of the law was hidden," they say (Rabbi Sotah 49). Their utmost severity is directed against Akibah, who, they say, "deserved to be burned by the fire of God for bearing to the great Rabbi the tidings of the ban," תלמיד אחד היה לו לר״א שנתחייב שריפה למקום. The expression שנתחייב שריפה למקום is not quite clear. If Akibah did his simple duty, why should he have merited punishment, and meriting punishment, why should it have been that of immolation (שריפה)? But in this seeming censure of the Rabbis there is at once expressed the high degree of Akibah's worth, and of the even greater worth of Rabbi Eliezer. So holy was the latter that none but an angel should have borne the message of his ban to him. In usurping to himself the right of an angel, Akibah became subject to the conditions governing a "service angel." The service angels are created in the fire stream (Nehar di Nur) for service unto

Jehovah and perish immediately after their work is accomplished, being engulfed in the Nehar di Nur (see Hagigah 13). Akibah, therefore, should have been burned by the heavenly fire. That which saved him was the distinction of having served and studied under Rabbi Eliezer. As such his physical condition became superior to that of a service angel, and his life was spared. "Leave him alone," the word went forth, "he hath served a great man," אמרו הניחו לו אדם גדול שימש (see Talmud Babli Erubin 54 *a*).

26. Talmud Babli Baba Metziah 59.
27. Ibidem Baba Kama 91.
28. Patristic Chapters II, 16.
29. Talmud Babli Sotah 48. The words, כל מי שיש לו פת בסלו, "He who hath bread in his basket," etc., seem to come from the same source whence came those lustrous sentences reported by Matthew (6, 26), "Behold the birds of the heaven, that they sow not, neither do they reap, nor gather into barns; and your heavenly Father feedeth them. Are ye not of much more value than they?" ... "Consider the lilies of the field, how they grow; they toil not, neither do they spin, yet I say unto you, that even Solomon in all his glory was not arrayed like one of these. But if God doth so clothe the grass of the field, which to-day is, and to-morrow is cast into the oven, shall he not much more clothe you, O ye of little faith?"

The utterances of Rabbi Eliezer and those of Jesus seem more than a coincidence, they are wonderfully alike, they could not be more so, in aim at least, if uttered by the same person or by one who was on terms of familiarity with the person and his thoughts. Did Eliezer repeat authentic utterances? It is more than probable. His master, Ben Zakkai, came upon the scene less than half a century after the birth of Christ; he knew; he had heard from eye-witnesses of the Man of Galilee. But it was a matter over which careful men spoke in hints and whispers, and the diplomatic Ben Zakkai was the last person to express himself in terms that would remind of Jesus or which might be construed as betraying a leaning toward the doctrines of the "Minim" (Christians). Eliezer, on the other hand, had no diplomatic considerations. In fact, he may have looked upon his excommunication as an unjust act equal to the condemnation of Christ by the Sadducees. To him the life, words, acts and sufferings of Jesus were intensely significant. He associated with the followers of Christ; he was, in fact, one of them, and he did not hesitate to promulgate doctrines which he thought fair and noble. It is not strange, therefore, to find him repeat almost verbatim the words of Jesus. If we compare a few of the maxims of Eliezer with the words of Christ, we are at once struck with their wonderful similarity, and no sane person will assert that Jesus repeated what Eliezer had said. Thus we find that Jesus warns against the putting away of a wife for any cause other than adultery (Matt. 5, 32), and in another place he praises the institution of marriage as a divine injunction. Rabbi Eliezer is ready with the same thought, in almost the same words, כל שאינו עוסק בפריה ורביה כאלו שופך דמים, "He who puts away his wife, and liveth not with her in accordance with the Law of God (and the law of nature), is as one who sheds (human) blood" (Babli Yebamoth 63). Jesus preaches forgiveness of sin, bliss of Paradise for the righteous and the repentant sinner, but punishment for the non-repentant. Eliezer says, "In the coming world the Lord will sit in the circle of the righteous, who will point with their finger at him, saying, 'He is our God, our hope and our salvation'" (Babli Taanith 31). And again (Shebuoth 39), "Those who repent, the Lord will cleanse; but he will not cleanse those who do not repent," ינקה לשבים לא ינקה לאינו שבים. Jesus condemns set phrases of prayers and showy devotion (Matt. 6, 5). Eliezer holds that prayers at set times and in public, spoken in set phrases, are not devotion, העושה תפלתו קבע אין תפלתו תחנונים (Berachoth 29). Jesus praises a heathen in whose heart the faith has taken firm root, holding that salvation is to be universal to those who come to God with a contrite heart. Eliezer says, "The dispersion of Israel was for the purpose of increasing the number of converts to the faith in the God of Israel," לא הגלה ישראל אלא כדי שיתוספו עליהם גרים (Pesachim 87). In another place (Kiddushin 31, 32), Eliezer tells of the filial devotion of a heathen who would not disturb his father's sleep, though by doing so he might have gained a large sum of money. Obviously Eliezer had found no such devotion to the Lord's commandment among the Israelites. Does not this strikingly remind of the words of Jesus, "Verily I say unto you, I have not found so great faith, no, not in Israel" (Matt. 8, 10)? And so these analogies run through the Talmud like a sparkling, murmuring brook 'midst green meadows. And if we follow the brook to its source, we are brought face to face with facts which set at rest many doubts, principal amongst which is the question as to the "Sermon on the Mount." Jesus actually delivered that wonderful form of divine truth in his own matchless manner, and while some of the thoughts had been with the learned men in Israel long before him, none had ever given or sought to give them as compactly and concisely and with such force as Jesus. Some gifted person had retained the form and context and repeated them to others. Ben Zakkai knew them, and Eliezer, through close contact with the Christians, absorbed them so thoroughly that he embodied most of them in his discourses. (Conf. what we wrote on this subject in Chapter II.)

30. The expression, אחד מתלמידי ישי הנוצרי, "one of the disciples of Jesus of Nazareth," does not necessarily mean that James (or Jacobus) was an immediate disciple of Christ; but in the sentence following that passage the expression is found, כך לימדני ישו הנוצרי, "thus taught me Jesus of Nazareth," and this certainly points to a personal intercourse with Christ. The non-expurgated editions of the Talmud and the En Yacobh have these references in full (vide Babli Abodah Zarah 17, edition 1520; En Yacobh II, p. 348, ed. 1415; Hagadoth ha-Talmud ad loco, ed. 1511, and in the En Yacobh, ed. Saloniki), the close contact of James with Jesus is emphasized by the words, כך אמר לי ישו הנוצרי, "So was I told by Jesus of Nazareth"; conf. also the Midrash Rabba Koheleth (ed. 1519),

where the term משום ישו is found and points to the authenticity of the words of James.

31. Midrash Rabba Genesis, div. 13; Talmud Jerusalemi Sanhedrin, div. VII.

32. Talmud Babli Abodah Zarah 16 and 17.

33. Ibidem.

34. The Talmudic commentators are sorely perplexed regarding the identity of the person designated as פלוני, "Somebody"; some believe him to be identical with Absalom, the rebellious son of David; others think it is Solomon, who had fallen from grace and whom they would not mention by name. Even Balaam and Titus come under speculative consideration. The truth of the matter is, the Rabbis of those days did mention the name of Jesus, and men like Eliezer and others had no hesitancy in referring to him by his name. Later the times and with them the sentiment changed, and some of the copyists substituted the pseudonym for Jesus. There are several such pseudonyms for Jesus, the "John Doe" terms, as it were; but the students had not the least doubt as to who the person so designated was. This fiction was resorted to by the Rabbis partly out of fear for the super-sensitive censor of Christian governments, to whom the "Jesus" in a Hebrew book seemed placed for blasphemy. The Jewish people had suffered so much at the hands of Christians in the name of Jesus that the name became significant of horror, and Jewish scholars refrained from mentioning it in their discussions (see Josts Geschichte des Judenthums und seiner Secten, Vol. I, p. 394). The question asked by the visiting Rabbis, whether "Peloni" had a share in the bliss of Paradise, certainly points to Jesus. Had they meant any other person Eliezer would not have evaded the question. But in his state of mind he was unwilling to give a definite answer.

35. Tosephtah Yebamoth III, 3; Talmud Babli Yoma 66 *a*.
36. Talmud Babli Sanhedrin 68 *b*.
37. Talmud Jerusalemi Sotah, at the end.
38. Talmud Babli Gittin 63.

CHAPTER VI

1. Talmud Babli Berachoth 27; Bechoroth 36.
2. Aboth de Rabbi Nathan 14.
3. Talmud Jerusalemi Yebamoth 3.
4. Talmud Babli Berachoth 58.
5. Ibidem Megillah 3.
6. Ibidem Pesachim 49. Aaron, the brother of Moses, was the ancestor of the priests.
7. Ibidem Kethuboth 12 and 13; ibidem Sotah 20.
8. Ibidem Sabbath 153; Jerusalemi Sabbath I, 6; Babli Abodah Zara 61; ibidem Baba Bathrah 60.
9. Babli Berachoth gives the impression that it was Akibah who assisted against Josua; but ibidem 28 it is stated that Simon ben Yohai, a disciple of Akibah, asked the question. The chances are that master and disciple had an understanding in the matter, to down Josua.
10. Ibidem Berachoth 27; Jerusalemi Bechoroth 36.
11. See supra.
12. Talmud Babli Pesachim 53.
13. Ibidem Taanith 7.
14. Megillath Taanith XII, 29.
15. Tosephtah 'Hagigah.
16. Ibidem.
17. Midrash Rabba Genesis div. 64.
18. Koheleth IX, 4.
19. Midrash Rabba Esther at the end.
20. Spart X, 11. Hadrian was afraid of the Parthians, and in order to prevent them from going to war with the Romans, he conceded to them two provinces.
21. We shall not repeat here the talmudical form, which though surpassing in poetic grace, must of necessity be substituted by our less perfect rendition. We refer the reader to either the original, Talmud Babli Chulin 59 and 60, or to Winter and Wuensche's excellent translation of these passages

in the German language (Geschichte der Jüdischen Literatur, Vol. I, p. 344).

22. Script. hist. Augusti, by Flavius Popiscus; Midrash Rabba Genesis div. 64.

23. Talmud Babli Bechoroth 8 and 9.

24. The Romans called the rebellious Hebrews, particularly the terrible Siccarees, snakes. Conf. also Chapter III, this volume.

25. We call attention to the fact that this conversation took place before the Bar Kochba revolution, about the year 123 A.C. The rebellion, started about 131 A.C., lasted a little over two years. This would bring Rabbi Josua's answer very near an exact statement of facts, namely that the Hebrews could not get on a war footing short of seven years. Hadrian's information was that the rebellion would take place in a shorter time. He did not believe it, because when he visited Syria a year or two before he had found everything in perfect order and so reported to the Senate (see Chapter VII). Did Rabbi Josua seek to mislead him by telling him the truth? We think so.

26. Rashi Bechoroth 8.

27. The text contains the expression אָמַר שֵׁם, "he uttered the tetragrammaton," by means of which he flew into the air. But in our presentation we have followed the commentator "M'harsha," who lays special stress upon the fact that "the Rabbi fought the battle of Israel's faith against the heathen philosophers, and that there was no folly in his speech," לא היה מוסר נפשו על דברי ריק והבל אלא בא לווכח עמהם בענין אמונתינו (M'harsha to Bechoroth 8).

28. Babli Berachoth 9.

29. Ibidem Bechoroth 9 *a*.

30. Midrash Rabba Echah XLIII. 4.

31. Ibidem.

32. Talmud Jerusalemi Sanhedrin IV.

33. Ibidem.

34. Talmud Babli Chulin 59.

35. Ibidem Yebamoth 87; Maaser Sheni div. 2 at the end.
36. Midrash Rabbi Genesis, div, 61.
37. Ibidem Leviticus, div. 34.
38. In the utterances of Rabbi Josua is found a remarkable similarity to those of Eliezer with whom he holds that one should have faith in God's Providence for sustenance (מאן דיהיב חיא יהיב מזאני). Evidently both men drank at the same fountain, one sooner, the other later.
39. Talmud Babli Sanhedrin 99; Tosephta Oheloth div. 16.
40. Ibidem Pesachim 68.
41. Ibidem Sotah 20 (פרוש מדוכיא—חסיד שוטה).
42. Ibidem Sanhedrin 105; Tosephta Sanhedrin div. 13.
43. Talmud Babli 'Hagigah 3 a; Aboth de Rabbi Nathan div. 18.
44. Ibidem 'Hagigah 5 (מה תהוי לן ממינין).
45. See Chapter X, this work.
46. Talmud Babli 'Hagigah 3 a; Aboth de Rabbi Nathan div. 18.
47. Ibidem Sotah 49 (משמת ר׳׳יהושע בטלה עצה ומחשבה).

CHAPTER VII

1. Talmud Babli Berachoth 58, "All the sages in Israel are like peelings of garlic in comparison with this bald one, and he is Rabbi Akibah son of Joseph, and his father was a righteous proselyte." (כל חכמי ישראל לפני כלקופת השום חוץ ממקרח זה והוא רבי עקיבא בן יוסף ואביו היה גר צדק).
2. Talmud Babli Pesachim 49.
3. Ibidem Nazir 35.
4. Ibidem Kethuboth 62; Nedarim 50.
5. She married him on condition that he become a student of the Rabbi (Eliezer ben Hyrkanos) אי מקדשנא לך אזלת לבי רב, and upon his promise she lived with him secretly, איקדשה

לי בצינעא. The marriage was legal, since the consideration might have been money, contract or coition, כסף שטר or ביאה. The knowledge of this fact caused Rachel's father to drive her from his house (Babli Kethuboth 62). The version in Nedarin 50 differs from the above in one particular. There it is said that she betrothed herself to him, איתקדשת ליה, and after her expulsion from her father's house went to live with Akibah, ואיתנסיבה ליה, consummating the marriage in legal form, גמרה ומקנה ליה נפשה (comp. Babli Kiddushin 3 a and Ibidem 8 b).

6. Talmud Jerusalem Sabbath IV, I.

7. The "Golden City" (עיר של זהב) was evidently a very large golden medallion on which in bas-relief were the pictures of Jerusalem and the Temple, brilliant with many precious jewels. This was worn upon the breast pendent from a golden chain around the neck. It was this jewel that excited the envy of Gamaliel's wife. This jewel was a mark of distinction, and was worn only by those who had merited the "Crown of the Law." By her devotion, Rachel had given to Israel a great Master of the Law and was therefore worthy to wear the "Golden City." This explanation seems to be confirmed by Nedarin 50, where the expression עיר של זהב is found instead of ירושלים דדהבא. Or is Akibah's promise to his wife indicative of his future revolutionary activity, of the time when a revolutionary coin—מטבע מרוד—shall have its value, Jerusalem be a city of gold, and Rachel a princess in Israel? Who could adequately measure the plans and ambitions of this strange character of that day?

8. The historian Graetz is wrong in stating that Akibah studied first under Nahum of Gimsu and then under Eliezer. Nahum's school was of a higher order. There the latest decisions were discussed, and a certain independent exegetical exposition taught for which a preparatory knowledge of the traditional law was required, and this Akibah could have gotten only in Eliezer's school. Afterwards he attended the lectures of Nahum, from whom he learned the method of apply-

ing certain grammatical rules in the explanation of Holy Writ. He then joined the two systems which constitute the characteristic features of his work. (Comp. Yebamoth 16; Josts Geschichte des Judenthums und seiner Secten, Vol II, p. 59.)

9. Talmud Babli Yebamoth 16.
10. Midrash Rabba Song of Songs I, 3.
11. Ibidem.
12. "With whom dost thou busy thyself?" מי מעכב על ידך.
13. שעתיד לדרוש על כל קוץ וקוץ תילין תילין של הלכות.
14. Talmud Babli Nazir 35.
15. Talmud Babli Yebamoth 62 speaks of three hundred disciples, while Nedarin 50 and Kethuboth 62 give the number of disciples that accompanied Akibah as twelve thousand. The latter statement seems impossible from the fact that such an army would have excited the suspicion of Rome and caused the instant arrest of Akibah. The references, therefore, must mean that Akibah had that many sympathizers, men he had prepared for the coming struggle with Rome.

16. From the Talmudic texts it is impossible to ascertain (without correction of the reading) the exact number of years Akibah studied at either of the schools. The historian Jost (Geschichte des Judenthums und seiner Secten, Vol. II, p. 59), maintains a lofty silence on this point. Perhaps he did not know and therefore did not attempt to draw the matter under historical consideration. The historian Graetz (History of the Jews, Vol. II, p. 351–352, English translation), assuming it to be of importance regarding the revolutionary activity of Akibah, refuses to accept the authority of 'Hagigah 12, where it is stated that he studied twenty-two years. There the number is given in the figures כ״ב שנים. But, according to Kethuboth 62, Akibah spent "twice ten years" (תרי סרי שנין) at each of the schools. Assuming that there is a mistake in the text, and that תרי סרי stands for תריסר, which is twelve, it would be incorrect grammatically, since תריסר is masculine and סרי is feminine, as is also שנין. The only place where Abikah's period of study at each school is given as twelve

years is found in Nedarim 50, תרתי סרי שנין, is more accurate. But how reconcile the different readings? I am inclined to look upon the figure סרי as a Rabbinical interpolation to exaggerate the constancy between Rachel and Akibah, and that the text should properly read תרתי שנין, "two years." For if we consider that Akibah went to Jerusalem about fifteen years before the destruction of the second Temple, how could he have studied twenty-two years in the holy city? How could he, after another twenty-two years, receive the greater part of the vast estate of Calbah Shebuah? For even if the latter survived the attack of the Roman destroyer, which is doubtful, there was no fortune left to him. He had no ships richly laden in the harhor, mention of which is made in the Talmud (Jerusalemi Nedarin 50). Whereas if Akibah had studied two years at each school and then returned a famous scholar, which, considering his fine mind, is quite possible, he would have found his father-in-law in possession of his great wealth. Besides, no man could have been active for nearly half a century, as Akibah is said to have been, and not be known to Calbah Shebuah, who hearing of his son-in-law's acquired fame would have hastened to take him to his heart.

17. Nahum was from the town of Gimsu, but was styled "Gamsu" because of his saying. (Talmud Babli Taanith 21.)

18. See Supra.

19. The expression גם זו לטובה seems to me to be the watchword of a class stoicism, more fatalistic than of pious resignation. It was just such a motto that was needed to encourage the supreme effort for the unequal struggle and fortify the patriots against torture and death; that is, "come what may, we will fight for freedom."

20. Talmud Babli Taanith 21; ibidem Sanhedrin 108; Jerusalemi Peah 88.

21. Talmud Babli 'Hagigah 12; Midrash Rabba Genesis I, 1.

22. Talmud Babli Nedarim 50.

23. Evidently Calbah Shebuah lived a secluded life in his

palace in the same town where his daughter lived in a hovel. The text has the word למתא, which means a small place. If it had been in the holy city itself, the word ירושלים would have been mentioned.

24. Talmud Babli Nedarin 50; ibidem Kethuboth 62.
25. Ibidem Zebachim 13; Tosephta to Sanhedrin div. 1.
26. Talmud Jerusalemi Shebiith V, 7.
27. Ibidem Nedarin IX, 5.
28. Ibidem Baba Kama VIII, 6.
29. Ibidem Nedarim IX, 5.
30. Patristric Chapters III, 13–16. There were evidently some Rabbis who objected to this rule, and one of them told a fine bit of satire against Akibah, who often jested about those unable to control their passions. One day, so the legend runs, Satan, in the form of a beautiful woman, approached Rabbi Akibah, to seduce him to sin. Akibah was seized with sinful desires and followed Satan. When they had gone some distance the seducer revealed his identity and said, "If the heavenly hosts had not enjoined upon me to spare thee for the sake of thy learning, I should have made of thy blood two running wells, שויתיה לדמך תרתין מעי; that is, I should have exposed thee to public ridicule and killed thee morally." (Talmud Babli Kiddushin 81.)

31. Patristic Chapters III, 13.
32. Ibidem III, 15.
33. Ibidem III, 18.
34. It was a great effort, and was called by Akibah's contemporaries "Mishnayoth de Rabbi Akibah," also "Middoth de Rabdi Akibah." This system was later adopted by all other writers, notaby Rabbi Juda, the Prince.
35. Talmud Jerusalemi Shekalim V, 1.
36. The word פרדס is held to be the Notarikon or initials of the words פרוש (plain interpretation), רמז (hint, an explanation based upon the intrinsic value, either in position or in numeric value of a letter or word, and is also termed נמטריא (geometric), דרוש (exegesis or homiletical explanation), and סוד

(secret or mystic interpretation) to which belongs the cabalistic form of placing the scattered letters of the Tetragrammaton, by means of which the adepts were thought to be able to perform miracles.

37. Talmud Babli 'Hagigah 14.
38. See "Josua ben Hananiah."
39. Talmud Babli Abodah Zara 55.
40. ההיא מתא seems to indicate some strategic point of the Romans, probably a town near a Roman camp.
41. כל דעביד רחמנא לטב עביד.
42. Talmud Babli Berachoth 60.
43. Ibidem Abodah Zara 54.
44. Ibidem 55.
45. Ibidem Sabbath 8.
46. Ibidem Baba Kama 113.
47. See "Josua ben 'Hananiah."
48. Talmud Babli Baba Bathra 10.
49. Talmud Babli Abodah Zara 20, שחק דעתידה למיניירה ונסוב לה; comp. Seder ha-Doroth ad loco.
50. Conversions of Romans to Judaism were not at all rare. Poppæa, the wife of Nero, was a Jewess, and was buried by that Emperor in accordance with Jewish rites (Tacitus Annalium Lib. XVI, 6, "Post finem ludicri, Poppæa mortem obiit... Corpus non igni abolitum, ut Romanus mos; sed regum externorum consuetudine, dissertum odoribus conditur, tumuloque Iuliorum insertur." Juvenal says, "They listen to the whisperings of old Jews, to the mumblings of old Jewesses, with devout attention" (VI, 541). "Those whom dreams have made anxious, seek consolation in the Jewish religion" (ibidem 544).
51. Talmud Babli Nedarin 66.
52. Talmud Jerusalemi Rosh ha-Shanah 56.
53. The Rabbinical legend of Bar Kochba's origin is very curious. According to it the Jewish leader was the child of a princess in Arabia of Jewish race as well as her husband, though both were black in color. The child, however, was

born white. The Moorish prince suspected his wife of infidelity, and debated whether he ought not to put both her and the child to death. Hadrian, before becoming Emperor, had been Governor of Syria and had visited the Jewish prince's house, and possibly had been unduly intimate with his wife. Still the Moor hesitated, and he consulted Akibah, who at the time happened to come to his house, as to what he ought to believe. The Rabbi was struck with the possible political advantages to be realized for his own plans from control of a son of the proudest house of Rome. Such a one, trained in the wild life of the desert, might become a suitable leader in mature life for his adopted countrymen against the Roman legions. His crafty mind soon suggested how this might be done, even while the distracted Moor was urgently asking what he thought. It was commonly said of him that he could find a reason for anything, and on this occasion he found a plausible one for the appearance of a white infant in a darkskinned household.

He asked if there were perchance statues or pictures of white color in the royal bedchamber, and when the Moor replied there were, the Rabbi quoted Jacob's stratagem for making Laban's sheep bring forth white or spotted sheep at his will. The simple warrior accepted the explanation and reared the boy as his own. When grown to manhood his mother, who possibly had been so instructed beforehand, sent her son to Akibah, whose plot was then ripe for an outbreak in Judea.

Akibah's keen vision at once recognized in him, who combined with gigantic physical powers a fervent patriotism implanted by his mother's teachings, a fitting leader for the Jewish rebels. He brought him out before the people as their heaven-sent leader, and the people obeyed his word.

The Unknown demanded a test of their sincerity. He required that all who were ready to go forth to battle should show their indifference to pain by cutting off a finger on the right hand of each. Two hundred thousand at once complied. Then the elder men remonstrated that it was not well to maim soldiers. They suggested that instead of mutilation each recruit should be required to tear a young cedar up by the roots as a test. Two hundred thousand more tore up cedars and piled them before their leader.

It may well be that people asked who is this man whom Akibah, the foremost sage in Israel, so honors? What is his name? Whence does he come? Akibah's answer silenced these inquiries as he had silenced the jealous fears of the Moorish prince. His name was Bar Kochba, the Son of the Star, the Star of Jacob, come according to prophecy to crush the enemies of the Lord and his people, the Messiah. It was enough to know that the "Star of Jacob" had arisen and to obey him. The Messiah had no birthplace; he needed no name; for all Holy Names were his.

None ventured to question this decree of the greatest sage in Israel, especially at a time when the coolest were throbbing with the hope of national freedom and glory. The people accepted the leader, though he looked rather a demi-god of the heathen pantheon than a Hebrew.

Some there were who knew Hadrian, and wondered in their hearts at the resemblance between the Roman persecutor and the supposed Messiah. Their suspicions spread among the people.

Bar Kochba was neither morally nor intellectually great. He was only a splendid warrior, fierce of soul, mighty of frame. When his power decayed the people began to call him not Son of the Star, Bar Kochba, but Son of Lies — Bar Kozeba. Akibah may well have reflected how much of truth was in the popular name; for was not Hadrian to himself the very Arch-Liar who had broken all promises to Israel?

In years long afterwards, when the aspiration for national independence had been long quenched in Jewish breasts, a man arose in the Council of Israel which still maintained a precarious authority under Roman rule. This was Rabbi Judah, the Prince, the lineal descendant of Hillel. Judah placed the solemn ban on any Jew who should henceforth presume to appropriate to mortal the title of "Star of Jacob" (see Midrash Rabba Genesis, Parshah 75; ibidem Numbers chapter V; ibidem Lamentations II, 2; Talmud Babli Gittin 57).

54. דרך כוכב מיעקב.
55. See Dio Cassius I, 69.
55 *a*. Midrash Rabba Echah II, 2, אל תקרי כוכב אלא כוזב.
55 *b*. Talmud Babli Sanhedrin 74, וחי בהם ואל שימות בהם.
56. Ibidem Berachoth 61; ibidem Pesachim 112.
57. Ibidem Berachoth 61.
58. Ibidem Berachoth 16. "With all thy soul, even if thy soul be taken from thee on account thereof." בכל נפשך אפילו נוטל את נפשך.
59. Ibidem.
60. "Monuments are not erected over the graves of the righteous; their sayings are their monuments." אין עושים נפשות לצדיקים דבריהם הם זכרונם (Midrash Rabba Genesis div. 82).
61. Ibidem div. 23.
62. גדולה מלאכה שמכבדת בעליה. Comp. Aboth de Rabbi Nathan div. II.
63. Talmud Babli Baba Metziah 62.
64. Ibidem.
65. Ibidem Yoma 85. This utterance is enhanced by the further statement that the sinner is not he who transgresses against the personality of the deity, by philosophical speculation, but he who sins against man by unkindness and injustice. The former finds forgiveness, if he seeks it, on the day of Atonement, יום הכפורים מכפר. The latter, that is he who offends his fellow-man, must ask his pardon ere he can hope to be forgiven, עד שירצה את חבירו.
66. Talmud Babli 'Hagigah 15.
67. Ibidem Sotah 17.
68. Ibidem Sanhedrin 77.
69. Aboth de Rabbi Nathan III.
70. Tosephta Berachoth 58.
71. Talmud Babli Kethuboth 62. Rabbi Akibah's daughter imitated the self-sacrifice of her mother for the sake of the

Law, living alone while her husband, Ben Azzai, devoted himself to study, ברתיה דרבי עקיבא עבדא ליה לבן עזאי הכי והיינו דאמרו אינשי רחילא בתר רחילא אזלא כעובדי אמה כך עובדי ברתא.

CHAPTER VIII

1. Talmud Babli 'Hagigah 15, משמת רבי עקיבא בטלו זרועי תורה ונסתתמו מעיני החכמה.
2. It is not certain what was his real name. Mair was merely titular and signified that he was "an Enlightener." He was also referred to by the Chaldaic-speaking Rabbis as "Nehorai," which also means a bearer of light, one who had intellectual ability to explain the Law. רבי מאיר היה נקרא גם (Talmud בן רבי נהוראי שהיה מנהיר עיני תלמידי חכמים בהלכה Babli Sabbath 147; ibidem, Erubin 13).
3. Ibidem Gittin 57; Tacitus historia I, 2; ibid. II, 8.
4. Rabbi Mair derives the word סורו (Lamentations 4, 15) from the Greek συρείν, to pull, to drag away (Midrash Rabba, Leviticus, chapter 14, 2).
5. Talmud Babli Erubin 13, שהוא אומר על טמא טהור ומראה לו פנים ועל טהור טמא ומראה לו פנים.
6. Vide Sepher Shaarai Teshubah by Rabbi Hai Gaon.
7. Midrash Rabba Koheleth 82, לעולם ילמד אדם בנו אמנת נקייה וקלה.
8. Talmud Babli Gittin 24. He is termed לבלר (from the Latin *libellarius* a writer of books); he was an author who wrote for others; that is, he cared more for the gain than the glory.
9. Midrash Rabba Koheleth II, 18.
10. Talmud Babli Erubin 13.
11. Ibidem Sanhedrin 14.
12. Ibidem Erubin 13.
13. Ibidem Sanhedrin 24, עוקר הרי הרים וטוחנן זו בזו.

NOTES

14. The dignity of "Haham," or academic reader, was evidently instituted by Simon the son of Gamaliel II. Before that time there was but a תורגן, interpreter, and this office did not equal the dignity of Haham (see Babli Berachoth 27; comp. Jost's Geschichte des Judenthums und seiner Secten II, 110).

15. Talmud Jerusalemi Moed Katon III, 1 fol. 81 *a*.
16. Talmud Babli Baba Bathra 8.
17. There never was a time in the history of the Jews when the עם הארץ — "das Landvolk," as the German has it — was educationally superior to the teachers of the Law, from Moses down to the last of the Rabbis, yet there is no record to show that they were condemned on account of their ignorance. "Am ha-Aretz" must mean, therefore, a materialist, a sensualist, a man whose mind centered on earthly pleasures, an Epicure.
18. Talmud Jerusalemi Tehoroth VIII, 18, המניח עם הארץ בבית ישן ומצאו ער הבית טמא.
19. Talmud Babli Berachoth 17.
20. Ibidem Sanhedrin, בזמן שאדם מצטער מה אומרת שכינה מח אומרת קלני.
21. Ibidem Abodah Zara 17.
22. Ibidem Berachoth 10.
23. Ibidem.
24. Ibidem Erubin 53.
25. Ibidem.
26. Yalkut Mishleh, paragraph 963.
27. Midrash Rabba Koheleth chapter VII, 12, and with some variations in Babli Abodah Zara 18.
28. Midrash Rabba Koheleth.
29. Ibidem Genesis div. 48, עילית לקרתא הלך בנימוסיה.
30. Ibidem Koheleth IV, 3.
31. Talmud Babli Yoma 83, "שמ אדם רשע הוא שנאמר כי דור תהפוכות המה.
32. Ibidem, חלמא דבי שמשי לית בהי מששא. The Rabbis believed in dreams as significant of coming events, but

dreams which were due to indigestion, that is immediately after eating, were not considered the workings of the *alter anima*, and were not looked upon as divine inspirations.

33. The term ונטריה (from the Latin *notarius*) means "he wrote"; but may here have the double meaning of watching; while writing he also watched the house of the untrustworthy host.

34. Ibidem.
35. Ibidem, Sanhedrin 11, אמרה לו רבי אחד מכם קדשני בביאה.
36. אחדות באשה ערוה. In Babli Minachoth 44 a story is told of the same disciple quite unfit for reproduction, as it fits more readily in the Decameron of Boccaccio, though the Talmudic writers would cloak the story as if the student had withstood the temptations of Satan, the trial of a Saint.
37. The Seder ha-Doroth refers to this fact.
38. Talmud Jerusalemi Sabbath I, 5.
39. Aboth IV, 12.
40. Talmud Babli Yebamoth 121.
41. Ibidem, Sabbath 25, כל מי שיש לו נחת רוח בעישרו.
42. Ibidem Yoma 86.
43. Aboth IV, 12.
44. Midrash Rabba Koheleth I; Babli Sabbath 153.
45. Midrash Rabba Genesis div. 9.
46. Talmud Jerusalemi 'Hagigah II, 1.
47. Talmud Babli 'Hagigah 15.
48. Ibidem, אחר זמר יווני לא פסק מפומיה.
49. Ibidem 14, ארבעה נכנסו בפרדס; comp. our note to "Akibah."
50. Ibidem 15. The resemblance of Achar to Paul has been remarked by many. The difficulties of the dates are not so serious as to be an obstacle to a favorable comparison. They were not over-accurate in those days. Facts are cognizable by certain references to some remarkable personage, and persons may be identified by a consideration of certain facts. Thus we recognize the character of Paul as described in the

NOTES   305

New Testament and Achar as described in the Talmud to be one. Paul was a learned Hebrew, who said of himself that he sat at the feet of Gamaliel. But Gamaliel was a contemporary of Rabbi Yochanan ben Zakkai, at whose feet sat Achar. Both are "Inquirers"—scholars in the rabbinic academy. Both are excellent Greek scholars. Both turn from the ancient conception that the Jew must suffer on account of the sins of the fathers, must suffer on account of "Exile"; suffer in hopes of the coming of a Messiah; suffer because the Jew was a creature apart; suffer because the small men in Judea had great ambitions, and through their bickerings brought down the wrath of Rome alike upon the just and the unjust. The whole life of the Jew was made up of "don'ts," which "the coming of the Messiah would abrogate." The esthetic mind of this man—call him Paul or Achar—revolted against this thraldom, against this religion of suffering called into existence by fanatics fighting for a dead cause. The Greeks adored beauty, which made them happy. The Romans loved strength, and lived for power and glory. The character of this man Achar and this man Paul seems to stand out as one viewed from the point of their thoughts for mundane convenience. Achar rode horseback on the Sabbath. Paul permitted the eating of the food of the Gentiles. Achar, it is said, loved Greek song, so did Paul. Achar, having delved deeply into the mysteries of the metaphysics of his day, believed, as the Talmud says, in a duality of divine persons—in the *alter ego.* Paul, too, "saw" and grew firm in the faith of Jesus as the Christ. That Paul, or rather Achar, firmly believed that the faith in Jesus, the Christ, would bring happiness to the Jewish people, is certain. It is evident that Paul desired to bring about a better understanding between Hebrew and heathen. To the Hebrew, by a better appreciation of the manners of the heathens, by a less strict observance of man-made laws, a newer and a freer spirit would come. To the heathen, if he could be brought to believe in the love and mercy of God, in a faith based on vicarious atonement, a nobler and more humane consciousness would be his. Both Hebrew and heathen might join hands in the knowledge that each had conceded to the other without loss to either, and with great spiritual and material gain to both. This appears to have been the character and the aim of Achar as described in the Talmud, and this precisely is the character of Paul as described in the New Testament. These analogies are striking, but more remarkable is the fact that Paul is the only personage of those times whose name becomes conspicuous as a great interrogation-point by its absence. Christ and his apostles are mentioned in the Talmud; in places some are mentioned distinctly and by name; in others again the disciples are mentioned under the general name *Talmidai*. All, or nearly all, the Roman Emperors and the governors of Judæa are mentioned by name; all—some directly, others *sub rosa*—all, except Paul, the very creator of dogmatic Christianity. But it is our firm belief—reasoning by the deductions from the above suggestions, that Saul—who became another in faith for which he became Pau-ul—a worker—is none other than ▸Elisha, whom the Rabbis stigmatized as Achar, Another in Faith.

51. Talmud Jerusalemi Hagigah II, 1;
52. Talmud Babli Sabbath 118; ibidem Chulin 2.
53. Midrash Rabba Koheleth 7.
54. Babli 'Hagigah 15.
55. Jerusalemi Kilayim at the end.
56. Babli Sotah 49.
57. Ibidem, Hagigah 15, כי נח נפשא דרבי מאיר סלוק קוטרא מקברא דאחר.
58. Aboth IV.
59. Babli Hagigah 15.
60. Aboth IV.

CHAPTER IX

1. Talmud Babli Sanhedrin 14.
2. Ibidem Abodah Zara 8.
3. Ibidem Berachoth 32.
4. Ibidem Sanhedrin 14.
5. Ibidem Sabbath 113; Midrash Rabba Leviticus div. 34.
6. Midrash Rabba Leviticus div. 21.
7. Talmud Jerusalemi Sanhedrin div. I, 2, fol. 19, חייך שאני ובוראך מכירין כוחך.
8. Talmud Babli Gittin 67, שמדותי תרומות מתרומות מדותו של רבי עקיבא.
9. Ibidem Rosh ha-Shanah 18; Sifri to Deuteronomy div. 31.
10. Midrash Rabba Leviticus div. 21.
11. Talmud Babli Succah 21.
12. Aboth de Rabbi Nathan 18, טוחן הרבה ומוצא קמעא.
13. Ibidem; comp. Babli Gittin 67, שנה הרבה ומשכח קמעא ומה שהוא משכח סובין של משנתו.
14. Talmud Babli Sabbath 33.
15. Ibidem.
16. Ibidem; comp. Midrash Rabba Genesis div. 79,
17. Talmud Jerusalemi Sabbath fol. 3.
18. Ibidem Shebbiith fol. 9.
19. Graetz, Geschichte, etc., Vol. IV, p. 492.
20. Talmud Babli Sabbath 33*b* and 34*a* says that the Prophet Elijah appeared at the mouth of the cave and told them that the Roman Emperor had died. The simple fact may be that Eleazer, who lived less secluded, had brought the news of the accession to the throne of Marcus Aurelius, and that it was now safe to return.
21. Ibidem Berachoth 31, אסור לאדם למלאות פיו שחוק בעולם הזה.
22. Ibidem Sabbath 33. Here we have another remarkable analogy to the words of Christ; comp. Matt. 10, 29.

23. Talmud Babli Sabbath 33.
24. Talmud Jerusalemi Shebiith 9.
25. Talmud Babli Sabbath 33.
26. Midrash Rabba Numbers div. 52.
27. Talmud Babli Sabbath 33.
28. Talmud Jerusalemi Shebiith 9, שמעת שטבריה עתידה ליטהר.
29. Talmud Babli Yoma 57. The Emperor's daughter mentioned here was the beautiful Lucilla, afterwards the wife of Verus. Jost (Geschichte des Judenthums und seiner Secten, Vol. II, p. 93, note) mentions Christian sources according to which this miracle was performed by Papis, the Bishop of Hierapolis.
30. Talmud Babli Megillah 12.
31. Ibidem Succah 30.
32. Midrash Rabba Genesis div. 86.
33. "Patristic Chapters."
34. Talmud Babli Sabbath 113.
35. Ibidem 118.
36. Midrash Rabba Leviticus div. 19.
37. "Patristic Chapters" III, 7.
38. Talmud Babli Berachoth 7, גדול שמושה של תורה יותר מלמודה; compare the maxim in the Patristic Chapters, ולא המדרש העיקר אלא המעשה—the principle of human effort is not centered in theorizing, but in practical righteousness.
39. Talmud Babli Baba Metziah 58.
40. Ibidem Berachoth 31, אסור לאדם למלאות פיו שחוק. The word שחוק means frivolous jest; "a loud laughter bespeaks a vacant mind."
41. The term יראת השמים must be understood in the sense of "love of Heaven," in contradistinction to the term יראת חטא, which means "fear of sin."
42. Talmud Jerusalemi Peah I.
43. Talmud Babli Pesachim 87.
44. Ibidem Baba Metziah 58.
45. Ibidem Kethuboth 67.

46. Ibidem Sotah 32.
47. Ibidem.
48. Where business is not the aim but the end of human effort, it is sinful.
49. Talmud Babli Sotah 32. This bit of sarcasm, keen and well applied, refers to the Patriarch Simon ben Gamaliel, who was proud of his position without having commensurate knowledge.
50. Midrash Rabba Numbers div. 11.
51. Ibidem Koheleth.
52. Talmud Babli Nedarin 49.
53. Aboth de Rabbi Nathan 50.
54. Talmud Babli Berachoth 55.
56. Midrash Rabba "Song of Songs."
57. Talmud Babli Baba Metziah 83.
58. Ibidem, אי צורבא מרבנן הוא וניים אקדומי קדים לגרסיה אי פועל הוא קדים קא עביד עבידתיה ואי עבידתיה בלילא רדודי רדיד ואי לא גנבא הוא ותפסיה.
59. By the term חומץ בן יין the Rabbi desired to put it to Eleazer that he was destroying the noble work of his father, who was like good old wine.
60. Talmud Babli Baba Metzia 83.
61. Ibidem.
62. Ibidem.
63. Ibidem Sanhedrin 65.
64. Midrash Rabba "Song of Songs," 6.
65. Talmud Babli Yebamoth 65.
66. Ibidem Baba Metziah 83.
67. Ibidem Yoma 85, עבירות שבין אדם לאדם אין יום הכפורים מכפר עד שירצה את חבירו.
68. Ibidem Taanith 20.
69. Ibidem Baba Metzia 83. Rabbi Samuel bar Nachmani said, "Rabbi Eleazer's wife told the mother of Rahbi Jonathan who told me, that Eleazer's body lay in the attic not less than eighteen years nor more than twenty years."
70. Ibidem.

71. Ibidem.
72. Ibidem.
73. Ibidem.
74. Ibidem.

CHAPTER X

1. Some of the writers on this subject, in the Middle Ages as well as in modern times, maintain that the Prince did not write the Mishnah, but that he compiled it mentally, and it was thus handed down from generation to generation, until the conditions in the sixth century made it necessary to commit it to writing. Their argument is based on the Talmudical principle that the oral law must not be written down, דברים שבעל פה אי אתה רשאי לאמרן בכתב (Babli Gittin 60 and Temurah 14). While others, like Maimonides, Samuel ha-Nagid, Rabenu Nissim, in the Middle Ages, and Geiger, Zacharias Frankel and I. H. Weiss in his excellent work Dor Dor ve-Dorshov (III, 244), hold that the Prince did write the Mishnah. We think this the correct opinion.

2. Talmud Babli Berachoth 28, כל תלמיד שאין תוכו כברו אל יכנס.

3. Ibidem Kiddushin 72. Akibah was executed in the year 137 A.C.

4. Ibidem Meilah 17.
5. Ibidem Rosh ha-Shanah 25 and 26.
6. Ibidem 26 *b* and Megillah 18.
7. Ibidem Pesachim 41 ; Baba Kamma 82.
8. Ibidem Pesachim 94; Yoma 25.
9. Ibidem Yebamoth 84; Menachoth 18; Erubin 13 ; Megillah 20; Shebuoth 13 ; Sabbath 147.
10. Talmud Jerusalemi Kilayim IX, 4. The Prince of the Captivity was of the tribe of Judah and from the male line of David, while Rabbi Juda was of the tribe of Benjamin and from the female line.

11. Ibidem.
12. Ibidem.
13. Talmud Babli Sanhedrin 38.
14. Ibidem Kethuboth 25 and 27; Taanith 17.
15. Ibidem Sabbath 11.
16. Ibidem.
17. Mechilta to Parshah Bo div. 18.
18. Patristic Chapters II, 1.
19. הלכה כרבי מחביריו; see Mebho ha-Talmud.
20. Talmud Jerusalemi Megillah I, 7; Babli Megillah 5.
21. Jerusalemi Kethuboth II, 6; Babli Megillah 22.
22. Talmud Babli Sanhedrin 5.
23. Ibidem Berachoth 30.
24. Ibidem Sabbath 46 and 48; Betzah 26.
25. Ibidem Taanith 14.
26. Ibidem Yebamoth 64.
27. Ibidem; Baba Bathrah 90; Yoma 83; Pesachim 90.
28. Ibidem Kethuboth 110.
29. There is no such book; but Samuel tried to show the Prince that he understood the motive clearly.
30. Talmud Babli Sanhedrin 5, אני מכירך זקן.
31. Ibidem Chulin 6. The Prince permitted bathing on certain fast days and the performance of labor on certain festivals (Megillah 5). He released farmers from paying tithes and stopping work on the Year of Rest (Shemitah) where certain lands were not formerly a part of the Holy Land.
32. Ibidem.
33. The Nethinim were of Gentile origin or of Hebrew mothers and Gentile fathers (see Babli Yebamoth 16; Jerusalemi Kiddushin IV).
34. Talmud Babli Kiddushin 71, קוצים אתם משימין בעיני.
35. Ibidem Baba Bathra 8.
36. Ibidem Makkoth 10.
37. By Artaban is probably meant one of the Nabathean Kings, Aretas, under whom the Judæans fought against the Romans.

38. The Script (Mezuzah) was probably sent in a case of precious metal. The word פול means a husk or shell, and the Heathen saw no particular value in the gift.

39. Talmud Jerusalemi Berachoth 89.

40. Talmud Babli Chulin 87.

41. Rappaport, Krochmal, Jost and other historians are in doubt about the identity of the Emperor who was the Prince's friend. We are less concerned about the man than about the fact that such an intimacy existed. Whether all the stories are true is also of small importance. That the Heathen Emperor consulted the Jewish sage about family affairs is probable; equally probable it is that the Roman Emperor, having confidence in the wisdom of the Patriarch, spoke to him of matters of state, as Hadrian with Rabbi Josua ben Hananiah.

42. By the term "Rabbi" or Master is always meant Juda the Prince (see Maimonides, Introduction to Mishnah Zeraim).

43. Talmud Babli Sanhedrin 91.

44. Ibidem.

45. Ibidem.

46. Ibidem 27; Yebamoth 49; Hagigah 14. Mention is made of Mishnath de Rabbi Akibah, Mishnath de Rabbi Eliezer ben Yacob and the seven hundred divisions of Tanaaim.

47. The word Mishnah, משנה, is from the root שנה, and, like the Aramaic תנא, means both to repeat, teach and learn, as the word Talmud, from the root למד, means to teach and to learn.

48. The word Gamarah, גמרא, from the root גמר, means to finish or to complete, the work of the Prince.

49. The full titles of the Mishnah, its divisions and sections, are as follows:

	Name of Series	Number of Divisions
I	Zeraim (זרעים), Seeds	XI
II	Moed (מועד), Festivals	XII
III	Nashim (נשים), Women	VII
IV	Nezikin (נזיקין), Damages	X
V	Kodashim (קדשים), Sacred Things	XI
VI	Teharoth (טהרות), Purifications	XII

NOTES

I. Zeraim

	Name of Division	Number of Section
I	Berachoth (ברכות), Prayers	IX
II	Peah (פאה), Corner	VIII
III	Demai (דמאי), Uncertain	VII
IV	Kilayim (כלאים), Mixtures	IX
V	Shebiith (שביעית), Sabbath Year	X
VI	Therumoth (תרומות), Offerings	XI
VII	Maaseroth (מעשרות), Tithes	V
VIII	Maaser Sheni (מעשר שני), Second Tithe	V
IX	Challah (חלה), Dough	IV
X	Orlah (ערלה), Buds, First Fruit	III
XI	Bikkurim (בכורים), First Fruit Offering	III

II. Moed

I	Sabbath (שבת), Sabbath	XXIV
II	Erubin (ערובין), Combinations	X
III	Pesachim (פסחים), Passover	X
IV	Shekalim (שקלים), Shekels	VIII
V	Yoma (יומא), The Day	VIII
VI	Succah (סוכה), Tabernacles	VIII
VII	Betza (ביצה), The Egg	V
VIII	Rosh ha-Shana (ראש השנה), New Year	IV
IX	Taanith (תענית), Fasts	IV
X	Megillah (מגילה), The Scroll	IV
XI	Moed Katon (מועד קטן), Minor Feast	III
XII	Hagigah (חגיגה), Feast of Offering	III

III. Nashim

I	Yebamoth (יבמות), Sisters-in-law	XVI
II	Khethuboth (כתובות), Marriage Deeds	XIII
III	Nedarim (נדרים), Vows	XI
IV	Nazir (נזיר), The Nazarite	IX
V	Sota (סוטה), Adulteress	IX
VI	Gittin (גיטין), Divorces	IX
VII	Kiddushin (קדושין), Betrothals	IV

IV. Nezikin

	Name of Division	Number of Section
I	Baba Kama (בבא קמא), First Gate	X
II	Baba Metziah (בבא מציעא), Second Gate	X
III	Baba Bathra (בבא בתרא), Last Gate	X
IV	Sanhedrin (סנהדרין), Courts	XI
V	Maccoth (מכות), Stripes	III
VI	Shebuoth (שבועות), Oaths	VIII
VII	Eduyoth (עדיות), Testimonies	VIII
VIII	Aboda Zara (עבודה זרה), Idolatry	V
IX	Aboth (אבות), Fathers	V
X	Horayoth (הוריות), Decisions	III

V. Kodashim

I	Zebachim (זבחים), Sacrifices	XIV
II	Menachoth (מנחות), Meat Offering	XIII
III	Cholin (חולין), Profane Things	XII
IV	Bechoroth (בכורות), The Firstborn	IX
V	Arachin (ערכין), Estimations	IX
VI	Themura (תמורה), Exchange	VII
VII	Kherithoth (כריתות), Excisions	VI
VIII	Meila (מעילה), Trespass	VI
IX	Thamid (תמיד), Daily Sacrifice	VII
X	Middoth (מדות), Measurements	V
XI	Kinnim (קנים), The Birds' Nests	III

VI. Teharoth

I	Khelim (כלים), Vessels	XXX
II	Ohaloth (אהלות), Tents	XVIII
III	Negaim (נגעים), Leprosy	XIV
IV	Parah (פרה), The Heifer	XII
V	Teharoth (טהרות), Purifications	X
VI	Mikvaoth (מקואות), Wells	X
VII	Nidda (נדה), The Menstruous	X
VIII	Machshirin (מכשירין), Preparations	VI
IX	Zabim (זבים), Persons with Fluxes	V

NOTES 315

	Name of Division	Number of Section
X	Tebul Yom (טבול יום), Immersed	IV
XI	Yadayim (ידים), Hands	IV
XII	Uktzin (עוקצין), Stalks of Fruit	III

To each of these sections a commentary by the name of Gemara is appended, and to it again are added countless other commentaries, to which again scholars in all ages have added and are adding still glosses and comments in an apparently endless chain.

50. Teharoth, Purifications, is a Talmudical euphemism, since it really refers to matters which are sacerdotally inadmissible, hence unclean for sacred uses.

51. See Jost's Geschichte des Judenthums und seiner Secten, Vol II, p. 202.

52. Midrash Rabba Lamentations II, 2.

53. The last of the princes was Gamaliel VI, who was deposed from the princely dignity by Emperor Theodosius II., in an edict dated October the 17th, 415 A.C. (see Cod. Theodosius XIV., 22); and in a decree of 426, that same Emperor ordered the subsidies which the Patriarch received from the Roman Jewish Congregations to be paid into the imperial treasury.

The Patriarchate embraced a period of 605 years from 180 B.C. to 425 A.C. and the reigning Patriarchs were as follows:

I	Antigonus of Socho	180	B.C.
II	Yose ben Yoezer	170–162	"
III	Josua ben Perachia	130	"
IV	Juda ben Tabbai	80	"
V	Shemaiah and Abtalion	60	"
VI	Sons of Bethyrah	35	"
VII	Hillel I.	30 B.C. to 10 A.C.	
VIII	Simon I.	10 A.C. to 30 A.C.	
IX	Gamaliel I.	30–50	A.C.
X	Simon II.	50–70	"

XI	Gamaliel II.	80–116 A.C.
XII	Simon III.	140–163 "
XIII	Juda I.	163–193 "
XIV	Gamaliel III.	193–220 "
XV	Juda II.	220–270 "
XVI	Gamaliel IV.	270–300 "
XVII	Juda III.	300–330 "
XVIII	Hillel II.	330–365 "
XIX	Gamaliel V.	365–385 "
XX	Juda IV.	385–400 "
XXI	Gamaliel VI.	400–425 "

Of all these Juda the First was the Prince who gave regal grandeur to his position, so that it was said of him, "From Moses the Lawgiver to Rabbi we have not found wealth and magnificence so combined," מימות משה רבינו עד רבי לא ראינו תורה וגדולה במקום אחד (Babli Gittin 59). The Patriarchs who succeeded him enjoyed also extraordinary privileges, and had the actual rank of princes of the empire. Emperor Julian addressed Hillel II as τὸν ἀδελφὸν (brother); and Emperor Theodosius the Great openly took sides with Gamaliel V, who was in feud with a Roman Governor in Syria (see Hieronymus, De Optimo, etc.).

54. Talmud Babli Succah 26, שנתיה דרבי הויה שיתין נשמין.

55. Haninah bar Hama, in deference to Rabbi Ephes, did not accept the office until two years later, and this only after the death of Rabbi Ephes.

56. That is what we understand by the phrase, זרוק מרה בתלמידים (see Rabbi Kethuboth 103).

57. Talmud Babli Kethuboth 104.

58. Moses bar Maimon, in his introduction to the Mishnah Zeraim, gives a fine eulogy of the Prince, and styles him "Our Master, the Holy One."

BOOKS AND MONOGRAPHS BY THE SAME AUTHOR

"The Monk and the Hangman's Daughter." (A Novel.)
" A Man, a Woman and a Million." (A Novel.)
" In the Confessional and the Following." (Short Stories.)
" Labor Unions and Strikes in Ancient Rome." (Mongr.)
"The Position of Laboring Men among the Ancient Hebrews." (Mongr.)
"Jesus, the Pharisee." (Mongr.)
"Oriental Aphorisms." (Mongr.)
"Two Great Jews." (Mongr.)

WORKS READY FOR THE PRESS

" Folk Lore of the Talmud."
" The Empire of the Ghetto."
" The Ghetto Apostate." (A Novel.)
"In His Image." (A Novel.)
"Semper Idem." (A Novel.)
" The Conquest of the Señoritas." (A Novel.)
" With Men and Women." (Short Stories.)
" The Red Hand of William Wallace." (A Drama in Four Acts.)
"Valera." (A Dramatic Libretto in Three Acts.)
Etc., etc., etc., etc., etc.

INDEX.

Aaron, High Priest, 11, 15, 38, 123
Abtalion, head of Sanhedrin with Shemaiah, 20; one of his sayings, 179
Abuiah, Rabbi, father of Elisha ben Abuiah, 204
Acher, signification of, 206, 208
Adultery, test for, 60
Agadah, or *Hagadah*, the parabolic exposition of the Pentateuch, the prophets, and the historic writings, 169
Antoninus, Pius, 185; revoked edicts of Hadrian, 245; conversations with Juda the prince, 257
Aquila, Roman convert to Judaism, 123, 133
Aramaic, the, 246, 261
Artaban, king, 256
Asmoneans, *Hashmoneans*, descendants of Hashmonai the priest, 3, 4

Babylonian, the, Hillel so called, 5, 9, 20, 211
Bar Illai, Rabbi Juda, 215
Bar Kappara, 253
Bar Kochba, the false Messiah, 42, 177, 271
Ben Abuiah, Rabbi Elisha, 204; his liking for Greek language and culture, 205; branded as traitor and called "Acher," 206; renounced Judaism and probably embraced Christianity, 208; his memory, 209
Ben Akibah, Rabbi, 89; favorite disciple of Eliezer, 109; volunteer messenger, 114; visit to Eliezer, 119; eulogy of, 121; view of evening prayers, 125; not a Jew, 152; incident that determined him to study, 153; love and marriage, 154; entered the school of Eliezer, 154; his modesty, his power of analysis, 155; his ability, 156; visit to his wife, 156; rules of interpretation, 160; joined the school of Nahum of Gamsu, 161; return to

INDEX

— *Continued :*

reconciliation with his father-in-law, 163 ; de-
judge, 164 ; his maxims, 166 ; his ambition, 167 ;
.d with Mohammed, 168 ; reduced the oral law to a sys-
, 169 ; arranged the Agadah, 169 ; study of magic, 169 ; his
teachings, 172 ; revolution against Hadrian, 173 ; takes wife of
Roman governor, 175 ; presents Bar Kochba as the Messiah,
177 ; evades Roman spies, 178 ; council at Lydda, 179 ; death
by torture, 181 ; one of his sayings, 183 ; his versatility, 267

Ben Amram, Rabbi Jonathan, rebukes Juda the prince, 254

Ben Arakh, Rabbi Elazar, 71 ; a good answer, 92 ; probably became a Christian, 96

Ben Azariah, Rabbi Elazar, president of the Sanhedrin, afterwards assistant, or vice-president, 127, 128, 152

Ben Azzai, Rabbi, son-in-law of Rabbi Akibah, 170

Benai (sons of) Bethyra, 8, 9, 107, 247

Ben Babba, Rabbi Judah, member of Sanhedrin at Yamnai, 188 ; rigid observer of the law, 212 ; ordained Mair and Simon, 212 ; slain by Roman soldiers, 213

Ben Betiach, 62, 63

Ben Dosa, Rabbi 'Haninah, compared with Ben Zakkai, 73 ; an ascetic and mystic, 75 ; his sayings, 77 ; his judgments, 78 ; his wife, her desire and dream, 81 ; tales of his miraculous power, 76, 81, 82, 84, 85, 88

Ben Elisha, Rabbi Ishmael, 176

Ben Gorion, Rabbi Juda, 218, 222

Ben Hananiah, Rabbi Josua ; decision against Eliezer, 113 ; defended him after his death, 121 ; his studies and subtlety, 122 ; his engagement and its rupture, 123 ; an artisan, 124 ; president of Court of Appeals, democratic spirit, 124 ; disputes with Gamaliel, 126 ; his travels, 128 ; put down by woman, girl, and boy, 129 ; in favor with Roman emperors, 130, 133-138 ; forbidding fire for three days, 134 ; carried sixty academicians to Hadrian for a wager, 138-142 ; contest of wits, 140 ; his sayings, 148 ; relations with Christians, 149, 150 ; his death, 151

Ben 'Hiyah, Rabbi Juda, revenges his father, 248

Ben Hyrkanos, Rabbi Eliezer, a scholar, brother-in-law of Gamaliel, 96, 97 ; stubborn in his views, 96, 106 ; excommunication, 96, 113 ; application to Ben Zakkai, 97 ; his father's visit to the school, 100 ; opened school at Lydda, 103 ; his famous trial and

INDEX 321

Ben Hyrkanos, Rabbi Eliezer—*Continued:*
    appeal to the walls, 104 ; interpretation thereof, 110 ; pleads for tradition, 106, 108 ; repudiates suicide, 115 ; charged with being a Christian, 116 ; his denial, 119 ; death, 120 ; ban removed by Rabbi Josua, and burial at Lydda, 120

Ben Illai, Rabbi, 217, 218

Ben Yohai, Rabbi Simon, son of a Jew in Roman service, 213 ; friend and disciple of Akibah, 213 ; left his wife in order to study, 214 ; established a school at Thekoa, 216 ; denounced the Romans, 218 ; betrayed by spy and fled to mountains, 218 ; life in cave, 219 ; mystic power, 221, 224 ; contempt of earthly things, 223 ; opened school at Tiberias, 223 ; mission to Marcus Aurelius, 224 ; cures the emperor's daughter, 224 ; sayings and maxims, 226, 228, 229 ; form of mental activity of the Jewish race, 231 ; decision in divorce, 231 ; buried in cave, 238 (A.D. 165)

Ben Zakkai, Rabbi Yochanan, favorite disciple of Hillel and founder of modern Judaism, 13 ; diplomat and scholar, 55 ; his patience, 56 ; virtual head of Sanhedrin, 58 ; his boldness, 60 ; abolished ordeal of "bitter waters," 37, 60 ; also "red cow" offering, 60 ; opposed to insurrection, 63 ; left doomed city in coffin, 65 ; sought refuge in the emperor's camp, 66 ; got permission to found a school at Yamnai, 67 ; formed a Sanhedrin, 69 ; mourns over ruin of the Temple and prophesies a spiritual temple, 68 ; consolations at death of son, 71 ; his death, 72 ; choice of disciples, 91 ; reception of Eliezer, 97

Ben Zoma, Simon, trusted agent of Josua, 131 ; parable, 132 ; his death, 132 ; one of the four mystics, 170

Beruriah, wife of Rabbi Mair, 191 ; her skill in controversy, 192 ; the student's stratagem, 202

Bethar, fortress, 178

Bible, translated by Aquila, 123

Cabalah, 169

Caiaphas, Joseph, 45–47

Calba Sebuah, father-in-law of Rabbi Akibah, 101, 153, 162

Captivity, the ; Introduction, x. ; the prince, or exilarch, of the Babylonian Jews, 247

Christianity, a historical fact, 34 ; it is Judaism developed, 71, 117

Circumcision, 245, 252

Cyrus, king of Persia, 1

Divorce, 201, 231
Domitian, 130

Eleazar, son of Ben Yohai, 218 ; made captain of Roman soldiers, 234 ; his death and disposal of his body, 238 ; sarcasms, 246 ; Rabbi Juda's suit of his widow, 239, 272
Exilarch, title of the prince of the Babylonian Jews, 247

Gamaliel I., Rabbi, president of Sanhedrin, 53, 58
Gamaliel II., Rabbi, president of Sanhedrin, 70, 84, 104, 110, 113, 215, 244
Gamaliel III., son of Juda the prince, 272
Gate, " the Death," 65
Gemara, commentary on the Mishna, 261–268

Hadrian, emperor of Rome, 131, 133, 174, 185, 245
Herod, leaned towards Sadducees, 4 ; ruled in Palestine, 5
Halakah, the oral teaching, 94
High Priests, their policy, 4 ; riches, 6 ; indifference to learning and religion, 35 ; no political power, 38 ; one of them slain, 39 ; Joseph Caiaphas, 45 ; intruding high priests, 3, 57 ; tyranny and corruption, 61
Hillel, Rabbi : Introduction, xii ; birth, 5 ; poverty, 6 ; elected president of the Sanhedrin, 9 ; Gentile teachers, 9 ; foresaw the exile, 10, 28 ; Davidic descent, 11, 240 ; doctrines and teachings, 11, 12, 14, 17, 20, 21 ; his policy, paving the way for universal faith, 13 ; foundation for the work of Jesus Christ, 13, 29, 32, 35 ; not a reformer, 14 ; the Prosbul Act, 14, 22 ; absence of the miraculous, 15 ; story of a heathen's visit to him, 15, 18 ; cared more for good men than scholars, 21 ; his knowledge, 24 ; his patience and meekness, 24 ; prepared the people for exile, 28 ; his tact, 29 ; his death, 29 ; analogy between his teachings and those of Christ, 36 ; Hillelism, 68 ; policy of his house, 240 ; transmitted presidency to his family, 211, 244
'Hiyah, the great Babylonian, offends Juda the prince, 248
Huna, the exilarch, or prince of the captivity, 247
Hyrkan, John, High Priest, 3
Hyrkanos, visit to his son Eliezer, 100

Ishmael, Phabi, High Priest, 38, 61

INDEX 323

James, disciple of the Christ, 116, 118, 119
Jesus of Nazareth, his history, from the Talmud, 30 ; his descent, 33 ; authentic history, 34 ; an exile, 35 ; his baptism, 41 ; how he began his mission, 42 ; the people not hostile to him, 43 ; the High Priests saw danger to themselves in his mission, 44 ; Galilean independence, 44 ; plot against him, 45 ; no crime to proclaim himself the Messiah, 47 ; Pilate examines him, 49 ; his death on the cross, 50 ; Jesus and Hillel compared, 51 ; his greatness, 52 ; who are responsible for his death, 49, 52
John the Baptist, 36, 41
Josua ben Perachia repulsed Jesus, 32
Juda the prince, Rabbi ; his title, 11, 242 ; his actual office, 243 ; son of Gamaliel II., 244 ; his birth, 244 ; education, 246 ; deference to Babylonian prince, 247 ; pride in his descent, 248 ; his policy that of Hillel, 249, 250 ; his sayings, 250 ; modified Sabbath observances, 252 ; opposition, 252, 254 ; rebuke of Jonathan ben Amram, 254 ; friendly to Christians, 256 ; relations with Roman rulers, 257 ; Jewish emigration, 258 ; efforts to create a Jewish literature, the Mishna, 259–269 ; systematized Jewish law, 261–269 ; other work, 270 ; office of patriarch abolished, 272 ; removed to Sephoris, 272 ; appointed his sons to office, his death, 273
Judean Christians and friendly Jews, 22, 150, 256
Julian, emperor, 271
Julianus, joint leader with Pappus of the rebellion against Trajan, 131, 173

Ki Dor, villainous innkeeper, 198
Ki Tobh, name given to the sun by Rabbi Mair, 197

Legends, Parables, etc.:
    A dangerous passenger, 230
    a Jewish Lucretia, 202
    Akibah shown to Adam, 156
    Artaban's gift, 256
    body and soul, 257
    cure of Marcus Aurelius's daughter, 224
    death of husbandmen, 221
    dream of 'Haninah ben Dosa's wife, 81
    failure of attempt to make Hillel angry, 25

Legends, Parables, etc.—*Continued*:
    Fifth Book of Moses, the, 227
    'Haninah ben Dosa and the block of marble, 82
    Josua and the sixty academicians, 137
    Ki Dor and the three Rabbis, 198
    king and his twin brother, the, 190
    lamp filled with vinegar, the, 83
    letters of Hebrew alphabet crowned, 156
    lion and the fox, the, 186
    lion with bone in throat, the, 133
    maiden's rescue, the, 88
    princess and the spindle, the, 147
    Rabbi Eleazar and the misshapen man, 236
    Rabbi Josua put down by woman, girl, and boy, 129
    Rabbi Mair and his friend the sun, 197
    Rabbi Mair and the woman's accusation, 201
    rescue of sister-in-law, 194
    serpents bite law-breakers, 222
    spell-bound sorcerer, the, 144
    tasting of swine's flesh, 196
    testimony of tree, brook, and walls, 104
    traitor turned to stone, 222
    two men and a dove, 258
    widow Ikho and the beams, the, 85
    Yokai and the bird, 220
Loans, innovations by Hillel, *see* Prosbul Act
Lydda, academic centre under Gamaliel II., 103, 116, 179

Maimonides, codified the Talmudic laws, 274
Mair, Rabbi, 181; enigmatical character, 185; his parables, 186; dialectitian, literary work, 187; made reader in Sanhedrin, 188; threatened with excommunication, 189; dislike for materialism, 189; his strictness, 190; his family life, 191; death of his sons, 192; other tales and legends, 194, 196–198; jealousies among students, 201; student tricking his wife, 202; goes to Sardes, 203; his sayings, 204; a woman's charge, 204; his friendship with Elisha made a charge against him, 208; his death, 209; his axiom, 210
Marcus Aurelius, 224
Mar Samuel, physician, 251, 253, 272

INDEX

Materialists, 189
"Men of miracles," 86
Mercabah, the, theosophy, or mystic lore, 93
Messiah, the, expected, 41, 159, 176; the highest ideal fulfilled in Jesus Christ, 50, 51; the false Messiah, 42, 177, 271
Minim, heretics, 33
Mishna, the, 260–269
Mohammed, Introduction, viii.; 168
Mosaic Law, the, 14, 20, 23, 48, 243

Nahum of Gamsu, a famous doctor and mystic, 159; fatalist, Hebrew of Hebrews, 160; legend showing his sanctity, 161; teacher of Rabbi Akibah, 161
Nasi, prince, 11

Oral law, or tradition, the, 31, 91, 169, 259
Ordination, by laying-on of hands, or by the kiss, forbidden by Hadrian, 181, 185, 188, 212, 213
Otho-ha-Ish, name given to Christ, 32

Parables, *see* Legends, Parables, etc.
Paradise, or *Pardes*, 170, 206
Pappus, leader of rebellion against Trajan, 131, 173, 180
Passover given precedence over the Sabbath, 8, 9
Patriarch, title of the president of the Sanhedrin, 5; abolished, 271
Patriarchate, the, 69, 211, 271
Paul of Tarsus, 57; his style reflects the Agadah, 169
Pharisees, the, their teachings, 5; meaning of the word, 35; corrupt, 39; "dyed Pharisees," 40; eight hundred crucified, 40; not responsible for death of Christ, 53
Pilate, Pontius, fifth procurator of Judea, 33; Christ brought before him, 48; examined and tries to save him, 49
Practice, a system of religious observance, 75
Prosbul Act, the, 14, 22

Rabbis, the, teachers of the Law and a sort of clergy, 2; intermediate between the Sadducees and Pharisees, 4; judges, 38; sometimes artisans, 6, 124
Rachel, wife of Ben Akibah, 154, 156, 162.

INDEX

Rufus, governor of Judea, 174 ; his wife left him for Ben Akibah, 175 ; he retreated to fortifications, 178 ; he tortured Ben Akibah, 181

Sabbath, the, 7–9
Sadducees, the, 3, 9 ; the tendency of their principles, 4 ; the local aristocracy of Palestine, 35 ; their doctrinal position similar to Puritans, 37 ; their main object, 39 ; loss of influence, 67
Sanhedrin, the, 2, 3, 5, 38, 40 ; the new one, 67, 69, 111 ; custom, 188 ; interpreters of the Law, 243, 271
Severus, Roman general, 178
Shammai, Rabbi, Introduction, xii. ; opposed Hillel, 10, 12 ; zealous nationalist, 14 ; hated foreign element, 17
Shemaiah, 6, 8, 20
Siccarees, the, 58, 62, 205
Simon I., Rabbi, president of the Sanhedrin and son of Hillel, 58
Simon II., Rabbi, son of Gamaliel II., 58, 189, 244
Simon III., Rabbi, president of Sanhedrin, 188 ; father to Juda the prince, 244
Sopherim, the, 4

Talmud, the, an encyclopedia, 31 ; Christ's name frequent in it, 32 ; its spirit, 93 ; its composition and arrangement, 261–274.
Tax, the, *fiscus judæus*, 130
Temple, the, 34, 36, 57 ; of hearts, 59 ; a spiritual, 68 ; prophecy ceased, 86 ; destruction ordered, 176

Vespasian, emperor, 66, 69

Yam Trajanus, Trajan's day, 131
Yamnai, school of, 67 ; seat of new Sanhedrin, 67, 69
Yannai, king, crucified eight hundred Pharisees, 40
Year of Release, 22, 221, 226